JOHN AND WILLIAM BARTRAM'S AMERICA

AMERICAN NATURALISTS SERIES
Farida A. Wiley, *General Editor*

Published

JOHN BURROUGHS' AMERICA
ERNEST THOMPSON SETON'S AMERICA
THEODORE ROOSEVELT'S AMERICA
JOHN AND WILLIAM BARTRAM'S AMERICA

John Bartram

William Bartram

*Both Portraits by
Charles Willson Peale*

JOHN AND WILLIAM BARTRAM'S AMERICA

SELECTIONS FROM THE WRITINGS OF THE PHILADELPHIA NATURALISTS

Edited with an Introduction by

HELEN GERE CRUICKSHANK

Foreword by B. BARTRAM CADBURY

Illustrated by

FRANCIS LEE JACQUES

DEVIN-ADAIR, PUBLISHERS

Greenwich, Connecticut

Library of Congress Catalog Card Number: 57-8862
ISBN: 0-8159-5118-3

Manufactured in the United States of America

FOREWORD

WILLIAM BARTRAM and perhaps more especially his father, John, were leaders in the early development of scientific thinking in America. John, a Quaker and a very simple person, in Philadelphia established the first botanical garden in the colonies, and to it he brought a wide selection of plants from many parts of the country. In the course of his pioneering, he made the acquaintance of many leading figures of the day, including Benjamin Franklin and Thomas Jefferson. He also carried on extensive correspondence with some of the leading European naturalists of that day, such as Dr. John Fothergill, Linnæus, and Peter Kalm, and sent them many samples of American plants for their collections.

It remained for William, however, to assume the task of writing the record of the Bartrams' work together. John's few written accounts are rather labored and indicate that he did not enjoy the pen as much as the soil. William not only wrote the account of their Florida journey but also illustrated it, and although the writing may sometimes be rather quaint, it has a spark of realism and appreciation spiced with gentle humor.

Although William was one of the foremost of the earliest generation of American writers on natural history and travel, his work has never been known and appreciated in America the way it was abroad. The first edition of the *Travels,* published in London in 1791, attracted a great deal of attention in Europe, where it was widely read. It exerted considerable influence on the writings of Coleridge and several other authors of the period. Now we are indebted to Helen Cruickshank for this republication of the best of the writings of both Bartrams.

The descendants of John Bartram have scattered by now quite widely, though some are still living in the Philadelphia area. I am not able to say how many have inherited the interest in natural science which John Bartram established and whose literary expression was carried out by William. I do know, however, that some members in the present generation, including myself, take pride in the heritage and are applying it to the study of the natural sciences in various ways.

We, in this age of wonders, who speed along over ribbons of concrete in high-powered cars can have little conception of the hardships involved in traveling into the South in the middle of the 18th century. Going horseback or on foot over the few roads or poorly marked trails, the naturalist of that day suffered many hardships and discomforts. The fear of unfriendly Indians constantly lurked in the back of his mind. I have retraced small portions of the Bartrams' route, and I have often wondered as I looked into some of the sloughs and swamps, with their thick underbrush and forbidding canopy of Spanish moss, how many present-day explorers of the wild would have the fortitude to undertake the risk of danger and disease that these intrepid travelers accepted with spirit and eagerness. It makes the reading of their adventures all the more worth while.

B. Bartram Cadbury

Farmington, Conn.

CONTENTS

ILLUSTRATIONS BY
FRANCIS LEE JAQUES

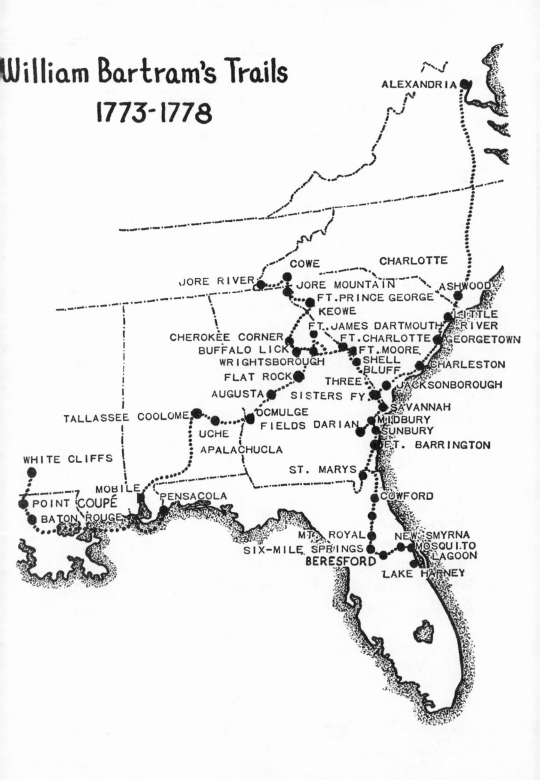

William Bartram's Trails
1773-1778

ALEXANDRIA

COWE CHARLOTTE

JORE RIVER JORE MOUNTAIN ASHWOOD

FT. PRINCE GEORGE

KEOWE LITTLE

FT. JAMES DARTMOUTH RIVER

CHEROKEE CORNER FT. CHARLOTTE GEORGETOWN

BUFFALO LICK FT. MOORE

WRIGHTSBOROUGH SHELL

BLUFF CHARLESTON

FLAT ROCK THREE JACKSONBOROUGH

AUGUSTA SISTERS FY.

TALLASSEE COOLOME SAVANNAH

OCMULGE MIDBURY

UCHE FIELDS DARIAN SUNBURY

APALACHUCLA FT. BARRINGTON

WHITE CLIFFS ST. MARYS

MOBILE

POINT COUPÉ PENSACOLA COWFORD

BATON ROUGE

MT. ROYAL NEW SMYRNA

SIX-MILE SPRINGS MOSQUITO

BERESFORD LAGOON

LAKE HARNEY

INTRODUCTION

IN THE YEAR 1699, ninety-two years after the first permanent English colony was established on the American continent, our first great American naturalist, John Bartram, was born. Forty years later, John's son William, who achieved distinction equal to or greater than his father's, was born. Their combined years spanned the middle and late colonial period and the early years of the United States as an independent country.

The Bartrams had before them an unmapped virgin country filled with quantities of unknown plants and animals. In that day the thoughts of most Americans were turned toward the conquest and taming of the wilderness; but the Bartrams looked upon it with the eyes of great botanists, of philosophers, explorers, historians, and ecologists.

While they wished to see new areas opened for settlement, they deplored the destruction of natural beauties that followed in the wake of the white man. Nearly two centuries ago William expressed the modern belief that man should use his environment wisely, and never abuse it, as indicated in the following quotation from his *Travels:*

I have often been affected with extreme regret at beholding the destruction and devastation which has been committed or indiscreetly exercised on those extensive, fruitful orange groves, on the banks of St. Juan, by the new planters under the British government, some hundred acres of which, at a single plantation, have been entirely destroyed to make room for the indigo, cotton, corn, batatas, &c. or, as they say, to extirpate the mosquitoes, alleging that groves near the dwellings are haunts and shelters for those persecuting insects. Some plantations have not a single tree standing; and where any have been left, it is only a small coppice or clump, nakedly exposed and destitute; perhaps fifty or an hundred trees standing near the dwelling house, having no lofty cool grove of expansive live oaks, laurel magnolias, and palms to shade and protect them, exhibiting a mournful, sallow countenance; their native, perfectly formed and glossy green foliage as if violated, defaced, and torn to pieces by the bleak winds, scorched by the burning sunbeams in summer and chilled by the winter frosts.

The way of these great naturalists was not easy. While exceptional opportunities lay before them, they had to face hazards difficult for us to comprehend. Travel was expensive and their funds were severely limited. In those far-off times, when settlements were few, except along the coast and for a short distance inland along the rivers, travel was rugged. Roads linking the remote settlements were often so primitive we would regard them today as mere trails. Now we can circumnavigate this earth with more ease and safety than the Bartrams could travel into the wilderness for a hundred miles. Camping equipment was limited to what could be carried before or behind the saddle. Insect repellents and mosquito netting were unknown. In the remote places, Indians and renegades lent danger to travel. Malaria, yellow fever, and other frequently mortal diseases were an ever-present threat. Hardships and dangers, however, did not stop the Bartrams.

As they discovered new species of plants and animals, they also observed the soil and ecological relationships existing between the animate and the inanimate. Information concerning Indians and their ways, plantation owners' methods of operation, birds, reptiles, insects, soil — as well as plants — were grist for their journals; blunt and brief as a captain's log were the entries by John; vivid and joyous were those by William.

During their early days of exploration there were neither laboratory nor museum collections to assist them in the identification of the plants and animals they found. They had comparatively few books at their disposal, and of those, since they were of Old World origin, almost none were of direct use to an American naturalist. No matter what field of natural history they investigated, they were pioneering.

Some three hundred and twenty species of plants were sent to England during the period that John ("The Truth Teller," to the Delawares) and William ("The Flower Hunter," to the Seminoles) were collecting and shipping specimens to Europe. It is safe to say the Bartrams sent the majority of all plants received there from America. Many of their preserved specimens are still in the British Museum (Natural History), as are many of their journals and numbers of William's drawings.

Strangely enough, even though the greatness of the Bartrams' contributions to science was recognized by their contemporaries, the scientists who named the new plants collected by them failed in most instances, as is the usual custom, to incorporate their names in the scientific names given to these plants.

When William was fourteen, his father took him on a trip

of exploration to the Catskills. While collecting plants, William also watched and sketched birds. He also collected birds, particularly the migratory species, which he called birds "of quick passage." He dried many of the bird skins and shipped them with his drawings to the English ornithologist George Edwards. Some of these same birds were later given by Edwards to Linnæus, who used them in naming new American species. William's observations and drawings of birds through the years became a valuable part of our ornithological history. They established him as the first of our native-born bird students. In several instances, when skins of birds new to science were lost, his drawings were kept as the example for the species. He listed two hundred and fifteen species of birds, noted their habits, discussed migration, and kept the first North American calendar of their arrivals and departures. It was William Bartram's influence that led Alexander Wilson to turn from the writing of poetry and teaching, in which fields he was undistinguished, to ornithology and fame. In 1806 Wilson urged Bartram to accompany him on an ornithological expedition down the Ohio and Mississippi to New Orleans. Ill health and eye trouble, however, compelled him to decline. Later these same frailties made it impossible for him to accept Thomas Jefferson's invitation to join the group which won everlasting fame as the Lewis and Clark Expedition.

For a while after his school years, William worked for a Philadelphia merchant. Later he became a trader at Cape Fear, North Carolina, where at an earlier time his explorer father had found and marveled at the "most wonderful plant" [Venus's-flytrap], an insectivorous plant which John had called "tipitiwichit." The leaves of this plant snap shut rather suddenly when an insect touches the upper surface of its leaves.

In the years when William was separated from his father, John continued to make his wishes known, as is indicated by the following letters:

In 176(1?) John wrote:

My dear Son

Cousin Billy tells me that your loblolly Bay or Alcea bears a very sweet blossom. I wish thee would look out for some of its seed. . . . I want seed of everything we have not & thee is a good judge of that. . . .

In another letter John wrote:

My dear Billy

I was lately tould by a man . . . that he saw in North Carolina not far from Cape Fear a strange plant as big as a dasy and much like it in flower . . . . who[se?] properties was such that if they looked earnestly at it the petals of the flower would close up . . . . if it is true it will be a fine curiosity . . . . pray gather every sort of seed that don't grow in our country . . . .

It is interesting to contrast the characteristics of this father and son. John, competent, sure and indefatigable, knew exactly what he wanted and drove straight toward his goal. Disappointments and disasters distressed him, but he shrugged them off and went right ahead with his plans. He was just and generous. There is little doubt that he would have been a success in any field to which he directed his vast energies. It is regrettable that many of the records of his findings are in a calendarlike form not suited for inclusion in this volume.

William inherited his father's intelligence, his appreciation of nature, and his great powers of observation. But his personality lacked the forcefulness of his father's, and he was gentle and pliable. He accepted direction from his father, for whom he had the most profound respect and love. For a time, he carried on a small business, in accordance with his father's plans for him. But he did so against an inner desire for quite a different kind of life. He had no interest in business and certainly no ability for it. Rather than deny his father's wishes he gave surface consent but put little of himself into his activities. At heart he was an artist and a naturalist with a poet's appreciation for nature.

In 1773, Dr. Fothergill, the English physician, agreed to finance William on a trip through Georgia and Florida. The doctor would have preferred that William search the northern colonies and Canada for plants that would grow out of doors in England, but William's dream of exploring the lush, exotic South to pursue the study of botany and animal life in some of its little-known regions was honored. This trip was to prove a memorable one. When William set out on this great adventure, he planned to be away for two years, but five were to elapse before his return. This journey resulted in the discovery of many plants new to science, including eared magnolia and the oak-leaf hydrangea, and in valuable information concerning Indians and their mode of life, birds, mammals, soil, and topography. His observations on Indians and Indian relics have become source material for history students of today. The report of his findings published in his book *Travels Through North & South Carolina, etc.,* gives the first genuinely artistic interpretation of the people and character of that part of our country. Moreover, if Gilbert White's *Natural History of Selbourne* (1791) establishes White as the first modern nature writer, William Bartram's *Travels* (1791) places him a close second.

James Madison, Alexander Hamilton, Benjamin Franklin, and other noted people sought Bartram's company. Many authors were greatly influenced by Bartram's writings, such as Wordsworth, in his poem "Ruth," or Coleridge, in much of his writing. Robert Southey, Thomas Campbell, and Felicia Hemans were among the English writers who fell upon William's *Travels* with joy.

In his later years, William Bartram was often to be found in shabby clothes, busy in the garden with spade and rake. It is said that one day he had just finished the description of a plant and was stepping into his beloved garden for a stroll when he died. It was July 22, 1823, and he was eighty-four.

Today, the paths which the Bartrams took through the wilderness areas are often obscure or lost, for these men frequently traveled in unmapped and then-unnamed territory. Some names used in colonial days have been forgotten or have been transferred to different localities. Yet Bartram enthusiasts, myself included, continue to search for the exact paths the naturalists followed.

I was fortunate in having grown up in a home where reading aloud on winter evenings was a favorite occupation. Of all the books read, none left a more lasting pleasure than William Bartram's *Travels,* and I have taken no trip into Bartram country in succeeding years without giving attention to his trails. Sometimes I have discovered a plant or some form of animal life in the exact locality where Bartram first recorded it.

At other times I have discovered a wilderness area, after this long lapse of time, still remaining as William Bartram described it nearly two centuries ago. Following his trail has given me such pleasure that I would urge our very mobile population to add this pursuit to their travels. (For the convenience of the reader, a map, showing as much of the William Bartram trail as it has been possible to disentangle, is shown on the endpapers.

Most of the wilderness areas that were unknown and untouched until the Bartrams explored them are now tamed and most of the forests destroyed. Some places are beneath the waters of reservoirs. Some of the birds, such as the Carolina paroquets and passenger pigeons which they watched, are now extinct.

In this volume, I have tried to collect those writings of the Bartrams which are the most interesting and informative. So far as possible, I have arranged the material in two sections; following William's report on his father, the first five chapters are by John Bartram and the last twelve by William. However, because of the similarity of material, some John Bartram material also appears in chapters six, twelve, and fifteen. The sources and authors of all selections are given near the end of the book ("Sources of Quotations," page 385); these are keyed to the text by reference numbers at the end of each group of selections taken from the same source.

For the sake of greater consistency and easier reading, it has been necessary to make changes in spelling and punctuation, for the 18th-century style is extremely difficult for the modern reader. These changes have been kept to a minimum, and basic style changes have not been made.

The scientific names of plants and animals which were used by the Bartrams are in parentheses, except those still in use. Scientific names not used by the Bartrams but in use today are italicized.

I have also included (page 3) the accurate biographical sketch of John and William Bartram written in 1896 by Dr. William Jay Youmans.

HELEN GERE CRUICKSHANK

Rockledge, Florida

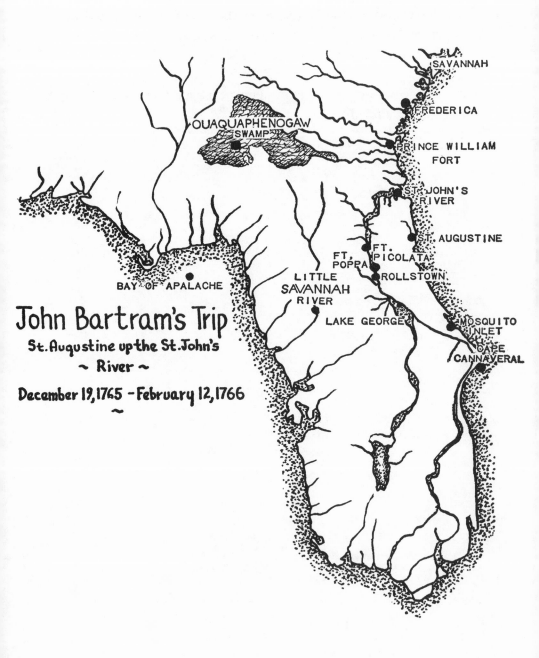

OUAQUAPHENOGAW
SWAMP

SAVANNAH

FREDERICA

PRINCE WILLIAM
FORT

ST. JOHN'S
RIVER

ST. AUGUSTINE

FT.
PICOLATA

FT.
POPPA

ROLLSTOWN

BAY OF APALACHE

LITTLE
SAVANNAH
RIVER

LAKE GEORGE

MOSQUITO
INLET

CAPE
CANNAVERAL

John Bartram's Trip

St. Augustine up the St. John's
~ River ~

December 19, 1765 - February 12, 1766
~

〇〉〇⟩

ACKNOWLEDGMENTS

To EDIT the best of the Bartrams' writings presented problems. Many of their notes, journals and letters, because of the age of the manuscripts, the lack of punctuation, and spelling typical of a day before Webster brought about standardization, are extremely difficult to read. Moreover, the location of places mentioned by the Bartrams on today's maps and the determination of our present names for plants and other forms of life they describe was not always possible.

The Historical Society of Pennsylvania kindly gave me permission to use any suitable material they had. The Trustees of the British Museum (Natural History) and Dr. G. Taylor, Keeper of Botany, permitted me to use parts of the William Bartram *Journal,* prepared for Dr. John Fothergill.

Monica de La Salle, librarian of the National Audubon Society; Helen Moore of the Pennsylvania Genealogical Society; Elizabeth Hall, librarian of the New York Botanical Garden; Ena Young, Curator of Maps at the American Geographical Society; the Staff of the Florida State Library at Tallahassee; Mr. Peter A. Brannon, Department of Archives and History of the State of Alabama; Dr. John Goff, Emory University; H. M. Haynes, Chief of the State Lands Section of Louisiana; Mr. Herbert Ravenel Sass, Mrs. J. C. Oliver, Dr. Frank Morton Jones, Dr. Malvina Trussell, and Mrs.

Fenley Hunter are among those who kindly helped me with plant puzzles or the tracing of the Bartram trails. Help and criticism given by Farida A. Wiley, editor of The American Naturalists Series, was invaluable.

I also thank my husband, Allan D. Cruickshank, for help in visiting Bartram haunts that were often difficult to reach; Francis Lee Jaques for the illustrations that so perfectly catch the wild spirit of the Bartrams' America, and B. Bartram Cadbury for his foreword.

H. G. C.

JOHN AND WILLIAM BARTRAM'S AMERICA

JOHN AND WILLIAM BARTRAM:
A Biographical Sketch*

John Bartram, 1699—1777
William Bartram, 1739—1823

During the century which preceded the American Revolution the science of the colonies, like their commerce, was tributary to that of the Old World. Fabulous reports in regard to the natural resources of America had been brought home by European voyagers, and the cultivators of all sciences and arts were looking to that vast unexplored region for products which should increase the knowledge of the naturalists, the resources of the physician and the agriculturalist, the profit of the merchant, and the enjoyment of the man of leisure. The function of those colonists who inclined to natural history was that of explorers and collectors, and among the earliest and most notable of these American collectors were the subjects of this sketch.

The grandfather of the elder Bartram, also named John, came from Derbyshire, England, to Pennsylvania in 1682. He brought his wife, three sons and one daughter and settled near Darby, in Delaware (then Chester) County. The third son, William, was the only one who married, his wife being Elizabeth, daughter of James Hunt. Both families belonged to the Society of Friends. The children of William were John (the botanist), James, William, and a daughter who died

* From *Pioneers of Science in America,* edited and revised by William Jay Youmans, M.D. (New York: D. Appleton and Company, 1896).

young. The second William went to North Carolina and settled near Cape Fear; John and James remained in Pennsylvania.

The date of John Bartram's birth was March 23, 1699 [as
reckoned by the Quaker calendar; now thought to be May
23, 1699. Ed.]. But little is on record concerning his early
years. Like the majority of the boys in the colonies, he was
brought up to a farming life, and his education was only such
as the country schools of the time afforded. After reaching
adult years he studied Latin a little, so as to be able to pick
out the descriptions of the plants in the Latin works of European botanists. In a sketch of John Bartram written by his
son William, it is stated that he had an inclination to the
study of physic and surgery and did much toward relieving
the ailments of his poor neighbors. In January, 1723, he
married Mary, daughter of Richard Morris, of Chester Meeting, by whom he had two sons — Richard, who died young;
and Isaac, who lived to old age. His wife Mary died in 1727,
and in September, 1729, he married Ann Mendenhall, of
Concord Meeting, who survived him. John and Ann Bartram
had nine children, five boys and four girls. Of these the third
son was William, he and his twin sister Elizabeth being born
February 9, 1739. The ground on which John Bartram laid
out the first botanical garden [probably the first to contain
both native and exotic species. Ed.] in America was on the
west bank of the Schuylkill River, at Kingsessing, near
Gray's Ferry [now within the limits of Philadelphia. Ed.],
and was bought by him September 30, 1728. "Here he built
with his own hands," says William, "a large and comfortable
house of hewn stone, and laid out a garden containing about
five acres." The year of its erection is shown by a stone on the
wall on which is cut "John — Ann Bartram, 1731." . . .

That the building was a labor of love is attested by the care bestowed upon the carved stonework around the windows and doors and the pillars under the porch. John Bartram must have been a good stonecutter and mason, for this is one of four stone houses that he built in his lifetime.

Nearly all the extant information concerning the lives of the two Bartrams has been embodied in the *Memorials of John Bartram,* by William Darlington, published in 1849. This volume contains the sketch of John Bartram by his son William, with some additions by the editor, and over four hundred pages of correspondence. About a fourth of these letters are from his friend Peter Collinson; the others are from eminent botanists in Europe and America, and from Bartram to these various correspondents. Darlington also reprinted a sketch of John Bartram which appeared in *Letters from an American Farmer,* by J. Hector St. John, published in London soon after Bartram's death. The "letter" describing Bartram purports to be written by a Russian traveler, who is evidently a myth, although in all important respects the account represents the botanist as he was. As to how Bartram's interest in botany was aroused, the "Russian gentleman" has a pretty story, telling of a sudden awakening after the botanist had married; but Bartram himself is better authority, and he writes to Collinson, May 1, 1764, "I had always since ten years old a great inclination to plants, and knew all that I once observed by sight, though not their proper names, having no person nor books to instruct me."

He was encouraged to study systematically by James Logan (founder of the Loganian Library, in Philadelphia), who gave him several botanical works. In order that his explorations, begun at his own expense, might be extended, Bartram's friends prompted him to seek the patronage of some wealthy and influential person in the mother country. Accordingly, a quantity of his specimens and a record of some of his observations were sent to Peter Collinson, a Quaker merchant in England, who was greatly interested in horticulture. Bartram's consignment secured his interest, and led to a correspondence which lasted nearly fifty years. The first letter in Darlington's collection is from Collinson under the date of January 20, 1734-'35, and refers to letters from Bartram of the preceding November; hence this correspondence probably began when Bartram was about thirty-five years of age. In his early letters Collinson makes many inquiries about American plants and requests for specimens. He sends Bartram seeds, roots, cuttings of trees, vegetables, and flowering plants cultivated in England, packages of paper in which to preserve specimens, and gives him directions for collecting and drying plants. From time to time he sends presents of cloth and other articles for the use of the botanist or his family. For Bartram's "improvement in the knowledge of plants" he early offers, if duplicate collections are sent, to "get them named by our most knowing botanists, and then return them again, which will improve thee more than books." In this way the learning of Dillenius, Gronovius, and other eminent men was brought to the aid of the humble colonist. Collinson obtained for Bartram many orders of seeds and roots of American plants, and early secured for him the patronage of Lord Petre, whose gardens and hothouses were probably the most extensive in the kingdom. This noble amateur ordered quantities of seeds from time to time, and when Bartram asked for a yearly allowance to enable him to extend his explorations, Lord Petre agreed to contribute ten guineas toward it. As much more was obtained from the Duke of Richmond and Philip Miller, and the twenty guineas were paid each year till 1742, when Lord Petre died. The first expedition that Bartram made with this assistance was an exploration of the Schuylkill River. He transmitted his journal of the trip and a map of the river to his patrons, and with both of these Collinson reported Lord Petre to be much pleased.

Besides plants, Collinson asks Bartram at various times to send insects, birds, and their eggs, and nests, terrapin and other turtles, snakes, shells, wasp's and hornet's nests, and fossils, which then were regarded as "evidence of the Deluge." "My inclination and fondness of natural productions of all kinds," he writes, "is agreeable to the old proverb *'Like the parson's barn — refuses nothing.'* " During the second year of his allowance Bartram complains that it does not recompense him for his labors, and he also finds fault with Collinson for giving him seeds and cuttings that he has already, and for not having answered some of his letters. Collinson, in a businesslike reply, shows that Bartram's complaints are due to his ignorance of commercial affairs, the difficulty of transatlantic communication, and to his exceeding the commissions of his patrons — whereupon the botanist promptly apologizes.

In 1738 Bartram made a journey of five weeks through Maryland and Virginia to Williamsburg, then up the James River, and over the Blue Ridge Mountains, traveling in all about eleven hundred miles. Most of his expeditions were made without any scientific companion. "Our Americans," he writes to a correspondent, "have very little taste for these amusements. I can't find one that will bear the fatigue to accompany me in my peregrinations."

In an undated letter, written probably in 1739, to Colonel Byrd of Virginia, Bartram reports that he had been making "microscopical observations upon the male and female parts

of vegetables." He had also made, he says, "several successful experiments of joining several species of the same genus,
whereby I have obtained curious mixed colors in flowers,
never known before." To this he adds: "I hope by these practical observations to open a gate into a very large field of experimental knowledge, which, if judiciously improved, may
be a considerable addition to the beauty of the florist's garden." It was in this "field of experimental knowledge" —
namely, cross-fertilization — that Darwin afterward won a
share of his fame. Bartram evidently discussed this subject
with Collinson, for the latter writes in 1742: "That some
variegations may be occasioned by insects is certain; but then
these are only annual, and cease with the year." Permanent
variegations, he says, are produced by budding — a sort of
inoculation.

That Bartram had a hostility to superstition, tempered
with much consideration for persons, is shown by a letter in
which he tells of a visit to Dr. Witt, of Germantown, another
of Collinson's correspondents. He says: "When we are on
the topic of astrology, magic, and mystic divinity, I am apt to
be a little troublesome, by inquiring into the foundation and
reasonableness of these notions — which, thee knows, will not
bear to be searched and examined into: though I handle
these fancies with more tenderness with him than I should
with many others that are so superstitiously inclined."

One of the botanists whom Collinson had enlisted in iden-
tifying Bartram's specimens was Prof. Dillenius, of Oxford,
and in 1740 Collinson writes for some mosses for him, saying,
"He defers completing his work till he sees what comes from
thee, Clayton, and Dr. Mitchell." In the same year a list of
specimens which had been named by Dr. J. F. Gronovius, of
Leyden, was returned, and contained this entry: "Cortusæ

sive Verbasci, Fl. Virg., pp. 74, 75. This being a new genus, may be called *Bartramia.*" The name *Bartramia* is now borne by a different plant, a moss growing in the Berkshire Hills of Massachusetts.

Bartram's correspondence with Gronovius began about 1743, and extends over a dozen years or more. Gronovius writes at length, very appreciatively, and makes many requests. He sends his books as they appear, and before the publication of his *Index Lapidæ,* sends a transcript of the passage, in Latin, in which he is to give Bartram credit for his finds of fossils.

Among the European scientists whom Collinson made acquainted with Bartram's work was Sir Hans Sloane, physician and naturalist, who succeeded Newton as President of the Royal Society. At his request Bartram sends him, in 1741, some "petrified representations of seashells." The next year Sloane sends to Bartram a silver cup inscribed:

> *The gift of Sr. Hans Sloane, Bart,*
> *To his Frd John Bartram.*
> *Anno 1742.*

A figure of this cup is given by Darlington. Sloane also sent Bartram his *Natural History of Jamaica,* in two ponderous folio volumes.

About this time a correspondence began between Bartram and Dr. John Fothergill, a wealthy physician and naturalist, who, like Sloane, had first received some of Bartram's specimens from Collinson. Dr. Fothergill wishes to know what mineral springs there are in America, and Bartram sends him what information he has and can get from others.

Bartram also exchanged letters with Philip Miller, author of the *Gardener's Dictionary;* with George Edwards, who in

1766 sends his book containing descriptions of birds that the Pennsylvanian had sent him; with Prof. John Hope, of Edinburgh; and with the ablest observers of Nature in the colonies, among whom were Dr. John Mitchell, Rev. Jared Eliot, John Clayton, Cadwallader Colden, and Dr. Alexander Garden.

In 1744 he writes, "Dr. Gronovius hath sent me his *Index Lapidæ,* and Linnæus the second edition of his *Characteres Plantarum,* with a very loving letter desiring my correspondence, and to furnish him with some natural curiosities of our country." The same year he sends to England his *Journal of the Five Nations and the Lake Ontario,* describing a journey he had made the preceding fall. It contained an account of the "soil, productions, mountains, and lakes" of those parts of Pennsylvania and New York through which the route lay; and gave the proceedings of a great assembly of Indian chiefs held to treat with the agent of the Province of Pennsylvania, whom Bartram accompanied. The journal was afterward published in London.

The visit of Peter Kalm to America took place in 1748 to 1751. He traveled through Canada, New York, Pennsylvania, and adjoining provinces; made the acquaintance of the Gray's Ferry botanist, and obtained much assistance from him. It has been alleged that Kalm took to himself the credit of some discoveries which rightfully belonged to Bartram. This would not be suspected from reading Kalm's *Travels,* in which he gives Bartram a page and a half of hearty commendation, saying, among other things: "We owe to him the knowledge of many scarce plants, which he found, and which were never known before. . . . I likewise owe him many things, for he possessed that great quality of communicating everything he knew. I shall, therefore, in the sequel frequently mention this gentleman." On nearly every one of the next twenty pages credit is given to Bartram for information.

In 1751 Benjamin Franklin and D. Hall published at Philadelphia an American edition of Dr. Thomas Short's *Medicina Britannica,* "with a preface by Mr. John Bartram, Botanist, of Pennsylvania. . . ."

John Bartram's son William begins to figure in his father's correspondence when about fifteen years old. At that time Bartram sent some of William's drawings of natural objects to Collinson, and took him on a trip to the Catskills. In 1755 Bartram writes: "I design to set Billy to draw all our turtles with remarks, as he has time, which is only on Seventh days in the afternoon, and First-day mornings; for he is constantly kept to school to learn Latin and French." This attention to the languages indicates that Bartram was determined that his son should not suffer from the lack of knowledge by which his own reading of works of natural history had been limited. William was then attending the old college of Philadelphia.

The same message also shows that Bartram's idea about Sunday occupations was somewhat unusual for that generation, and in fact it is stated that he was excommunicated by his brother Quakers about this time for his independent religious views. The question of an occupation for William now came up, and in the letter just quoted his father asks Collinson's advice in the matter. "My son William," he writes, "is just turned sixteen. It is now time to propose some way for him to get his living by. I don't want him to be what is commonly called a gentleman. I want to put him to some business by which he may, with care and industry, get a temperate, reasonable living. I am afraid that botany and drawing will not afford him one, and hard labor don't agree with him. I have designed several years to put him to a doctor, to learn physic and surgery; but that will take him from his drawing, which he takes particular delight in. Pray, dear friend Peter, let me have thy opinion about it." Franklin offered to teach William the printing trade, but Bartram was not quite satisfied with the prospects for printers in Pennsylvania, and Franklin then suggested engraving. But William became neither printer nor engraver. At the age of eighteen he was placed with a Philadelphia merchant, Mr. Child, where he remained for four years.

Bartram's science was largely practical. He wrote to Dr. Alexander Garden, of Charleston, in 1755, suggesting a series of borings on a large scale, to search for valuable mineral products. He gives as a reason the satisfaction to be derived from knowing the composition of the earth, and adds, "By this method we may compose a curious subterranean map." "This scheme of John Bartram's," says Darlington, "if original with him — would indicate that he had formed a pretty good notion of the nature and importance of a geological survey and map, more than half a century before such undertakings were attempted in our country, or even thought of by those whose province it was to authorize them."

Bartram was evidently much interested in geological subjects; thus, in 1756 he writes, "My dear worthy friend, thee can't bang me out of the notion that limestone and. marble were originally mud, impregnated by a marine salt, which I take to be the original of all our terrestrial soils."

In 1760 he made a trip through the Carolinas, his journal of which he wrote out and sent to England. The following summer, William, then twenty-two years old, went to North Carolina and set up as a trader at Cape Fear, where his uncle William had settled as a young man. That year John Bartram makes a journey to Pittsburgh and some way down the Ohio River, keeping a journal, as usual, which is sent to his English friends. Nearly all these trips were made in autumn, so as to get ripe seeds of desirable trees and plants.

Bartram had too tender a feeling toward animal life to be much of a zoölogist. He says on this score: "As for the animals and insects, it is very few that I touch of choice, and most with uneasiness. Neither can I behold any of them, that have not done me a manifest injury, in their agonizing mortal pains without pity. I also am of the opinion that the creatures commonly called brutes possess higher qualifications, and more exalted ideas, than our traditional mystery-mongers are willing to allow them." His ideas concerning animal psychology were thus clearly in advance of his time.

The war with France, known to Americans as the French and Indian War, resulted in extending the British possessions in America as far west as the Mississippi River. Immediately a desire was expressed in England for a thorough exploration of this great accession of territory. Bartram writes in 1763 that this could not be made without danger from the Indians. His own expeditions had been very short during the hostilities. The late war had shown the colonists what atrocities the savages were capable of, and the prevailing feelings toward the red men had become dread and hatred. "Many years past in our most peaceful times," writes Bartram, "far beyond the mountains, as I was walking in a path with an Indian guide, hired for two dollars, an Indian man met me and pulled off my hat in great passion, and chawed it all round — I suppose to show me that they would eat me if I came in that country again." In two other letters he declares that the only way to keep peace with the Indians "is to bang them stoutly." The

question arises whether the combative disposition of the botanist thus revealed might not have been one of the reasons
for his exclusion from the Society of Friends.

In 1764 Bartram sends to England his *Journal to Carolina
and New River*. In this year, one Young, of Pennsylvania,
managed to gain the favor of the new king, George III, by
sending him some American plants, and obtained sudden pre-
ferment. It was said that all the plants had been sent to England before — many of them by Bartram. The friends of our
botanist, feeling that he was much more deserving of such favor, urged him to send specimens to the king, which he does
through Collinson, desiring that he may be given a commission for botanical exploration in the Floridas. April 9, 1765,
Collinson writes, "My repeated solicitations have not been in
vain," and reports that the king has appointed Bartram his
botanist for the Floridas, with a salary of fifty pounds a year.
This appointment continued till the death of the botanist,
twelve years after. Bartram accordingly made an expedition
in the South the next fall. He was then sixty-five years old;
and, although his eagerness for exploring was undiminished,
he felt the need of a companion on this trip, and got William to go with him, the latter closing out his not very successful business at Cape Fear in order to do so. In his sketch
of his father, William states that he had been ordered to
search for the sources of the river San Juan (St. John's), and
that he ascended the river its whole length, nearly four hundred miles, by one bank and descended by the other. He explored and made a survey of both the main stream and its
branches and connected lakes, and made a draft showing
widths, depths, and distances. He also noted the lay of the
land, quality of the soil, the vegetable and animal productions, etc. His report was approved by the governor of the

province, and was sent to the Board of Trade and Plantations in England, by which it was ordered published "for the
benefit of the new colony." Bartram collected a fine lot of
plants, fossils, and other objects of interest on this trip, which
were forwarded to the king, who was reported to be much
pleased with them. His journal is still extant, in a volume
with an *Account of East Florida,* by William Stork, published
in England. It is evident from this production that the botanist was not a ready writer. His observations are minute and
sagacious, and his language is simple, but his sentences are
loosely strung out, and the record is the barest statement of
facts. His *Journal to the Five Nations,* however, is much
more readable.

William seems to have been much taken with Florida, and
accordingly his father helped to establish him as an indigo
planter on the St. John's River. After about a year of disas-
trous experience he returned to his father's home and went to
work on the farm in the vicinity of Philadelphia. Collinson
had been watching for an opening for William in England,
but so far nothing had come of it. The next year he writes
that the Duchess of Portland, a "great *virtuoso* in shells and
all marine productions," had just dined at his house, and,
having seen William's drawings, "she desires to bestow
twenty guineas on his performances *for a trial.*" The kind of
objects she wants drawn are told. The same month, July 18,
1768, Collinson writes to William that he had also secured an
order from Dr. Fothergill for drawings of shells, turtles, terrapin, etc. This was probably the last letter of Collinson to
the Bartrams, as he died on the 11th of the following month.
During his long friendship with John Bartram the two men
had never met.

William now began to send drawings and descriptions to

Dr. Fothergill from time to time. In 1772 he began explorations in the Floridas, Carolina, and Georgia, the expense of
which for nearly five years was borne by Dr. Fothergill, and
to him William's collections and drawings were turned over.
William made many contributions to the natural history of
the country through which he traveled, and in 1791 published
his *Travels Through North and South Carolina, Georgia, East
and West Florida,* etc. His opinion of the red men is much
more favorable than that of his father. The volume contains
many engravings of plants and birds from the author's own
drawings. Of this book, Coleridge said: "The latest book of
travels I know written in the spirit of the old travelers is
Bartram's account of his tour in the Floridas. It is a work of
high merit in every way."

Among the influential friends of the elder Bartram was
Benjamin Franklin. While in England, Franklin writes to
him and sends him seeds of garden vegetables at various
times; and when the Revolution had stopped Bartram's sending seeds to England for sale, Franklin offers to sell them for
him in France.

Among the testimonials to his botanical achievements that
Bartram received was a gold medal, weighing 487 grains,
from a society in Edinburgh, founded in 1764, for obtaining
seeds of useful trees and shrubs from other countries. This
medal is inscribed, "To Mr. John Bartram, from the Society
of Gentlemen in Edinburgh, 1772"; and on the reverse,
"Merenti," in a wreath. The medal is figured in Darlington's
Memorials, and when that book was published was in the
possession of a Mrs. Jones, a descendant of the botanist.

April 26, 1769, the Royal Academy of Sciences of Stockholm, on the proposal of Prof. Berguis, elected Bartram to
membership. Another honor that he received from the same

country was a letter from Queen Ulrica, and with this may be mentioned the opinion passed upon him by Linnæus, who called Bartram the greatest natural botanist in the world. Bartram was one of the original members of the American Philosophical Society, and contributed many papers to its *Transactions*.

The closing years of Bartram's life were the opening years of the Revolution. He was living when independence was declared in the neighboring city of Philadelphia, but died the following year, September 22, 1777, at the age of seventy-eight. A granddaughter who remembered him distinctly has stated that he was exceedingly agitated by the approach of the British army after the battle of Brandywine, and that his days were probably shortened in consequence. The royal troops had been ravaging the country, and he was apprehensive lest they should lay waste his darling garden. . . .

He was of an active temperament, and often expressed the wish that he might not live to be helpless. This desire was gratified, for he died after only a short illness. . . .

Concerning Bartram's ability as a naturalist there are enthusiastic opinions extant in letters by Franklin, Collinson, Colden, and others well qualified to judge.

William Bartram, after the death of his father, continued in the pursuit of natural history. The Botanic Garden was inherited by his brother John, who took William into a partnership which lasted many years. After their arrangement terminated, William continued to assist his brother until the death of the latter, in 1812. The garden then descended to John's daughter Anne, the wife of Colonel Robert Carr, in whose family William resided from that time until death. He was never married. In 1782 William Bartram was elected Professor of Botany in the University of Pennsylvania, but declined the position on account of ill health. He became a member of the American Philosophical Society in 1786, and was elected to other learned societies in both Europe and America. He was an ingenious mechanic, and, as before intimated, was skillful in drawing and painting. Most of the illustrations in Prof. Barton's *Elements of Botany* were from his drawings. His botanical labors brought to light many interesting plants not previously known. But this was not his only field. He made the most complete and correct list of American birds before Wilson's *Ornithology,* and, in fact, his encouragement and assistance was largely instrumental in making that work possible. Among William Bartram's scientific correspondents were the Rev. Henry Muhlenberg and F. A. Michaux, to whom he furnished seeds. A manuscript diary kept by him, which was presented to the Academy of Sciences of Philadelphia in 1885, by Mr. Thomas Meehan, is rich in ornithological, botanical, and meteorological notes, also records of personal experiences, all of which are of great interest. His death occurred suddenly from the rupture of a blood vessel in the lungs, July 22, 1823, in the eighty-fifth year of his age.

Besides his *Travels,* William Bartram was the author of *Anecdotes of a Crow* and *Description of Certhia.* In 1789, he wrote *Observations on the Creek and Cherokee Indians,* which was published in 1851, in the *Transactions of the American Ethnological Society,* Vol. III. . . .

In the old stone house the great fireplace has been filled up, although but few other changes have been made. The building is full of curious turns and cubbyholes. Connected with a cupboard in the sitting room is a recess running behind the chimney, which furnished a safe depository in winter for specimens that frost would injure. Back of the sitting room, in the wing of the building, is an apartment with large windows looking toward the south, which was the botanist's conservatory. Here were reared such plants as could not stand a Pennsylvania winter — gathered in Florida or the Carolinas, or sent from Europe. In the grounds close to the river is a great imbedded rock, hewn flat, in which is cut a wide, deep groove. This is the nether stone of John Bartram's cider mill. The Botanic Garden remained in the possession of Colonel Carr till about 1850, when it became the property of Mr. A. M. Eastwick. This gentleman had derived much pleasure from visiting it as a boy, and was resolved to preserve it without the sacrifice of a tree or shrub. In 1853 a *Handbook of Ornamental Trees,* by Mr. Thomas Meehan, was published, the main purpose of which, as stated in the preface, was to describe the trees then in the Bartram garden. After Eastwick's death, the fate of the garden was somewhat dubious. His executors saw no duty but to get as much money out of the estate as possible. About 1880 Prof. C. D. Sargent, of Harvard University, obtained the promise of a private subscription to buy the old garden, and a price was agreed upon, but the executors withdrew from the agreement. In 1882 Mr. Thomas Meehan became a member of the Common Council of Philadelphia and at once introduced a scheme for small parks for the city, in which the Bartram place was included. Repeated re-elections enabled him to follow the matter up, and finally, in the spring of 1891, the city took possession of the property, and put a superintendent in charge of it. The great gale of September 1875 and some fifteen years of neglect had had their effect among the trees, but many planted by the botanist's own hands yet remain (1896). It should be a source of gratitude to all cultivators of science that this relic of the beginnings of botany in America is now assured of preservation.*

* Now, in 1957, the Bartram house and grounds are owned by the City of Philadelphia and are under the custody of the Fairmount Park Commission. . . . The house and gardens are open to the public and there is a telephone listed under City of Philadelphia, Bartram's Garden. [Ed.]

1. Son William Reports on the
Life of His Father*

RICHARD BARTRAM, the grandfather of the subject of this sketch, came from England to America with the adherents of the famous William Penn, proprietor of Pennsylvania, towards the close of the seventeenth century. He settled a plantation in the township of Marpole, and county of Chester, at the distance of twelve miles from Philadelphia.

From Richard descended two sons, John and Isaac. The former inherited the paternal estate in Marpole, and the latter settled upon another plantation in Darby, a few miles distance. John, the elder, had two sons by his first marriage, namely, James and John, early in the beginning of the eighteenth century; and by his second marriage, a son and daughter, named William and Elizabeth. Soon after his second marriage, he removed to North Carolina, where he settled a plantation at a place called Whitoc, and there, with the greatest part of the settlement, fell a victim to the rage of the Whitoc Indians. The widow and her two children were carried away captives by the Indians, but were afterwards redeemed, and returned to Pennsylvania.

John, the celebrated botanist and naturalist, inherited the estate in Darby, which was left to him by his uncle Isaac.

* The sources of all Bartram material in this book are given on pages 385 to 388. The reference numbers, as at the end of this chapter, are keyed to the sources found on those pages. [Ed.]

Being born in a newly-settled colony, of not more than fifty years' establishment in a country where the sciences of the old continent were little known, it cannot be supposed that he could derive great advantages or assistance from school learning or literature. He had, however, all or most of the education that could, at that time, be acquired in country schools; and whenever an opportunity offered, he studied such of the Latin and Greek grammars and classics as his circumstances enabled him to purchase. And he always sought the society of the most learned and virtuous men.

He had a very early inclination to the study of physic and surgery. He even acquired so much knowledge in the practice of the latter science as to be very useful; and, in many instances, he gave great relief to his poor neighbors, who were unable to apply for medicines and assistance to the physicians of the city (Philadelphia). It is extremely probable that, as most of his medicines were derived from the vegetable kingdom, this circumstance might point out to him the necessity of, and excite a desire for, the study of botany.

He seemed to have been designed for the study and contemplation of Nature, and the culture of philosophy. Although he was bred a farmer or husbandman, as a means of procuring a subsistence, he pursued his avocations as a philosopher, being ever attentive to the works and operations of Nature. While engaged in ploughing his fields and mowing his meadows, his inquisitive eye and mind were frequently exercised in contemplation of vegetables; the beauty and harmony displayed in their mechanism; the admirable order of system, which the great Author of the universe has established throughout their various tribes, and the equally wonderful powers of their generation, the progress of their growth, and the various stages of their maturity and perfection.

He was, perhaps, the first Anglo-American who conceived the idea of establishing a botanic garden, for the reception and cultivation of the various vegetables, natives of the country, as well as of exotics, and of traveling for the discovery and acquisition of them. He purchased a convenient piece of ground, on the banks of the Schuylkill, at the distance of about three miles from Philadelphia; a happy situation, possessing every soil and exposure, adapted to the various nature of vegetables. Here he built, with his own hands, a large and comfortable house of hewn stone, and laid out a garden containing about five acres of ground.

He began his travels at his own expense. His various excursions rewarded his labors with the possession of a great variety of new, beautiful, and useful trees, shrubs, and herbaceous plants. His garden, at length, attracting the visits and notice of many virtuous and ingenious persons, he was encouraged to persist in his labors.

Not yet content with having thus begun the establishment of this school of science and philosophy, in the blooming fields of Flora, he sought farther means for its perfection and importance, by communicating his discoveries and collections to the curious in Europe and elsewhere, for the benefit of science, commerce, and the useful arts.

Having arranged his various collections and observations in natural history, one of his particular friends* undertook to convey them to the celebrated Peter Collinson, of London. This laid the foundation of that friendship and correspondence which continued uninterrupted, and even increasing,

* Joseph Brentnal, Merchant, of Philadelphia.

for near fifty years of the lives of these two eminent men. Collinson, ever the disinterested friend, communicated from time to time, to the learned in Europe, the discoveries and observations of Bartram. It was principally through the interest of Collinson that he became acquainted, and entered into a correspondence, with many of the most celebrated literary characters in Europe, and was elected a member of the Royal Society of London, of that of Stockholm, &c.

He employed much of his time in traveling through the different provinces of North America, at that time subject to England. Neither dangers nor difficulties impeded or confined his researches after objects in natural history. The summits of our highest mountains were ascended and explored by him. The lakes Ontario, Iroquois, and George; the shores and sources of the rivers Hudson, Delaware, Schuylkill, Susquehanna, Allegheny, and St. Juan were visited by him at an early period, when it was truly a perilous undertaking to travel in the territories, or even on the frontiers, of the aborigines.

He traveled several thousand miles in Carolina and Florida. At the advanced age of near seventy years, embarking on board of a vessel at Philadelphia, he set sail for Charleston, in South Carolina. From thence he proceeded by land, through part of Carolina and Georgia, to St. Augustine, in East Florida. When arrived at the last-mentioned place, being then appointed botanist and naturalist for the King of England, for exploring the provinces, he received his orders to search for the sources of the great river St. Juan.

Leaving St. Augustine, he traveled by land to the banks of the river and, embarking in a boat at Picolata, ascended that great and beautiful river (near 400 miles) to its sources, attending carefully to its various branches and the lakes connected with it. Having ascended on one side of the river, he descended by the other side, until the confluence of the Picolata with the sea.

In the course of this voyage, or journey, he made an accurate draught and survey of the various widths, depths, courses, and distances, both of the main stream and of the lakes and branches. He also noted the situation and quality of the soil, the vegetable and animal productions, all of which were highly approved by the Governor, and sent to the Board of Trade and Plantations, in England, by whose direction they were ordered to be published, for the benefit of the new colony.

Mr. Bartram was a man of modest and gentle manners, frank, cheerful, and of great good nature; a lover of justice, truth, and charity. He was himself an example of filial, conjugal, and parental affection. His humanity, gentleness, and compassion were manifested upon all occasions, and were even extended to the animal creation. He was never known to have been at enmity with any man. During the whole course of his life, there was not a single instance of his engaging in a litigious contest with any of his neighbors, or others. He zealously testified against slavery; and, that his philanthropic precepts on this subject might have their due weight and force, he gave liberty to a most valuable male slave, then in the prime of his life, who had been bred up in the family almost from his infancy.

He was, through life, a striking example of temperance, especially in the use of vinous and spirituous liquors; not from a passion of parsimony, but from a principle of morality. His common drink was pure water, small-beer, or cider mixed with milk. Nevertheless, he always kept a good and plentiful table. Once a year, commonly on a New Year's day, he made a liberal entertainment for his relations and particular friends.

His stature was rather above the middle size, and upright. His visage was long, and his countenance expressive of a degree of dignity, with a happy mixture of animation and sensibility.

He was naturally industrious and active, both in body and mind; observing, that he never could find more time than he could employ to satisfaction and advantage, either in improving conversation, or in some healthy and useful bodily exercise: he was astonished to hear men complaining that they were weary of their time, and knew not what they should do.

He was born and educated in the sect called Quakers. But his religious creed may, perhaps, be best collected from a pious distich engraven by his own hand in very conspicuous characters upon a stone placed over the front window of the apartment, which was destined for study and philosophical retirement.

> *'Tis God alone, Almighty Lord,*
> *The Holy One by me ador'd.   J.B.*
> *1770.*

This may show the simplicity and sincerity of his heart, which never harbored, or gave countenance to, dissimulation. His mind was frequently employed, and he enjoyed the highest pleasure, in the contemplation of Nature, as exhibited in the great volume of Creation. He generally concluded the narratives of his journeys with pious and philosophical reflections upon the Majesty and Power, the Perfection and the Beneficence, of the Creator.

He had a high veneration for the moral and religious

precepts of the Scriptures, both old and new. He read them often, particularly on the sabbath day; and recommended to his children and family the following precept, as comprehending the great principles of moral duty in man:

Do Justice, love Mercy, and Walk Humbly before God.

He never coveted old age, and often observed to his children and friends that he sincerely desired that he might not live longer than he could afford assistance to himself: for he was unwilling to be a burthen to his friends, or useless in society; and that when death came to perform his office, there might not be much delay. His wishes in these respects were gratified in a remarkable manner, for although he lived to be about eighty years of age, yet he was cheerful and active to almost the last hours. His illness was very short. About half an hour before he expired he seemed, though but for a few moments, to be in considerable agony, and pronounced these words, "I want to die." [1]

2. John Bartram's Report of a Trip Taken in 1743

[*John Bartram, the outstanding botanist of his period, had contemplated a trip into central Pennsylvania and New York for the purpose of collecting seeds and specimens, the former for the London market and the latter for his own Botanical Garden in Philadelphia.*

[*In 1743, Conrad Weiser was ordered to make a treaty of peace between the Iroquois and Virginia, and Bartram took this opportunity to accompany him to the Iroquois Castle. These two men were accompanied by the cartographer Lewis Evans. They set out in July and traveled west and north to Oswego, New York. This chapter relates the adventures of the party. It contains a graphic picture of the country through which they passed, together with the flora which Bartram observed.* Author unknown.]

[*This visit to the Central Council Fire of the Six Nations, is especially interesting, not only as having been made at so early a date, but it affords us a plan and view of the Long-House, peculiar to the tribes of that Confederacy.* Field.]

[*The following journal was kept by Mr. John Bartram in his travels from his house near Philadelphia to Onondago, and Oswego on the Cadarakin on Ontario Lake. It is a misfortune to the public that this ingenious person had not a liberal education; it is no wonder, therefore, that his style is not so clear as we would wish. However, in every piece of his, there is evident mark of much good sense, penetration, and sincerity, joined to a commendable curios-*

*ity. It was to gratify this disposition and that of his correspondents'
requests in England that he undertook, after other expeditions, to
accompany Mr. Weiser on the business of government, and was
honored with the encouragement of some very judicious and generous noblemen here, since dead, and the friendship of the skill-
fulest botanists in Europe.*

[*It may be proper to inform the reader that the negotiations set
on foot in the conferences here related, produced a congress at
Lancaster in Pennsylvania, begun the 22nd of June following,
which was attended with the wished for success, in an amicable
adjustment of all differences between the parties, under the media-
tion of the governors of Pennsylvania.*

[*This journal was by several accidents prevented from arriving
in England till June 1750, and is now made public without the
author's knowledge, at the instance of several gentlemen who were
more in number than could conveniently peruse the manuscript.
Had he intended it for publication he would have made it probably more entertaining and perhaps retrenched parts that made
the least figure in it.*

[*The friend to whom he sent it thought himself not at liberty to
make any material alterations. . . . But when it is considered how
great importance an intimate acquaintenance with the natural
state of this vast wilderness and its capacity of further improvement
is to Great Britain, and how little the endeavors of our countrymen have yet advanced this work, while we are indebted to our
most dangerous rivals (the French) for the little we do know, who
will, if possible, repay themselves by excluding us from all we do
not actually cultivate, and leave us that only while they want
power to take it from us; I cannot but think this plain but sensible piece merits attention. . . .*

[*Knowledge must precede a settlement, and when Pennsylvania
and Virginia shall have extended their habitations to the branches
of the Mississippi that water these provinces on the west side of
the Blue Mountains, we may reasonably hope to insure a safe and
early communication with the remote known parts of North America, and to secure the possession of a domain unbounded by any*

present discoveries. Preface to the *Journal,* editor's name unknown.]

The 3d of July 1743, I set out from my house on the Schuylkill River . . . and traveled beyond Perkiomy Creek the
first day.* The weather was exceeding hot. The 4th we set out
before day . . . crossed the Schuylkill, and rode along the
west side over rich bottoms, after which we ascended the
Flying Hill (so called from the great numbers of wild turkeys
that used to fly from them to the plains). Here we had a fine
prospect of the Blue Mountains, and over the rich vale of
Tulpehocken, the descent into which is steep and stony.
Through this vale we traveled west, and by the way observed
a large spring sixteen foot deep and about twenty yards wide,
which issued out of a limestone rock. At night we lodged at
Conrad Weiser's, who is the general interpreter, and who
went with us. . . .

July 5th . . . Having called on a man who was to go with
us and carry part of our provisions to Shamokin (he could
not get his horse shod that day), we rode to William Parson's
plantation, who received and entertained us very kindly. His
house is about six miles from the Blue Mountains.

The 6th, we set forward and ascended the first Blue Ridge.
. . . We were warned by a well-known alarm to keep our
distance from an enraged rattlesnake that had put himself
into a coiled posture of defense within a dozen yards of our
path, but we punished his rage by striking him dead on the
spot: he had been highly irritated by an Indian dog that
barked eagerly at him but was cunning enough to keep out

* John Bartram's record now begins. [Ed.]

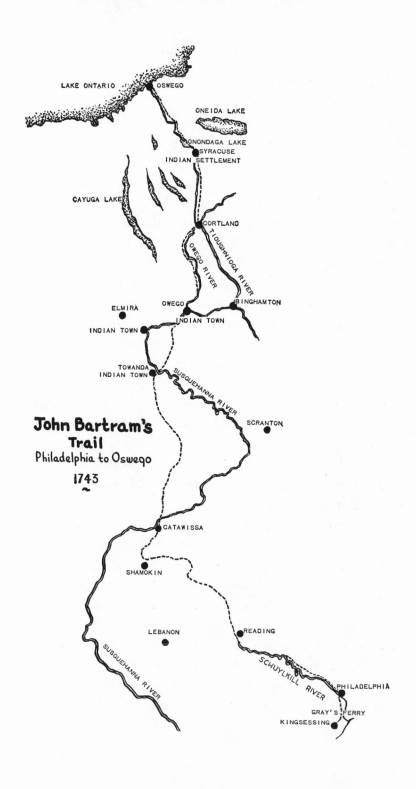

John Bartram's Trail
Philadelphia to Oswego
1743
~

of his reach, or nimble enough to avoid the snake when he sprung at him. We took notice that while provoked, he contracted the muscles of his scales so as to appear very bright and shining, but after the mortal stroke, his splendor became much diminished. This is likewise the case of many of our snakes. . . .

July 8th. [Town of Shamokin, Pa.] It contains eight cabins near the river's bank right opposite the mouth of the west branch that interlocks with the branches of the Allegheny. It is by means of this neighborhood that we may reasonably hope, when these parts shall be better known, that a very beneficial trade may be extended through the Hokio into the Mississippi and its branches among the numerous nations that inhabit their banks. It is to be wished that the English government in these parts had been more diligent in searching and surveying the heads of their own rivers and the sources of the others that run westwards from the backs of their respective provinces. Yet enough is already known to justify the surmises of Mr. de la Salle, who in his *Journal* addressed to the Count de Frontenac, expresses his fears lest the English, from their settlements, should possess themselves of the trade on the Mississippi.

I quartered in a trader's cabin, and about midnight the Indians came and called up him and his squaw, who lay in a separate part where the goods were deposited, whether together or no I did not ask. She sold the Indians rum, with which being quickly intoxicated, men and women began first to sing and then dance round the fire. Then the women would run out to other cabins and soon return, leaving the men singing and dancing the war dance, which continued all the next day. An Englishman, when very drunk, will fall fast asleep for the most part, but an Indian, when merry, falls to

dancing, running, and shouting, which violent action probably may disperse the fumes of the liquor, that had he sat still
or remained quiet, might have made him drowsy. . . .

As soon as we alighted they showed us where to lay our
baggage, and brought us a bowl of boiled squashes, cold; this
I then thought poor entertainment, but before I came back
I had learnt not to despise good Indian food. This hospitality
is agreeable to the honest simplicity of ancient times, and is
so punctually adhered to, that not only what is already
dressed is immediately set before a traveler, but the most
pressing business is postponed to prepare the best they can
get for him, keeping it as a maxim that he must always be
hungry. Of this we found the good effects in the flesh and
bread they got ready for us.

July 9th. After breakfast Lewis Evans and myself went to
the point of the mountain, close to the northeast branch, a
mile and a half up the river from our lodging. Good, level,
rich land all the way. We walked thither, carrying our blankets with us, and slept nearly three hours. Here we regulated
our journey, and having taken a pleasant view of the range
of mountains, and the charming plain of Shamokin, two
miles long and above one broad, skirted west and north by
the river and encompassed east and partly south with lofty
hills beside a fine vale bordering the northwest branch. We
returned to town and dined. In the afternoon we borrowed a
canoe, and paddled up the west branch. It is near two-thirds as
broad as the northeast or main river. I went ashore on the
south side to a point of a hill to look for curiosities but found
none; the rock consisted of a dark-colored shelly stone. Then
we diverted ourselves by swimming. The water was chin deep
most of the breadth, and so clear one might have seen a pin
at the bottom. At night I hung up my blanket like a ham-

mock, that I might be out of the reach of the fleas, troublesome and constant guests in an Indian hut; but I found my
contrivance too cool for a place open on all sides, tho' covered
with a kind of granary, especially with the wind blowing cold
from the northwest.

10th. We departed in the morning with Shickalamy and
his son, he being the chief man in the town, which consisted
of Delaware Indians. He was of the Six Nations, or rather a
Frenchman, born in Montreal and adopted by the Oneidoes,
after being taken prisoner. But his own son told me he was
of the Cayuga Nation, that of his mother, agreeable to the
Indian rule *Partus sequitur ventrum,* which is as reasonable
among them as among cattle, since the whole burden of bringing up falls on her. Therefore, in the case of separation, the
children fall to her share.

We had many advantages from the company of these
guides. They were perfectly acquainted with that part of the
country, and being of the Six Nations they were both a credit
and protection; and also as we went to accommodate the
differences and allay the heartburnings that had been raised
by a late skirmish on the back of Virginia, between some of
these nations and the English, we could not but derive a
confidence from the company of a chief. . . .

July 11th. About break of day it began to rain, and the
Indians made us a covering of bark got after this manner.
They cut the tree round through the bark near the root and
made a like incision about seven feet above it. These horizontal ones are joined by a perpendicular cut, on each side of
which they after loosen the bark from the wood. Hewing a
pole at the small end, gradually tapering a wedge about two
feet, they force it in till they have completed the separation
all round. The bark parts whole from the tree, one of which,

a foot in diameter, yields a piece seven feet long and about three wide. And having now prepared four forked sticks, they are set into the ground, the longer in front. On these they lay the crosspoles and on them the bark. This makes a good tight shelter in warm weather. The rain was quickly over, but as it continued cloudy, we did not care to leave our shed. Here the Indians shot a young deer that afforded us a good feast. . . .

12th. . . . Descending down a steep hill northeast, we came to a rich bottom by the river; hence north after northwest to a creek, and so through a grove of white walnut and locust; now onto some higher level land half a mile broad, and now some higher level land affording oak, hickory, walnut, locust, and pitch pine. Our course generally north-northwest till riding over a hazel plane we met eight Shawanese Indians on horseback coming from Allegheny, and going to Wiomick upon an important account, as they said. We turned back with them to the adjacent wood and sat down together under a shady oak. The squaws which they brought to wait upon them kindled a fire to light their pipes. Our interpreter and Shickalamy sat down with them to smoke, the customary civility when two parties meet. Conrad Weiser, understanding they were some of the chiefs of the Shawanese, acquainted them with our business at Onondago, a compliment they were so well pleased with that they gave us the *tohay,* a particular Indian expression of approbation, and which is very difficult for a white man to imitate well. After a half hour's grave discourse, several of them went to catch the horses, and one of the principal men made a handsome speech, with a pleasant, well-composed countenance, to our interpreter, to the following effect: "That they were sensible with what unwearied diligence he had hitherto been instrumental in preserving peace and good harmony between the Indians and white people, and that as they could not but now commend the prudence and zeal with which he had effected this laudable purpose, so they earnestly entreated and fiercely hoped he would still persevere in the same endeavors and with the same success, and that his good offices may never be wanting on any future occasion. . . ." [That night] we lodged within about fifty yards of a hunting cabin, where there were two men, a squaw and a child. The men came to our fire and made us a present of some venison, and invited Mr. Weiser, Shickalamy, and his son to a feast at their cabin. It is incumbent on those who partake of a feast of this sort to eat all that comes to their share or burn it. And Weiser, being a traveler, was entitled to a double share, but he, being not very well, was forced to take the benefit of a liberty indulged him, of eating by proxy, and called me. But both being unable to cope with it, Lewis came to our assistance, notwithstanding which we were hard set to get down the neck and throat, for these were allotted to us. Now we had experienced the utmost bounds of their indulgence, for Lewis, ignorant of the ceremony of throwing the bone to the dog — tho' hungry dogs are generally nimble, the Indians are more nimble — laid hold of it first and committed it to the fire, religiously covering it over with hot ashes. This seems to be a kind of offering, perhaps first fruits to the Almighty Power to crave future success in the approaching hunting season, and was celebrated with as much decency and more silence than many superstitious ceremonies. . . .

14th . . . We kept generally a north-northeast course, mostly along rich bottoms interspersed with large spruce and white pine, oak, beech, and plane tree, ginseng, and many more. We frequently passed the creek (which was very strong) for the mountains often closed on one side. [The creek] was big enough to turn two mills. At 9 o'clock the Indians fished for trout, but caught none, being provided with no other means of taking them but by poles sharpened at the end to strike them, and the water was deep. At the foot of a hill we crossed the creek once more, and rode along a fine bottom full of great nettles. The timber was sugar birch, sugar maples, oaks, and poplar. Our course, northwest, continued till after 12 o'clock, then followed the east branch north-northeast about a mile along a rich bottom until we found a licking pond, where we dined. The back parts of our country are full of these licking ponds. Some are of black sulphurous mud, some of pale clay. The deer and elk are fond of licking this clay, so that the pond becomes elongated to a rood or half an acre. The soil, I suppose, contains some saline particles agreeable to the deer, who come many miles to one of these places. There had been a great elk there that morning, but the Indians told us that many years ago some Indians quarreled there, in the squabble one lost his life, and that this made the deer keep from thence for many years. . . .

16th. We began our journey up a little hill, steep and somewhat stony, and then through oak, chestnut, huckleberries, and honeysuckle, the land poor, sometimes white pine, spruce and laurel. At half an hour after seven northeast through a great white pine and spruce swamp, full of roots and an abundance of old trees lying on the ground, or leaning against live ones. They stood so thick that we concluded it almost impossible to shoot a man at 100-yards' distance, let him stand never so fair. The straight bodies of these trees stood so thick a bullet must hit one before it could fly 100 yards in the most open part. . . . We dined at half an hour

after twelve and set out again at three, course north along a
steep hillside full of excellent flat whetstones of all sizes,
from half a foot to four feet long, and two inches to a foot
wide, and from half an inch to a foot thick. I brought one
home which I have used to whet my ax, scythe, chisels, and
knife, and it is yet very little the worse for wear. It is as fine
as the English rag, but of a blackish color. . . . [A town
called Tohicon] lies in a rich neck between the branch and
main river . . . the Indians welcomed us by beating on their
drums as soon as they saw us over by the branch (of Cayaga),
and continued beating after the English manner as we rode
to the house. Laid in our luggage and entered ourselves. The
house is about thirty feet long and finest of any I saw among
them. The Indians cut long grass and laid it on the floor for
us to sit or lie on. Several of the men came and sat down and
smoked their pipes, one of which was six foot long, the head
of stone, the stem a reed. After this they brought victuals in
the usual manner. Here I observed for the first time in this
journey, that the worms which had done much mischief in
several parts of our Province, by destroying the grass and
even corn for two summers, had done the same thing here,
and had eaten off the blades of their maize and long white
grass, so that the stems of both stood naked four foot high.
I saw some of the naked dark-colored grubs half an inch long;
tho' most of them were gone, yet I could perceive they were
the same that had visited us two months before. They clear all
the grass in their way in any meadow they get into, and seem
to be periodical as the locusts and caterpillars, the latter of
which I am afraid will do us great mischief next summer. . . .

July 17th. [An Indian pawawing.] They cut a parcel of
poles about the bigness of hop poles, which they stick in
the ground in a circle about five foot diameter, and then

bring them together at the top and tie them in the form of an oven, where the conjurer placeth himself. Then his assistants cover the cage over close with blankets and, to make it more suffocating, hot stones are rolled in. After all this the priest must cry aloud, and agitate his body after the most violent manner, till nature has almost lost all her faculties before the stubborn spirit will become visible to him, which they say is generally in the shape of some bird. There is usually a stake driven into the ground about four foot high, and painted. I suppose this they design for the *winged airy Being* to perch upon while he reveals to the invocant what he has taken so much pain to know. However, I find different nations have different ways of obtaining the pretended information. Some have a bowl of water into which they often look when their strength is almost exhausted and their senses failing, to see whether the spirit is ready to answer their demands. I have seen many of these places in my travels. They differ from their sweating coops in that they are often far from water and have a stake by the cage, yet both have a heap of red-hot stones put in. At eleven we dressed our dinner, and found an Indian by the river side resting himself. All his provision was a dried eel. This he made us a present of, and we gave him a share of our dinner.

Their way of roasting eels is thus: They cut a stick about three foot long and as thick as one's thumb. They split it about a foot down, and when the eel is gutted, they coil it between the two sides of the stick and bind the top close, which keeps the eel flat, and then stick one end in the ground before a good fire. . . .

18th. This morning we sent an Indian with a string of wampum to Onondago, to acquaint them with our coming, and the business we came about, that they might send mes-

sengers to the several nations as soon as possible, for this
town serves the five nations as Baden does the thirteen can-
tons of Switzerland, with this difference, that Onondago is at
the same time the capital of the canton. . . .

19th. . . . After dinner we soon began to mount up a
pretty steep hill, covered with oak, birch, ash, and higher up
an abundance of chestnut and some hickory. This is middling
land, the produce the same for three miles as our land bears
with us. It lies very high, and when cleared will have an
extensive prospect of fertile vales on all sides. We then rode
down a long rich hill of moderate descent where grew an
abundance of gooseberries. All the trees were crowded with
wild pigeons, which, I suppose, breed in these lofty trees. I
found many fossils on this hill. . . .

20th . . . After dinner we passed a branch of the great
Susquehannah, down which lake canoes may go quite to
where the river is navigable for boats. On the banks I found
Gale [a shrub] like the European. This is the nearest branch
of the Susquehannah river to that of Onondago. Leaving this
on our right, to our left we perceived a hill where the Indians say corn, tobacco, and squashes were found on the
following occasion: An Indian (whose wife had eloped) came
hither to hunt and to purchase another wife with his skins.
He espied a young squaw alone at the hill. Going to her and
asking where she came from, he received for an answer that
she came from heaven to provide sustenance for the poor
Indians, and if he came to that place twelve months after,
he would find food there. He came accordingly and found
corn, squashes, and tobacco which were propagated from
thence and spread through the country. . . . This silly story
is religiously held for truth among them. . . .

In the afternoon it thunder'd hard pretty near us, but

Passenger Pigeons

rained little. We observed the tops of the trees to be so close to one another for many miles together, that there is no seeing which way the clouds drive nor which way the wind sets, and it seems almost as if the sun had never shone on the ground since the creation. About sunset it cleared up and we encamped on the left branch of the Susquehannah. The night following, it thundered and rained very soft, and took us at a disadvantage for we had made no shelter to keep off the rain, neither could we see it till just over our heads, and it began to fall.

One of our Indians cut four sticks five feet long and stuck both ends in the ground, at two-foot distance, one from another. Over these he spread his match coat and crept through them, and then fell to singing. In the meantime we were setting poles slantwise in the ground, tying others across them, over which we spread our blankets and crept close under it with a fire before us and fell asleep.

I waked a little after midnight, and found our fire almost

out, so I got the hatchet and felled a few saplings which I laid on and made a rousing fire, and lying down once more, I slept sound all night.

21st. In the morning, when we had dried our blankets, we kept along the side of the hill, gradually ascending, the soil good, timber tall, and an abundance of ginseng. Here the mosquitoes were very troublesome, it being foggy. . . . We stopped at half an hour after eleven. This hill was a little sandy, with some large pines growing upon it. Here we walked and looked about us, not having had such an opportunity for two days. We had a fine prospect over the vale of the great mountain we had just crossed and which differed so remarkably from all I had ever been upon before, in its easy and fruitful ascent and descent, in its great width, everywhere crowned with noble and lofty woods, but above all, in its being entirely free from naked rocks and steep cliffs. . . . After having enjoyed this enchanting prospect, we descended easily for several miles over good land producing sugar maples, many of which the Indians had tapped to make sugar of the sap. There were also oaks, hickory, white walnuts, plums and some apple trees, full of fruit. The Indians had set long bushes all round the trees at a little distance; I suppose to keep the small children from stealing the fruit before they were ripe. Here we halted and turned our horses to grass, while the inhabitants cleared a cabin for our reception. They brought us victuals, and we dispatched a messenger immediately to Onondago to let them know how near we were, it being within four miles. All the Indians, men, women, and children, came to gaze at us and our horses. The little boys and girls climbed on the roofs of their cabins, about ten in number, to enjoy a fuller view. We set out about ten and traveled over good land all the way, mostly an easy descent, some limestone, then down the east hill, over ridges of limestone rock, but generally a moderate descent into the fine vale where this capital (if I may so call it) is situated.

We alighted at the council house, where the chiefs had already assembled to receive us, which they did with a grave cheerful complaisance, according to their custom. They showed us where to lay our baggage and repose ourselves during our stay with them, which was in the two end apartments of this large house. The Indians that came with us were placed over against us. This cabin is about eighty feet long, and seventeen broad. The common passage six feet wide. The apartments on each side five feet, raised a foot above the passage by a long sapling hewed square and fitted with joists that go from it to the back of the house. On these joists they lay large pieces of bark, and on extraordinary occasions spread mats made of rushes; this favor we had. On these floors they sit or lie down, everyone as he will. The apartments are divided from each other by boards of bark, six or seven foot long, from the lower floor to the upper, on which they put their lumber. When they have eaten their hominy, as they sit in their apartments before the fire, they can put the bowl overhead, having not above five foot to reach. They sit on the floor, sometimes at each end, but mostly at one. They have a shed to put their wood into in winter or, in the summer, to sit in to converse or play. This has a door to the south. All the sides and roof of the cabin are made of bark, bound fast to poles set in the ground, and bent round at the top, or set aflat for the roof as we set our rafters. Over each fireplace they leave a hole to let out the smoke, which in rainy weather they cover with a piece of bark, and this they can easily reach with a pole to push it on one side or quite over the hole. After this model most of their cabins are built.

The fine vale of Onondago runs north and south, a little inclining to the west, and is nearly a mile wide where the town is situated, and excellent soil. The river that divides this charming vale is two, three, or four foot deep, very full of trees fallen across or driven into heaps by the torrents. The town in its present state is about two or three miles long, yet the scattered cabins on both sides of the water are not above forty in number. Many of them hold two families, but all stand single, and rarely more than four or five near each other, so that the whole town is a mixture of cabins, interspersed with great patches of high grass, bushes, and shrubs, some of peas, corn and squashes; limestone bottom composed of fossils and sea shells. . . .

At night, soon after we were laid down to sleep, and our fire almost burnt out, we were entertained by a comical fellow, disfigured in as odd a dress as Indian folly could invent. He had on a clumsy vizard of wood color'd black, with nose four or five inches long, a grinning mouth set awry, furnished with long teeth. Round the eyes circles of bright brass, surrounded by a large circle of white paint; from his forehead hung long tresses of buffalo hair. From the catch part of his head, ropes were made of the plaited husks of Indian corn. I cannot recollect the whole of his dress but it was equally uncouth. He carried, in one hand, a large staff; in the other a calabash with small stones in it, for a rattle, and this he rubbed up and down his staff. He would sometimes hold up his head and make a hideous noise like the braying of an ass. He came in at the further end and made this note at first; whether it was because he would not surprise us too suddenly I can't say. I asked Conrad Weiser, who as well as myself lay next to the alley, what noise that was and Shickalamy, the Indian chief and our companion, who I supposed thought me somewhat scared, called out, "Lie still, John." I never heard him speak so much plain English before.

The jack-pudding presently came up to us, and an Indian boy came with him and kindled our fire, that we might see his glittering eyes and antic postures as he hobbled around the fire. Sometimes he would turn the buffalo's hair on one side that we might take a better view of his ill-favored phys. When he had tired himself, which was some time after he had tired us, the boy who had attended him struck two or three smart blows on the floor, at which the hobgoblin seemed surprised, and on repeating them he jumped fairly out of doors and disappeared. I suppose this was to divert us and get some tobacco for himself, for as he danced about he would hold out his hand to any he came to, to receive this gratification which as often as anyone gave him he would return an awkward compliment. In this I found it no new diversion to any but myself. In my whim I saw a vizard of this kind hang by the side of one of their cabins to another town. After this farce we endeavored to compose ourselves to sleep but toward morning were again disturbed by a drunken squaw coming into the cabin frequently, complimenting us and singing.

23rd. We hired a guide to go with us to the salt spring, four or five miles off, down the river on the west side of its mouth, being most of the way good land, and near the mouth very rich; from whence it runs westward near a quarter of a mile, a kind of sandy beach adjoining to the bank of the river, containing three or four acres. Here the Indians dig holes, about two foot deep, which soon fill with brine. They dip their kettles and boil the contents until salt remains at bottom. There was a family residing [there] at the time. The boys in the lake fishing, the squaw fetching water, gathering wood, and making a fire under the kettle, while the husband was basking himself on the sand under the bushes. We filled our gallon keg full of water and brought it back to town, where we boiled it to about a pound of salt.

24th. Lewis and I hired a guide to go with us to Oswego for 16s. Our intention was more to get provisions for our journey home than to gratify our curiosity. In the meantime, Conrad stayed at Onondago to treat with the Indian chiefs about the skirmishes in Virginia, with a view to incline them singly in favor of our application before they assembled in council. Here I cannot help observing, it was scarcely ever known that an Indian chief or counselor, once gained so far as to promise his interest, did break his promise, whatever presents have been offered him from another quarter.

30th. . . . This afternoon the chiefs met in council, and three of them spoke for near a quarter of an hour each. Two of these, while speaking, walked backward and forward in the common passage, near two-thirds of its length, with a slow, even pace and much composure and gravity in the countenance. The other delivered what he had to say sitting in the middle, in a graceful tone exhorting them to a close, indissoluble amity and unanimity; for it was by this perfect union their forefathers had conquered their enemies, were respected by their allies, and honored by the world; that they were now met according to their ancient custom, tho' several imminent dangers stood in their way, mountains, rivers, snakes and evil spirits, but that by the assistance of the great Spirit they now saw each other's faces according to appointment.

This the interpreter told me was the opening of the diet, and was in the opinion of these people abundantly sufficient for one day, since there is nothing they hold in contempt so much as precipitation in public councils. Indeed they esteem it at all times a mark of much levity in anyone to return an immediate answer to a serious question, however obvious, and they consequently spin out a treaty, where many points are to be moved, to a great length of time; this is evident from what our conference with them produced afterwards at Lancaster which began the 22nd of June, 1744.

This council was followed by a feast, after 4 o'clock. We all dined together upon four great kettles of Indian corn soup, which we soon emptied, and then every chief retired to his home.

31st. About noon the council sat the second time, and our interpreter had his audience, being charged by the governor with the conduct of the treaty. Conrad Weiser had engaged the Indian speaker to open the affair to the chiefs assembled in council. He made a speech near half an hour and delivered three broad belts and five strings of wampum to the council, on the proper occasions. There was a pole laid across from one chamber to another over the passage; on this their belts and strings were hung, that the council might see them, and here have the matters in remembrance, in confirmation of which they were delivered. The conference held till 3 o'clock, after which we dined. This repast consisted of three kettles of Indian corn soup, or thin hominy, with dried eels and other fish boiled in it, and one kettle full of young squashes and their flowers boiled in water, and a little meal mixed. This dish was but weak food. Last of all was served a great bowl full of Indian dumplings, made of new soft corn, cut or scraped off the ear, then with the addition of some boiled beans lapped well up in Indian corn leaves. This is good hearty provisions. After dinner we had a favorable answer, corroborated by several belts of wampum, with a short speech to each. These we carried away as our tokens of peace and friendship. The harangue concluded with a charge to sit still as yet, for tho' they had dispatched our business first, it was not because they were weary of us, but to make us easy. This compliment preceded other business, which lasted till near sunset, when we regaled on a great bowl of boiled cakes six or seven inches in diameter and about two thick, with another of boiled squash. Soon after, the chiefs in a friendly manner took their leave of us and departed every one to his lodging. This night we treated two of the chiefs that lived in the council hall which, as I mentioned, was our quarters. They drank cheerfully, wishing a long continuance of uninterrupted amity between the Indians and the English.

August 1st. Six of the Antioque Indians had an audience, but when they came to it, could not make themselves understood, tho' provided with an interpreter brought near 700 miles (they said more); he could not understand the Mohawk language but only the Delaware and middling English, so they contrived he should direct his speech to Conrad Weiser in English, and interpret this to the council. They gave broad belts of wampum, three arm belts, and five strings. One was to wipe clean all the blood they had spilt of the five nations; another to raise a tumulus over their graves, and to pick out the sticks, roots or stones, and make it smooth on the top; a third, to cleanse the stomach of the living from gall or anything else that made them sick. A fourth was a cordial to cheer up their spirits; a fifth, to clothe their bodies and keep them warm; a sixth, to join them in mutual friendship; a seventh, to request them to let them settle on a branch of the Susquehannah, another to entreat the five nations that they would take a little care to protect their women from insults while out hunting, and the rest for such like purposes.

This business lasted for four hours. Then we dined on Indian corn and squash soup and boiled bread. . . . These two days the wind was south and warm and several showers to the southeast. The council met at 9 o'clock, and the kettles of soup and a basket of dumplings were brought in for dinner. After dinner the Antioques delivered a belt and a string of wampum, with a complaint that the Marylanders had deposed their king, and desired leave to choose one for themselves. To this, as well as all the articles opened yesterday, the chiefs returned plausible but subtile answers. Then they gave us two strings withal, telling us now that they had thrown water on our fire and we were at liberty to return home when we pleased. They all took their leave and bid us adieu by shaking hands very kindly, and seemingly with much affection. This night the young men got into liquor, kept shouting and singing till morning.

3rd. We prepared for setting forward, and many of the chiefs came once more to take their farewell. Some of them brought us provisions for our journey. We shook hands again and set out at nine.

It was greatly to my mortification that I was forced to return for the most part the same way I came.

19th. Before sunset, I had the pleasure of seeing my own house and family. I found them in good health, and with a sincere mind I returned thanks to the Almighty Power, that had preserved us all.[1]

3. John Bartram's Introduction to Short's
*Medicina Britannica**

THE FIRST MAN that was famous for the practice of physick in the Grecian history was Aesculapius, the son of Apollo, who practiced an age before the Trojan War and, as they say, was so skillful in his applications as to cure diseases and raise the dead. Whereby he gained so great a fame as to have a temple built to him, where those people that were afterwards cured of their infirmities, either by his former directions or their own discoveries, wrote their method of cure particularly and reposed it in that temple. From whence, after six hundred years, and about the time of the captivity of the Jews, the famous Hippocrates, who was born and lived near the temple, in the Island of Coos, searched the medicinal receipts and by those informations and his own ingenuity so enlarged his knowledge in practice of physick as to be, to this day, called the Divine Hippocrates. But the Christians say that he learned his wonderful knowledge from the writings of Solomon and his treatise of plants, which was procured from the captive Jews, or the Chaldeans, after they had burnt the Temple. However, it is certain that most nations, tho' never so barbarous, have made use chiefly of vegetables for the cure of their diseases, and doubtless with good success. And certainly we have in our country a great variety of good

* Published in 1751 by Benjamin Franklin and D. Hall.

50

medicinal plants which may be administered to the people with great advantage, if properly adapted to the season, age, and constitution of the patient, and to the nature, time, and progress of the disease; without which caution, it is not likely that the practice should succeed generally. But it is very common with our people, when a root or herb hath been given with good success several times in a particular disease, and the patient recovered soon after the taking of the medicine, to applaud that medicine exceedingly. Then many that are sick of the same disease, or any other that hath near the like symptoms, apply directly to this famed specific, expecting immediate relief; which often failing by reason of its improper application, as to time, constitution, or nature of the disease, many choice medicines grow out of repute again, are disregarded and little use made of them, especially if they are common and easy come at; whereas, if their virtues were well known, and a skillful person had the administering of them, who knew how to properly correct and fit them to the constitutions of the patients, and join suitable vehicles or companions with them, to lead them to the parts of the body where the distemper lies, then those very herbs or roots, I suppose, might continue or increase their reputation.[1]

4. John Bartram Reports on His Trip to St. John's River, Florida, 1765

Letter from John Bartram to his wife

Savannah, September 4th, 1765

My Dear Spouse:

This day we arrived at Savannah town, in Georgia, by ten o'clock. This was reckoned a very hot day, here, with thunder and showers, thermometer 86°. They have had here, as well as at Charleston, the hottest summer and dryest and wettest August that hath been for many years. Many great bridges are broken down, and we are forced to swim our horses over; but, God Almighty be praised, we are got safe into Georgia; and strange it is, that in all this dreadful season for thunder and prodigious rain, we have not had occasion to put a great coat on, in both the Carolinas, nor rested a day, on account of rain. But we can't be expected to be favored so long; however, God's will be done.

We are hardy and have a good stomach. The people say that if we can weather this month, we need not fear. We have been pestered, these two mornings, with very large mosquitoes; but their bite is not near so venomous as the small sort at Charleston.

The land, in general, is pretty good most of the way from Charleston to this town, and the people very civil to us. We have just been with one of the Governor's council, Mr.

Habersham, to whom our worthy friend, Dr. Wangel, recommended me, to wait on the Governor; who received us with exceeding civility, offering to do me all the kindness that lay in his power; nay, that if any unforeseen accident should happen, if I wanted anything that he could help me to, he would immediately do it.

We design to set out tomorrow toward Augusta, one hundred and fifty miles up the river, where I have many great recommendations from the chiefs in Charleston; but, whether I shall set out from there, through part of the Creek Nation to Augustine, or come back again to this town, I can't say until I consult some very knowing gentlemen at or near Augusta.

We are obliged to be at or near Augustine by the first of October, or thereabouts; so that we have about a month to travel five hundred miles in.

My dear love, my love is to all our children, and friends, as if particularly named, which I have not time nor room, at present, to do. It is by the Governor's favor, as well as information, that I met with this opportunity to deliver it to his care, in a letter to Mr. Lamboll.

Our son Billy, I hope, if we have our health, will be of great service to me. He desires to be remembered to his mother, brothers, sisters, and friends.

September the 5th. Thermometer 80°. Just ready to set out toward Augusta, when we have breakfast. Perhaps the next letter may be dated from Augustine; but if we come back to this town, we shall be writing here.

However, dear love, in the meantime, I remain thy affectionate husband,

John Bartram,
In great haste.

This town is prettily situated on dry sandy ground, and generally good water. Great ships lie close, too, and safe harbor.[1]

On St. John's River, Florida

December the 19th, 1765. Set out from St. Augustine early in the morning, which was frosty, the ground being covered with a white hoar frost. We traveled to Greenwood's house, where we lodged. The roads were very wet, by reason of much rain that lately fell. Here I observed very large oaks, magnolias, liquidamber, near 100 foot high, and guilandina thirty. These grew on a high bluff eight or ten foot above the surface of the river, which rises here eighteen inches at high water, and in dry season is sometimes brackish, but in wet is drinkable to Cowford, which is twelve miles below this, and about twenty-four from its mouth.

20th. Set out for Robert Davis's, whose son the Governor had ordered to take us up to search for the head of the river St. John's; and having necessaries provided, I, my son William, Mr. Yates, and Mr. Davis embarked in a battoe.* Mr. Davis was not only to conduct us but to hunt venison for us, being a good hunter, and his Negro was to row and cook for us all, the Governor bearing all our expenses.

22nd. Thermometer 70, wind southwest. Cleared up, and we set out from Mr. Davis's, but the wind turning south again and blowing hard against us, we rowed but a few miles, then landed and walked on shore, found a pretty evergreen which produces nuts or stones as big as acorns and good to eat, and perhaps may be improved by culture to be near as

* A dug-out canoe. [Ed.]

good as almonds. It bears plentifully, grows eight or ten foot high. The people call them wild limes,* for this shrub much resembles that tree. Here grew chinquapins, the middling ground being generally 300 yards broad to the higher land, some little swamps bordering the small rivulets. We encamped, saw a large alligator. . . .

24th. Cold morning, thermometer 50, wind northwest. Blowed pretty fresh but ceased towards night; landed, and Mr. Davis shot a deer, and his Negro a turkey. I and my son walked in the wood to observe the soil and plants with a man that went to fell some trees for honey; he felled one that contained only some yellow wasps that had taken up their winter quarters in a pine tree. We then walked to another hollow tree, wherein was a swarm of bees and some honey; but both the white people and Indians often meet with such good success as to find great quantities of honey and wax, even ten gallons, more or less, out of one tree; the Indians eat much of it with their venison and sour oranges, of which they cut off one end, then pour the honey into the pulp, and scoop both out as a relishing morsel. . . .

25th. . . . After several miles, by choice swamps near the river, we landed at a point of high ground, which had been an ancient plantation of Indians or Spaniards. Many live oaks grew upon it near two foot in diameter, and plenty of oranges; the soil was sandy but pretty good. We walked back from the river, the ground rising gradually from the swamp on the right hand, where grow small evergreen oaks, hickory, chinquapins, and great magnolias, and in the swamp grows the swamp or northern kind eighteen inches diameter and sixty foot high, liquidamber and red maple three foot diameter, elm, ash, and bays. . . .

* Tallow nut. [Ed.]

27th. Thermometer 50, fine morning. Set out from the Store* and about five miles above landed on a high bluff on the east side of the river at Johnson's Spring, a run of clear and sweet water. Then traveled on foot along thick, woody, but loamy ground, which looked rich on the surface by reason of the continual falling leaves and by the constant evergreen shade rotting the soil, as the sun never shines on the ground strong enough to exhale their virtue before their dissolution, as under deciduous trees. We crossed several small rivulets of clear, sweet water and as many narrow moist swamps. 'Tis diverting to observe the monstrous grapevines, eight inches in diameter, running up the oaks six foot in diameter, swamp magnolia seventy foot high, straight, and a foot in diameter. The great magnolia very large, liquidamber, white, swamp, and live oaks, chinquapins, and cluster cherry all of an uncommon size, mixed with orange trees, either full of fruit or scattered on the ground, where the sun can hardly shine for the green leaves at Christmas, and all in a mass of white or yellow soil sixteen foot more or less above the surface of the river. We came down a steep hill twenty foot high and about 400 or 500 yards from the river, under the foot of which issued out a large fountain† (big enough to turn a mill) of warm, clear water of a very offensive taste, and smelt like bilge water, or the washings of a gun barrel. The sediment that adhered to the trees fallen therein looked of a pale white or bluish cast like milk and water mixed. . . .

January 4th, 1766. Pleasant morning; thermometer 50. Set out from Whitlow's Bluff. The river makes a great, easy bend, and sends out a branch, then the course is from east to south, then southeast. The east banks are sandy, eight or ten foot perpendicular, full of live and swamp oaks, great magnolia,

---

* Spalding's Lower. [Ed.]   † Beecher's Spring. [Ed.]

bay, and liquidamber, but none of them very large. Then pineland to the south bend, then lower ground but on the west side very good swamp. The river then takes a contrary bend to the south, then east, where there is a fine orange grove on each side of the river. At the corner of the south bend, the mouth of a lake appears,* one mile wide and two or three long, which we entered. The course is near south and north; the east side is lined with a narrow cypress swamp and live oaks alternately, the west side with pines; but above, the marshes are very rich, full of water reeds and elders on both sides of the river, which is about thirty yards broad and near three fathom deep. We landed where a sandy bluff joined the river; it produced live and water oak, palms, and bay. Coasting the east side, we soon came to a creek, up which we rowed a mile, in four or six foot of water and thirty yards broad. It was the color of the sea, smelled like bilge water, tasted sweetish and loathsome, warm and very clear, but a whitish matter adhered to the fallen trees near the bottom. The spring† head is about thirty yards broad and boils up from the bottom like a pot. We plumbed it, and found about five fathom of water. Multitudes of fish resort to its head, such as very large gar, cats, and several other sorts; the alligators very numerous either on the shore or swimming on the surface of the water, and some on the bottom, so tame or rather bold as to allow us to row very near them. What a surprising fountain it must be, to furnish such a stream, and what a great space of ground must be taken up in the pinelands, ponds, and savannahs and swamps to support and maintain so constant a fountain, continually boiling right up from under the deep rocks, which undoubtedly continue under most of the country at uncertain depths. . . .

---

* Lake Beresford. [Ed.]   † Blue Springs, west of Orange City. [Ed.]

January 10th. Pleasant morning; thermometer 50. The wolves howled, the first time I heard them in Florida. Here we found a great nest of a wood rat, near four foot high and five in diameter, built of long pieces of dry sticks, all laid confusedly together. On stirring the sticks to observe their structure, a large rat ran out, and up a very high sapling with a young one hanging to its tail.*

January 12th. Fine, clear morning; thermometer 44. Set out, and rowing southeast soon came to a little lake,† which we headed. It seemed surrounded with marsh; some few pines appeared in the distance. We turned back and within a mile came into the main river, which turned various courses southeast and north, but generally east by north; it sends out on each side lagoons and branches that drain those extensive marshes. We came now to a large lake ‡ five or six miles long and near one wide. A long tongue of low marsh comes from the northeast end, where a long hammock of oaks runs a south course. We then rowed out of the lake and between several islands, and came again into the main river, which runs in general an east-and-west course on a sandy bottom, shoaling gradually until the weeds and reeds stopped our battoe in such a manner that it was impossible to push her any farther, though the water was three foot deep, and a small current against us. This we suppose was the draining of the extensive marshes which opened towards the southeast, how far beyond our view we could not determine. The water reeds grew here in the current as thick and close together as on the marsh, that is, as close as hemp; yet the current forceth its way through, and also under the great patches of the pistia, the water persicaria, and other water plants, which are

---

* This is the earliest known description of the wood rat. [Ed.]
† Lake Ruth. [Ed.]   ‡ Loughman. [Ed.]

all entangled together, covering many thousands of acres of the St. John's and its branches, which heads in numerous rich swamps and marshes. We returned to the rich hammock,* where we lodged last night.

January 13th. Fine, pleasant morning; thermometer 54. Set out homeward from the rich hammock, the highest up the river we could land at. Thermometer 79. About one o'clock we came to Round Lake,† so we called it, it being one of the roundest I ever saw, almost surrounded with palmetto, pine, and scrub oak. The lake is six miles more or less in diameter, and generally all over the lake about nine or ten foot deep.

January 14th. Clear morning; wind north. Set out from Coffee Bluff, thermometer 52. . . . Our hunter killed a large he-bear, supposed to weigh 400 pounds; was seven foot long, cut four inches of fat on the side, its forepaw five inches broad, his skin when stretched measured five foot and a half long, and four foot, ten inches in breadth, and yielded fifteen or sixteen gallons of clear oil. Two of us had never eat an ounce of bear's meat before, but we found it to our surprise to be very mild and sweet, above all four-footed creatures, except venison. Although it was an old he-bear, his fat, though I loathed the sight of it at first, was incomparably milder than hog's lard and near as sweet as oil of olives. It was not hunger that engaged us in its favor, for we had a fat young buck and three turkeys fresh shot at the same time, and some boiled with the bear, but we chose the last for its sweetness and good relish.

January 15th. This morning was very warm and a little showery; the mosquitoes were troublesome last night, and

---

* Baxter Mound in Persimmon Hammock. [Ed.]

† Lake Harney. The Bartrams were probably the first Europeans to reach this high point on the St. John's. [Ed.]

this morning the flies blowed our meat before 10 o'clock; the ticks creeping and lizards running about our tent. We stayed here all day to barbecue our meat to serve us down the river, which would soon spoil if not preserved either by fire or salt, and of the last we had only enough to season our victuals with. It rained fast, yet we walked to see several warm springs on the west end of the lake. . . .

January 16th. Very cold, windy day, the lake* being so rough we could not stir; so our hunters rendered the bear's oil and stretched and dried the skin.

January 17th. . . . We cut down three tall palm or cabbage trees and cut out the top bud, the white, tender part, or the rudiments of the great leaves, which will be six or seven foot long when full grown, and the palmed part four in diameter. This tender part will be three or four inches in diameter, tapering near a foot, and cuts as white and tender as a turnip. This they slice into a pot and stew with water; then, when almost tender, they pour some bear's oil into it, and stew it a little longer, when it eats pleasant and much more mild than cabbage. I never eat half as much cabbage at a time, and it agreed the best with me of any sauce I ever eat, either alone or with meat. Our hunters frequently eat it raw and will live upon it several days. The small palmetto or Chamaerops yields a small white bud no bigger than one's finger, which is eaten by men, bears, and horses, in case of great need. This situation pleased me so much we called it Bartram's Bluff, and for an industrious planter with a few hands may be a pretty estate.†

January 19th. Fine, warm morning, birds singing, fish jumping, and turkeys gobbling. Set out and presently came to a rich island, and ran between it and the Indian land, which

---

* Lake Jessup. [Ed.]   † About four miles below Lake Monroe. [Ed.]

Black Bears

is high and shelly, then lower, and very good on each side. We soon came into the river again and rowed down it till we came to a small branch on the east side, down which we rowed near half a mile, where we were entirely stopped by the pistia and persicaria growing all in a mat. We then turned back, concluding it to run on the east side of an island and to join the river below in some of its eastern lagoons to the river; down which we proceeded, and crossed the mouth of the east lake.* In an hour or two arrived at Spalding's Upper Store, where we stayed all night, which was very warm, and the mosquitoes very troublesome, as much so as any time since I left Charleston.

* Lake Dexter. [Ed.]

January 20th. Fine, warm morning, but the southwest wind soon blew so hard that we durst not venture to sail on the great lake,* and our pilot wanted to dry his skins. So we stayed here all day, but in the afternoon our host went over the river to shoot geese in the pineland ponds, where they generally feed on the grass growing there. For they don't frequent the river, as we did not see one all the way, but multitudes of ducks. . . . We landed on a bank of the river† a little above the place where the Indians swim their horses over, about four foot above the water. The bank was composed of snail and mussel shells, a stratum of which, that was even or under the surface of the river, was converted into concrete as hard as a soft stone, as are most of the banks of the upper part of the river, which will burn to lime. . . .

January 24th. Moderate, clear morning; rowed early by a bank of pineland for several miles and some cypress swamps; then came to a large creek called Johnson's Spring.‡ The west end of the lake about eighty yards . . . broad, but after, it widens to about 200. The pineland comes pretty close to its banks, then a narrow, low marsh interposes, and after we rowed higher up we saw narrow cypress swamps, loblolly bays, and some few oak hammocks. The creek abounds with fish, many stingrays near its mouth. It is supposed to run seven miles from its head to the lake,§ where the bar is about eighteen inches deep, but the creek is three, four, and five foot up to the spring, which is nearly level with the lake and full of grass and weeds at the bottom; many of which reach to the top of the water and are a great obstruction to boats in going up, without they keep directly in the channel. On the north side, towards its head, a large marsh

* Lake George. [Ed.] † Site of Volusia. [Ed.]
‡ Later, William calls this Six Mile Creek. Today it is known as Salt Springs. [Ed.]
§ George. [Ed.]

brancheth out. We came at last to where the cattails and bulrushes grew so thick that we could not force the battoe
through them, though it was 100 yards broad and three or
four foot deep, so clear we could see the mussel shells on its
shelly bottom in patches three or four foot in diameter between the great patches of grass and weeds.

We landed to search the head springs and passed through
an orange grove and an old field of the Florida Indians, then
came to the main springs, where a prodigious quantity of very
clear, warm, brackish water boiled up between vast rocks of
unknown depth. We could not reach the bottom with a very
long pole. This was on the north bank about twelve foot high
above the water, which spreads immediately fifty or sixty
yards broad. We walked round the west end towards the
south bank, where the bare flat rocks appeared above water
and a great stream boiled up of a salt and sourish taste but
not near as loathsome as several before described, nor had it
any bad smell, or whitish sediment as they. We examined the
composition of the rocks, and found some of them to be a
concrete reddish sand, some whitish mixed with clay, others
a ferruginous, irregular concrete, and many a combination
of all these materials with sea shells, clams, and cockles. We
found in the bank an ash-colored, tenacious earth, and a
stratum of yellow sand beneath.

Near here my son found a lovely sweet tree* with leaves
like the sweet bay, which smelled like sassafras and produced
a very strange kind of seed pod, but the seed was all shed; the
severe frost had not hurt it. Some of them grew near twenty
foot high, a charming bright evergreen, aromatic. . . .

January 25th. Fine, pleasant morning, although a little
frost in the pinelands; saw several flocks of pigeons flying

* Star anise. [Ed.]

about both yesterday and today. About noon we landed at Mount Royal and went to an Indian tumulus, which was about 100 yards in diameter, nearly round, and near twenty foot high; found some bones scattered on it. It must be very ancient, as there are live oaks growing upon it three foot in diameter. What a prodigious multitude of Indians must have labored to raise it. To what height we can't say, as it must have settled much in such a number of years, and it is surprising where they brought the sand from, and how, as they had nothing but baskets or bowls to carry it in. There seems to be a little hollow near the adjacent level on one side, though not likely to raise such a tumulus the 50th part of what it is. But directly north from the tumulus is a fine straight avenue about sixty yards broad, all the surface of which has been taken off and thrown on each side. This makes a bank of about a rod wide and a foot high, more or less, as the unevenness of the ground required, for the avenue is as level as a floor from bank to bank, and continues so for about three quarters of a mile to a pond of about 100 yards broad and 150 long north and south, which seemed to be an oblong square. Its banks, four foot perpendicular, gradually slope every way to the water, the depth of which we could not say, but do not imagine it deep, as the grass grows all over it. By its regularity it seems to be artificial; if so, perhaps sand was carried from hence to raise the tumulus, as the one directly faces the other end of the avenue. On the south side of the tumulus I found a very large rattlesnake sunning himself. I suppose this to be his winter quarters. Here had formerly been a large Indian town; I suppose there are fifty acres of planting ground cleared and of a middling soil, a good part of which is mixed with small shells. No doubt this large tumulus was their burying place or sepulcher. Whether the

Florida Indians buried the bones after the flesh was rotted off them, as the present southern Indians do, I can't say. We then rowed down the river and encamped at Spalding's Lower Store, opposite a small, rich island on the west side. . . .

January 27th. . . . Set out early and landed on a small island* of near 100 acres, part cypress swamp, part marsh, and piney palmetto, a very rotten black soil, mixed with white sand. We landed on a low bluff of mussel and snail shells, generally broken and powdered by the surges of the lake. Here, as well as in most other places on any high dry bank on the river or its branches where the soil is good, are found fragments of old Indian pots and orange trees, which clearly demonstrates that the Florida Indians inhabited every fertile spot on the St. John's River, lakes, and branches. . . .

January 29th. Fine, clear morning and warm day like the first of our May. Walked all about the town† and adjacent

* Bear Island in Lake George. [Ed.]
† Rollestown on the east bank of the St. John's between East Palatka and San Mateo. [Ed.]

St. John's River

woods. Near the banks of the river are the remains of an old
Spanish entrenchment, twelve yards one way and fourteen
the other, about five foot high; three sides being open to the
river. The town is half a mile long, with half a score of scattered houses in it, built of round logs. The streets are laid
out at right angles; one of them is 100 foot broad, the other
sixty. The land back is all pine and scrub oaks. The bluff continues half a mile down the river, which is seven fathom deep
near the town, but towards the opposite shore there is a sand
bar. It is not above half a mile wide here, but soon widens
above.

February 11th. Northwest wind very high; could not venture on the river, so walked all over the island,* observing
the improvements and the curiosities, both natural and artificial, of the Indians and Spaniards. Of the former, were several middling tumuluses or sepulchers of the Florida Indians,
with numerous heaps of oyster shells, which one may reasonably suppose were many hundred years in collecting by as
many thousands of Indians, also variety of old broken Indian
pots. 'Tis very demonstrable that the Spaniards had a fine settlement here, as there still remain their cedar posts on each
side of their fine straight avenues, pieces of hewn live oaks,
and great trees girdled round to kill them, which are now
very sound, though above sixty years since they were cut.
This rich island, though it appears sandy on the surface, yet
hath a clay bottom, above which in some places there is a
dark-colored stratum of indurated sand rock.[2]

* Fort George Island near the mouth of St. John's River. [Ed.]

5. John Bartram Corresponds with Benjamin Franklin and Other Famous People

Peter Collinson to John Bartram

London, January 20, 1734–5.

My *Good* Friend John Bartram:

I now do myself a further pleasure to consider thy curious entertaining letters of November 6. I am afraid, in doing me a pleasure, so much time was lost which would turn to a more profitable account in thy own affairs.

Thee writes for some botanical books; and indeed I am at a loss which to recommend, for, as I have observed, a complete history of plants is not to be found in any author. For the present, I am persuaded the gentlemen of the Library Company, at my request, will endulge thee the library, when thee comes to town, to peruse their botanical books; there is Miller's *Dictionary,* and some others.

Please to remember those Solomon's Seals, that escaped thee last year.

The great and small Hellebore are great rarities here, so pray send a root or two of each next year. Please to remember all sorts of lilies, as they happen in thy way; and your spotted Martagons will be very acceptable.

The Devil's Bit, or Blazing Star, pray add a root or two, and any of the Lady's Slippers.

My dear friend, I only mention these plants; but I beg thee not to neglect thy more material affairs to oblige me. A great

many may be put in a box 20 inches or 2 feet square, and
15 or 16 inches high; and a foot in earth is enough. This may
be put under the captain's bed, or set in the cabin, if it is
sent in October or November. Nail a few small narrow laths
across it to keep the cats from scratching it. . . .

I hope thee had mine, per Captain Davis, with a box with
seeds in sand, and two parcels of seeds per my good friend
Isaac Norris, Jr. . . .

Pray what is your Sarsaparilla? The May apple, a pretty
plant, is what I have had for some years sent me per Doctor
Witt. It flowers well with us; but our summers are not hot
long enough to perfect the fruit. . . .

The Ground Cypress is a singular pretty plant. If it bears
berries or seeds, pray send some; and if it bears flowers or
seeds pray send some specimens in both states.

Pray send me a good specimen or two of the shrub, 3 feet
high, that grows by the water courses.

The shrub that grows out of the sides of rocks, sometimes
five or six feet high, bearing red berries hanging by the
husks, is called *Euonymous,* or Spindle tree. We have the
same plant, with a small difference; grows plenty in England.

Your Wild Senna, with yellow flowers, is a pretty plant.
Send seeds of both this and Mountain Goat's Rue.

Thee need not collect any more of the White Thorn berries, that has prodigious long, sharp, thorns. It is what we
call Cock-spur Thorn. I had a tree last year, that had at least
a bushel of berries. But haws of any other sort of Thorns will
be acceptable.

Pray send me a root or two of cluster-bearing Solomon's
Seal. It is in all appearances a very rare plant — as is the
Panax. . . .

When it happens in thy way, send me a root or two of the little tuberous root called Devil's Bit, which produces one or two leaves yearly.

I only barely mention these plants; not that I expect thee to send them. I don't expect or desire them, but as they happen to be found accidentally: and what is not to be met with one year, may be another.

It happens that your late ships, in the autumn, come away before a great many of our seeds are ripe, and the spring I don't approve as the best season to send them; but it rarely happens otherwise. I have taken a method to send some in paper, and some in sand. . . . I have raised a great many pretty plants out of your earth. I lay out a bed 5 or 6 feet wide; then I pare off the earth an inch or two deep, then I loosen the bottom, and lay it in very smooth again, and thereon (if I may use the term) I sow the sand and seed together as thin as I can, then I sift some good earth over it about half an inch thick. This bed ought to be in some place that it may not be disturbed, and kept very clear from weeds; for several seeds come not up till the second year.

I have put [in] some hard-shelled Almonds of my own growth, and some soft-shelled from Portugal: they are easily distinguished. The almond makes a fine pie, taken whilst a pin can be run through them; for you eat husk, shell, and kernel altogether, before the shell is hard.

I have put in the sand some vine cuttings, and some of the great Neapolitan Medlar, which we always graft on white thorns, and so must you. . . .

Send a quantity of seed of the Birch or Black Beech; it seems to be new. Send me a good root of Swallow-wort, with the narrow leaves and orange colored flowers; and of the pretty shrub called Red Root, and of the Cotton-weed or Life-everlasting, and some more seeds of the perannual Pea, that grows by rivers; this year, or next, as it happens.

Pray send me a walking-cane, of the Cane-wood.

Peter Collinson

Peter Collinson to John Bartram

[Not dated; Dec. 10, 1738? Ed.]

Dear Friend John:

Lord Petre has ordered me to give thee two guineas, for thy extraordinary trouble about the specimens. The Laurels are perfectly fine. That and the White Cedar are very acceptable. Thee shall not lose thy reward.

Dear friend, I must beg the favor of thee to remember what I have formerly requested, in behalf of a curious naturalist who, to engage thy memory, sends thee a specimen of his performance. He neglected, when in Virginia, to draw the Papaw; and as this is a curious plant, in flower and fruit, and not figured by anybody, now there is no way to convey to us perfect ideas of this plant but by gathering the blossoms and leaves and drying them between paper; but as the color and figure of the flower is liable to change, then he begs a short description of its colors; or else, to prevent further trouble, if some of the flowers growing on a small twig were put into some rum, one small twig would be enough; but thee may put several loose flowers in the jar of spirits, and then a couple of fruit, full ripe; and if it was not too remote, a couple of half ripe — for I am informed they grow in couples.

It is observed that spirits do very little to alter the color of fruits. If they do before thee sends it, pray give a little description of its color. Now, by these helps, my ingenious friend will be able to delineate the plant and fruit: and if thee will further assist him in the height of its growth, and the size of its stem, and what soil and place is most natural to it — we shall all be much obliged to thee. Pray fail not, and thee will oblige thine,

Peter Collinson

Peter Collinson to John Bartram

London, Dec. 20 [?], 1737

Dear Friend John:

I have thine of August 12th, which gives me both pleasure and pain. I dreaded to go on board to see the disaster, and so much labor and pain thrown away by such a swarm of pestilent beetles. As we say by a fine old woman, "There's the ruins of a fine face," and such as I never saw before. Pray next time divide the precious from the vile; I will send thee boxes enough. Keep the butterflies, or day-flies, by themselves, and these devouring beetles by themselves, but drown them in rum, or heat them in a gentle oven will stop all their further progress. Moths are sometimes subject to breed insects which will eat up their bodies, but the heat of a very slack oven kills them. Butterflies are not liable to these accidents, but at the proper time of sending, they may be collected all in one box, and desire the captain to set it in any dry place in the cabin; for the last, being put in the Lazaretto, under the cabin, narrowly escaped all being spoilt by a bag or barrel of salt being put over them, which came through the box. . . . As thee intends to repair that loss, which is very obliging, I only just give this hint, that I prefer butterflies and moths before beetles; and good reason, for there is ten times the beauty and variety in one as the other.

I shall now tell thee something which very much pleased me, and will surprise thee. The box of turtle eggs (which was an ingenious thought of thine to send), on the day I brought it from on board ship, being the 20th of October, I took off the lid, having a mind to see the eggs, and on peeping about I saw a little head just above ground, and while I was look-ing, I saw the ground move in a place or two more. In short, in the space of three or four hours, eight tortoises were hatched. It was very well worth observing how artfully they disengaged themselves from the shell, and then with their fore feet scratched their eyes open. They have had many visi-tors; such a thing never happened, I dare say, in England be-fore.

They seem to be all of one sort, but thee mentions two. I tried if they would eat, with lettuce leaves, etc., or if they would drink, but they regarded neither. But after they had been crawling about three or four days, they buried them-selves in the earth in the box, where they continue. Early in the spring I design to turn them out at Lord Petre's, who has large ponds, if they are water turtles. I believe it was providential that this box was put in the Lazaretto, for the warmth of the ship supplied the sun's heat and brought them to perfection. But the luckiness of the thing was their hatch-ing the day they were brought home. I have specimens of four sorts of American turtles, but these seem different from them all, by the length of their tail, and figure of their shell. . . .

The shells, with the likeness of large snails, are peculiar to your part of the world, but the small scallop, found on East Jersey, are found at New and Old England. But the present is not less esteemed, because it shows the produce of your shores. . . .

I am thine,

Peter Collinson

Peter Collinson to John Bartram

London, April 6, 1738

Dear Friend John:

The first thing I have to desire of thee is to send three or four or six specimens of the Sweet Gum, in blossom. This being a very extraordinary plant, some curious botanists in Holland beg this favor in order to settle its botanical character.

I desire specimens of these others — two or three of a sort: Black Gum and Black Haw — these we desire in blossom, and in fruit and leaf, as it happens; Sugar Birch, Black Thorn, and sorts of White Thorn, in blossom and fruit. . . .

Pray look out for a plant of White Cedar, for I am afraid that last sent me will go off, though it has a clod of its own earth about it. The smell of the leaves, a little dried, smells like a cinnamon. It is a fine plant. If mine stands, it will be the only one in England; though I have hopes to raise it from seed this year. Set half a dozen young plants in a box, and let them stand a year or two, to strike root, before they are sent.

Renew thy collecting of acorns; and if thee can, send specimens to each which is a great curiosity. Get what sassafras berries thee can; and send as many Red Cedar berries, in a little box by themselves, as thee can afford for half a guinea — being for [a] particular person; and send some more, what thee can, for thy three correspondents. Send some Sugar Maple seed and Rose Laurel cones; and send a specimen or two of the Upland Rose and the Marsh Rose. Try what thee canst do to send us some cones of the Long-cone White Pine. It is a very remarkable pine — having five leaves in a sheath; and the other, from Jersey, has two leaves. I have great hopes most of the plants will grow. They promise well; but I shall defer giving thee an account till next opportunity.

The Terrapins came very safe and well: but I have lost all the young ones from the eggs, which were fifteen, which is a great loss. If I ever have any more, I will take another method with them. But the curiosity was great, and admired by many; and it was very lucky that the first peeped its head out of the earth the very day I brought the box from on board — which I think was the 21st of October. If I had sent them then directly into the country, I had saved them; but I thought keeping them in town, I could better secure them from the cold, and so I lost them all, which I was sorry for; being, I am persuaded, the first that ever hatched in England. . . .

Peter Collinson

John Bartram to Peter Collinson

May, 1738

Dear Friend

I am exceedingly pleased with thy long letters, as thee calls them; but I wish they had been as long again. I shall make my observations on them, as follows: *December the 10th.* I am almost overjoyed in reading the contents of this letter — wherein thee acknowledges thy satisfaction of my remarks on the Locusts, Caterpillars, Pigeons, and Snakes. I am very thankful to thee, and the Royal Society, for taking so much notice of my poor performances. It is a great encouragement for me to continue my observations of natural phenomena. If I see any Locusts this year, I shall be very particular in my remarks; as also the Papaw, to gratify the curious friend who, thee says, will send me a specimen of his performances; which will be very acceptable. *December the 14th.* I am glad my map of the Schuylkill pleases thee and Lord Petre.

The panthers have not seized any of our people, that I have heard; but many have been sadly frightened with them. They have pursued several men, both on horseback and foot. Many have shot them down, and others have escaped by running away. But I believe, as a panther doth not much fear a single man, so he hath no great desire to seize him; for if he had, running from him would be a poor means to escape such a nimble, strong creature, which will leap about twenty feet at one leap. I know a man that was riding home when a panther met him, sometimes leaping before and sometimes behind and shaking his tail. When the man shouted for help, the panther was so enraged the man thought he should be torn off his horse. At length taking a leap behind, the man whipped his horse and escaped, being frightened almost to death.

In thy letter of *December 20th* thee supposes me to spend five or six weeks in collections for thee, and that ten pounds will defray all my annual expenses; but I assure thee, I spend more than twice that time, annually; and ten pounds will not, at any moderate expense, defray my charges abroad — beside my neglect of business at home, in fallowing, harvest, and seed time. Indeed, I was more than two weeks' time in gathering the small acorns of the Willow-leafed Oak, which are very scarce, and falling with the leaves — so that daily I had to rake up the leaves and shake the acorns out, before

they were devoured by the squirrels and hogs; and I reckoned it good luck if I could gather twenty under one tree —
hardly one in twenty bore any. Yet I don't begrudge my labor; but would do anything reasonable to serve you. But by
the sequel of thy letter, you are not sensible of the fourth
part of the pains I take to oblige thee. . . .

John Bartram[1]

John Bartram to Peter Collinson

December, 1738

Dear Friend:

I have performed my journey through Maryland and Virginia, as far as Williamsburg, so up James River to the
mountains, so over and between the mountains, in many very
crooked turnings and windings, in which according to the
nearest computation I can make, betwixt my setting out and
returning home, I traveled 1100 miles in five weeks' time,
having rested but one day in all that time, and that was at
Williamsburg. I happened to go in the only time for gathering of seeds — the autumnal — both in Maryland and Virginia; and the exceeding mild fall favored the opportunity
upon and between the mountains, whereby I gathered abundance of kinds of seeds in perfection, which have not ripened
for several years because of the early frosts, which came a
month or six weeks sooner than they did this year. . . .

I sent, by friend Thomas Bond, a box of turtle eggs and several roots packed up carefully; but the captain was so long
before he started, after he talked of sailing within two or
three days, that I am afraid they were damnified. I sent a box
of insects and a jar of Papaw flowers and fruit, which I hope

have come safe to hand. This hath been but a scarce year for several kinds of forest seeds, so could not procure several which thee sent for; but I have made it up, in a great variety of seeds of curious plants which grow between and upon the mountains. Next year, there may [be] more plenty of several kinds which you want; so please to let me know what sort will be acceptable: and if you please to order me to New England, next fall, I am not much against it — having health and prosperity also. I shall be glad to have letters of recommendation to thy friends there.

I received thy letter of July the 10th, with the names of the plants I sent last year, with the seeds and Tulip roots: all which I am obliged to thee for. I wish there may be some, differing from what we have already; for we have a great variety obtained from the breeders, which we have had there many years. . . .

This year the Medlar bore, which thee sent me for the Neapolitan — but I believe it is the English kind. However, one of our Persimmons is worth a dozen of them, for goodness in eating, and as big. But we have great variety of them; some are ripe in the middle of September, others not till Christmas. They are extremely disagreeable to eat until they are thorough ripe and will fall with shaking the tree; then their pulp is delicious. But their skin, which is thin as the finest paper, still retains an astringent bitterness; yet many of our country people are so greedy of them that they swallow down skin, pulp and seeds, all together. . . . They make an excellent liquor, or wine for pleasant drinking. . . .

I think to be diligent in my observations on the flower of our Sweet Gum, to gratify thee and thy curious friends. It seems strange that some accurate botanist hath not already taken notice of it; but I suppose the difficulty of procuring the flowers hath been some reason of the neglect — for the tree generally groweth straight and tall, and seldom bears seeds before the tree is forty or fifty feet high. . . .

John Bartram

John Bartram to Mark Catesby

[Not dated; 1740 or 1741. Ed.]

Friend Mark Catesby:

I received thy kind letter of the 29th of November, but thee not having inserted when or where it was writ, I am at a loss to know where to direct my answer, otherwise than to thee, and to the care of our well-beloved friend, Peter Collinson, who merits the esteem and friendship of most of the curious. The reading of thy acceptable letter incited in me the different passions of joy, in receiving a letter of friendship and request from one so much esteemed, and sorrow, in considering what time we have lost, when we might have obliged each other. It is a pity thee had not wrote to me ten years ago. I should by this time have furnished thee with many different species of plants and perhaps some animals; but the time past can't be recalled; therefore, pray, write often to me, and inform me in every particular what thee wishes of me, and wherein I can oblige thee; for when I am traveling on the mountains or in the valleys, the most desolate, craggy, dismal places I can find, where no mortal ever trod, I chiefly search out. Not that I naturally delight in such solitudes, but entirely to observe the wonderful productions in nature. . . .

Before Doctor Dillenius gave me a hint of it, I took no particular notice of mosses, but looked upon them as a cow looks at a pair of new barn doors; yet now he is pleased to say, I have made a good progress in that branch of botany, which really is a very curious part of vegetation.

I am exceedingly pleased with thy proposals; and shall do what I can conveniently, to comply with them. I have a great value for thy books, and esteem them as an excellent performance, and as an ornament for the finest library in the world. . . .

John Bartram

John Bartram to Thomas François Dalibard, French Botanist

[Not dated; about 1751. Ed.]

To Monsieur Dalibard, *à* Paris:

Our very worthy friend, *Benjamin Franklin,* Esq., whom I have the pleasure (as well as honor) to be intimately acquainted with, showed me a letter wherein thee mentioned a book thee designed to send me, which will be very acceptable, for I love Botany and Natural History exceedingly.

I shall be well pleased to correspond with one so curious, and shall make use of all opportunities to oblige; and as an introduction I have sent a little parcel of seeds and specimens which I have gathered. . . . I suppose it will be difficult to send you any plant that you have not, although I believe we have several which you want; but the difficulty is to know which they are. If I had a catalogue either of what you have, or what you want, I will endeavor to supply you, which I suppose must be carried on by the good offices of *Benjamin*

Franklin here, or my first correspondent in London, the generous Mr. Peter Collinson, who is ready to oblige all men. . . .

John Bartram[2]

John Bartram to Peter Collinson

March the 14th, 1752

Dear Friend:

I received thy kind letter June 16th, 1751, and thy Index with the *Bibliotheca Botanica* of Linnæus with the curious specimens of fishes, all which I am very thankful to thee for. I designed to have answered this last fall by a ship bound from Philadelphia to Rotterdam, but she went sooner than I expected, while I was up at our great mountains, beyond which I was thrice this fall and twice at or near the sea.

I should have been for above a month and still am weak by reason of a cough and fever that I can hardly hold my pen. I have sent thee, within a little box directed to thee at large, several strange sea shells, belemnites, and besides several different stones which I gathered on the ridges of our mountains which I hope may meet with thy acceptance. I am heartily sorry I had not more acquaintance with Mr. Slater before he went to Holland. I should have endeavored to have sent thee many curiosities by him, who seems to be a good sort of a man.

There [are] in Jersey, our low country [of] Maryland, Virginia, North and South Carolina great strata of strange sea shells of prodigious size and various forms at uncertain depths from twenty to forty foot under the surface and the strata in depths from one to two foot thick, which demonstrates that the sea once flowed there and that those strange shells lay either on its bottom or shore, and that it flowed quite to the hills which was then its bounds. Now the query is when this time was and how it came to be covered with such an even bed of sand, loam, or clay as to overspread them for near 1000 miles in length and in many places above 100 [miles] in breadth — so much for our low lands.

But when we ascend to our mountainous country, then we view nature in her ragged, torn, and tattered crags, in beholding the exalted rocky towers, those dreadful precipices of rocks washed bare, many undermined by furious torrents and tumbled down into the water courses; others hanging over or standing tottering on the other's shoulders, [in] deep valleys more of the solid rock the mighty ridges move through, that vast bodies of water might pass through with their sandy or muddy contents; vast lakes drained dry, at the bottom of which is now excellent rich soil and many that is so filled up by the wash of the adjacent mountains as to become marshes of large extent, many great lakes very much diminished in depth and extent by wearing the falls below deeper, so as to drain the water so much off, the adjacent shores is now become rich low land.

Your opinion of these great mutations would much oblige your friend,

John Bartram[3]

John Bartram to Charles Linnæus

[Not dated; 1752 or 1753. Ed.]

Respected and Worthy Friend:

I received about two months past, a letter from thee dated

August 10, 1750 [The letters from Linnæus to John Bartram are all missing. Ed.]. I was exceedingly pleased to receive so kind a letter from one [who] so deservedly bears so superior a character for learning; but was much concerned that I could not have had it sooner than about two years after it was wrote; and much the same misfortune happened to several pamphlets thee sent to Dr. Colden and Mr. Clayton, which our worthy friend *Benjamin Franklin* showed me last week, which he had just received, and intended to send according to direction by the next post.

I traveled in 1751 most part of the autumn, and found several new species of plants and shrubs, which I should have sent to thee if I had known they would be acceptable.

We have four or five beautiful species of *Jacobæa* (*Lilium*) that you have not in Europe. One species grows in our marshes, another on flat, stiff ground, another on cold, shady banks, by the rivers, another on loose, slaty soil on the great mountains; and most of these species are much valued by the Indians and back inhabitants, for the cure of the same diseases that the ancients used their Jacobæa for, though not one of them knew the name of the plant. . . .

John Bartram

John Bartram to Peter Collinson

August the 20th, 1753

Dear Peter:

I am now very intent upon examining the true distinguishing characters of our forest trees, finding it a very difficult task — and can have no help from either ancient or modern authors, they having taken no particular observation worth notice. I expect, by our worthy friend *Benjamin* [Frank-lin], specimens of the evergreens of New England — which I intend to compare with ours, and those of York government; so I may give a particular account of the evergreens natural to our northern parts, which I hope to send thee, this fall or next spring — with a fuller account of our Oaks and Hicko-ries. . . .

John Bartram

John Bartram to Peter Collinson

November 3, 1754

Dear Peter:

I received thy kind letter of July the 30th. Good grammar and good spelling may please those that are more taken with a fine superficial flourish than real truth; but my chief aim was to inform my readers of the true, real, distinguishing characters of each genus, and where, and how, each species differed from one another, of the same genus; and if you find that my descriptions are not agreeable with the specimens, pray let me know where the disagreement is, and send my descriptions back again that I may correct them — or if they prove deficient, that I may add farther observations; for I have no copy, and you have the original. So, by all means, send my descriptions back again by the first opportunity; for I have forgot what I wrote. The microscope I like very well; it is prettily adapted to the observation of plants. . . .

The great Water Turtle of New England, I take to be our great Mud Turtle [snapping turtle. Ed.] which is much hunted for, to feast our gentry withal; and is reckoned to be as delicious a morsel as those brought from Summer Islands.

. . . They are very large — of a dark muddy color — large round tail, and feet with claws — the old ones mossy on the back, and often several horse leeches sucking the superfluous blood; a large head, sharp nose, and mouth large enough to cram one's fist in — very sharp gums, or lips, which you will, with which they will catch hold of a stick, offered to them — or, if you had rather, your finger — which they will hold so fast that you may lift the turtle by it as high as your head, if you have strength or courage enough to lift them up so high by it. But as for their barking, I believe thy relator *barked*, instead of the turtle. They creep all over, in the mud, where they lie *perdu;* and when a duck, or fish, swims near them, they dart out their head as quick as light, and snap him up. Their eggs are round as a bullet, and choice eating.

As for the Opossums, I can't endure to touch them — or hardly look at them, without sickness at stomach; and I question whether any beast of prey is so fond of them as to kill them for food; and as they make but little resistance, but by their loathsome scent, few creatures will kill them for sport, except dogs. But if wolves or panthers should chase them, they can creep into less holes — in a hollow tree, or between rocks — than their pursuers can; or if suddenly surprised, there is a tree or bush mostly at hand, where they can be secure; for they can run to the extremity of a horizontal branch, and lap their tail-end round a slender twig, by which they will hang, pendulous, out of the reach of larger animals. . . .

John Bartram[4]

John Bartram to Peter Collinson

June the 24th, 1760

Dear Peter,

I have now my dear, worthy Peter's letter before me of February the 10th. I am very sorry that the seeds was damaged by the rotten squash. It seemed when I put it in the box to be ripe enough and I thought to oblige my dear friend with the best sort I ever ate. But I believe misfortune will pursue me to the grave, let my intention and care be ever so good.

The seeds that I collected on the south mountains on the branches of James River was excellent good. Those that I sowed are come up as close as they can grow except the mountain Angelica, which Clayton tells me will never come up. But I hope to find him mistaken, though he is a worthy, ingenious man. I took such care to gather the seeds in several degrees of ripeness. If none of mine come up I shall be almost ready to believe it will not come up in a garden.

I have received the laurel berries and arbutus in good order. The acorns was every one rotten. The packet of seeds was good. I sowed them directly after receiving, which was a week in June.

The seed thee sent last fall was choice good and most of them come up. The ranunculus and anemone root grows finely and several bore fine flowers. The flags — iris — grow well and two of the bulbous is ready to flower. Many aconites is come up and the polianthus by hundreds. Balm of Gilead and a pretty annual linaria hath been long in flower, sowed last February.

I hope the yellow digitalis and double-blossom celandine is

come up. But how glad, glad should I be if the doronicum gentian and laurels would come up which I sowed carefully last winter under shelter. All these are very acceptable. Above thirty carnations grows finely. Several of the bulbous roots and polianthus flowered pretty, as my wife told me, while I was gone.

Dear friend, I am going to build a green house. Stone is got and [I] hope, as soon as harvest is over, to begin to build it — to put some pretty flowering winter shrubs and plants for winter's diversion; — not to be crowded with orange trees or those natural to the torrid zone but such as will do being protected from frost.

The pretty little flower rudbeckia is a charming flower but difficult to raise by seed. I have often sent it. It improves prodigiously being in a garden. In the woods commonly it sends up but one stalk to a root and but one (or two) flower on it. But one I have hath now about 100 stalks on one root so I transplanted a pretty oenothera out of a meadow and it hath now shot up thirty-six stalks, each being full of flowers, and [I] hope these will continue to flower till frost. My aconite that I brought from James River last fall, if it be it grows finely and though in its native place sends forth but one stalk from one root, yet mine hath now five stalks and by its forward growth it may flower two month sooner than it did last fall, yet I hope to continue it in flower till frost if I don't let it seed to send to you. . . .

John Bartram

John Bartram to his son William, at Cape Fear

December the 27th, 1761

My dear Son:

Cousin Billy tells me that your loblolly bay or Alcea bears a very sweet blossom. I wish thee would look out for some of its seed. Perhaps it is not all shed, nor the water tupelo. I want seed of everything we have not, and thee is a good judge of that. The Alcea and the horse sugar I want much. They are very difficult to transplant. I had them from Charleston but they are gone off. Perhaps your northern one may do better. It is strange that the red sweet bay, some of which grows naturally in Virginia, should not bear our frost, and yet the great magnolia that grows naturally on the south of the Pedee seems to bear our frost tolerably. What havoc our present frost will make with the rest, I can't say. But, however, I want to try all, to be enabled to judge which of your plants will bear our vigorous frost and which will not.

Thee disappointed my expectation much in not sending me any seeds by Capt. Sharpless. [I] know your seeds were some or other ripening from the day thee set thy foot on Carolina shore to Sharpless's departure, and such as was within a mile or two of thy common walks, or most of them within sight. And yet I have not received one single seed from my son who glories so much in the knowledge of plants and whom I have been at so much charge to instruct therein, and fall being the best time to sow the native seeds. Spring may do, but many misseth coming up that year. I don't want thee to hinder thy own affairs to oblige me, but thee might easily gather a few seeds when thee need not hinder half an hour's time to gather them or turn twenty yards out of thy way to pluck them. I remain thy loving father,

John Bartram

John Bartram to Mr. Philip Miller

November 4, 1756

Respected Friend Miller:

. . . . Last year I found growing in an old drained beaver pond near [the] Connecticut River in New England a fine dwarf Crataegus [*hawthorn*] about two foot high, exceeding full of large, sweet, very juicy black fruit of an excellent taste, but a little rough. I put the berries in a bag and squeezed out the juice (as red as claret) that I might carry the seeds home, the better to send to my correspondents. I brought a small root home which now hath shot forth four or five stems, one about a foot high with thick, finely crenated leaves, and pedicle and middle nerve is all a deep purple color. . . . A few miles from the Blue Mountains in East Jersey, in a black larix [*larch*] and spruce swamp, I found a curious species of Crataegus growing five or six foot high, bearing a prodigious quantity of large, black, sweet juicy fruit a little roughish in taste. They grew on the tops of the branches in such bunches that I could pull them off by double handfuls. I gathered as many as a proportionable share with the other seeds to carry home. I and my little son John ate our belly full of them. They was very wholesome and quenched our thirst finely, it being an extreme hot day and no water near. . . .

John Bartram

John Bartram to Peter Collinson

[*Written upon Bartram's return from the botanical trip to Florida on behalf of the king of England. Ed.*]

Schuylkill, at my own house, June 4, 1766

Dear Peter:

I am now returned to my family, all whom I found in good health. God Almighty be praised for his favor. I am at present tolerable well but can hardly yet get over the dreadful seasickness and the southward fever.

I have left my son Billy in Florida. Nothing will do with

Florida

him now but he will be a planter upon the St. John's River
about twenty-four mile from Augustine and six from the fort
of Picolata. This frolic of his, and our maintenance, hath
drove me to great straits, so that I was forced to draw upon
thee at Augustine and twice at Charleston, all of which I
sent thee letters of advice . . .

I have packed up in a little box directed to thee . . . the
seeds I brought from Florida, which I should have sent sooner
but had not a good opportunity, but yet they are good. Don't
despair of their coming up, if not this year yet may come in
three years; many of the southern plants . . . I brought from
New River . . . three years past and sowed directly when
I came home is come up this spring, and some others every
spring since I sowed them. Many of my Florida plants and
those of Georgia is come up but I don't expect they will all
come up in less than one or two springs more.

The undermost seed I send for the king and those above
the partition is for thyself except the little . . . bag directed to John Web, who hath sent a fine collection of curious
garden seed by Captain Frend. . . . Pray send the little bag
to him or let him know of it. If the vessel sails tomorrow I
have time to write to him. I am grateful the cargo my son
John sent last fall is come safe and in good order. . . .

I have brought home with me a fine collection of strange
Florida plants which perhaps I may send sometime this summer, some for the king and some for thyself, but I want to
know how those I sent from Charleston and Georgia is accepted, or those I sent last spring for the king from home.

I hope what specimens I sent for thyself will give thee
great pleasure, as many of them is entirely new, the collecting of which hath cost thy friend . . . pain and sickness
which fret me constantly near or quite two months in Flor-

ida [with] a fever and jaundice. . . . Yet somehow or other
I lost not many hours time of traveling through those proc-
esses, and when at Augustine with fever and jaundice, I traveled both by water and land around the town for many
miles, and to Picolata to the congress, although so weak
[that] during the meeting of governor and Indians in the
pavilion, was forced to sit or lie down upon the ground close
by its side that I might observe what passed. . . .

John Bartram

John Bartram to Peter Collinson

August the 26, 1766

Dear Peter:

. . . I have forgot what part of my journal I sent thee
from Augustine, except the thermometrical observations. I allow that these flowering trees thee mentions, in Carolina, is
very fine, most of which grow in Georgia and Florida; but
then there grow, in both these last places, many more curious
evergreen trees and shrubs which, if not so beautiful in flowers, comes fully up with those and perhaps surpass them in
beauty of fruit and sweet scent as may be observed by my
specimens gathered on the banks of St. John's River. I am
obliged to thee for sending the specimens to the king. I sent,
last spring, the seeds I collected in east Florida.

Augustine, now, is in a very ruinous condition to what it
was when the Spaniards lived there. The soldiers have
pulled down above half the town for the sake of the timber
to burn. Most of the best houses stand yet, several of which
are much altered by the English, who drive the chimney
through the tops of the house roofs, and the sun begins to

shine through glass where before its light was admitted between bannisters. And where the well-cultivated gardens
were, it is now grown over with weeds and is the common
pasture for cattle.

Many of the orange trees and figs, near or quite a foot
diameter [are] cut down or grubbed up for fire wood, for the
English don't make such use of the sour oranges, as the
Spaniards, nor of citrons or sweet lemons. But now the
sweet, bitter-sweet lemons, limes, and guavas is chiefly taken
care of, but the two latter is most of them killed, especially
the branches, last winter. So were the bananas. As for the
figs and pomegranates, the English is not very fond of them.

I saw two of the opuntias as thick as my middle and six
foot high, much branched. They seemed to be near the same
kind with ours, but I am apt to think the fruit the Spaniards
eat so much of was the species of huica, with terrible sharp
spines at the ends of their leaves which some calls Adam's
needles, others palmetto royal, and some bananas, from their
fruit which is sweet with a little bitterness; and [the huica]
is the chief fencing about Augustine, both against man and
beast, and is frequently planted on their sandy ditches and
banks.

As for the Spanish improvements, I suppose formerly they
had made some both considerable and extensive, there being
the vestiges of large roads to several distant parts of St.
John's River and many miles beyond it. But since the Creek
Indians, by the help of the English, turned their arms against
the Spaniards, they have been cooped up within their own
fortifications and could not till any ground out of the reach
of their cannon balls. Neither could they keep any cattle out
of sight or cut a stick without a guard.

The Indians in both these provinces profess a strict friend-ship and perhaps will keep to it if the English don't give them just occasion to break out.

There is but very few Spaniards at Augustine, I think but one of any account. There was four churches belonged to the town, two was in it and the other very near. One was the Dutch church, with a steeple and stone cupola, this built of hewn stone. A more particular description of them is in my *Journal*.

I am glad the Pittsburgh iris pleaseth thee. I like it. So doth the sweet Carolina sort. Perhaps I may send thee a slip of it next fall. . . .

John Bartram[5]

John Bartram to Benjamin Franklin

November the 11th, 1772

My dear ould worthy Friend:

I have here before me thy kind letter of August 22, 1772. I sowed the rhubarb seed in two places, the one in the sun, the other in a shady cool place. That which was in the cool place growed. The leaves was as big as the palm of my hand but not palmated. Perhaps it may be next year.

The turnip seed came up well, growed large and tasted well and is by some admired and expect it may be a fine improvement.

I hear no more of the medal from Edenboro nor from Dr. Hope.

We have had several bright Aurora Borealis last summer and in the heat of harvest, which is very uncommon at that season, and we have had two slight shakes of an earthquake, very little thunder or rain but much hail in several parts distant from Philadelphia.

A late cold dry spring, temperate summer, and now a warm, dry fall. Very few troubled with agues. Some bad nervous fevers but not very mortal. But the favorablest Measels I ever knew and as yet the slowest in spreading. Perhaps when cold weather approacheth it may be more severe and spread more.

I remain, dear friend, with much love and respect thy sincearly well wisher as formerly.

John Bartram

I can hardly see to write or read.[6]

6. John and William Bartram Discover and Record Some Wonders of the New Continent

The Franklinia Alatamaha, or Lost Camellia

[*By John Bartram. The discovery of this beautiful shrub, or small tree, named in honor of Benjamin Franklin, is passed over lightly in John Bartram's* Journal. *Somewhere close to the Altamaha River, not far from old Fort Barrington, enough plants, cuttings, and seeds were collected to enable the tree, never found in the wild since 1790, to be preserved through cultivation. It will thrive in a variety of situations and should be more widely planted. The following two paragraphs are by John Bartram. The rest of the present book is by William Bartram, unless otherwise noted. Ed.*]

October 1, 1765. Fine, clear, cool morning. Thermometer 56., P.M. 68. This day's riding was very bad through bay swamps. Tupelos of both sorts, and cypress in deep water, some of which on the borders was very full of brush and briars, yet [we] got safe through all. This day's journey of twenty miles was all low, flat ground, the highest piney ground seldom above three or four foot perpendicular above the swamps. The trees generally very tall, straight, and pretty close together at twenty to one hundred yards distance. . . . And exceeding tall grass . . . very thick like a meadow, generally covered the ground. Unless in ponds, thickets of brush, or some sand hills interspersed towards the river, or where small palmettos growed, which generally is between the swamps and higher piney ground, though it commonly grows in the moister piney soil. We saw several deer, two or three together, both young and old, and several turkeys. In dry seasons hardly any water is to be found all this way, but in wet seasons most of it is covered with water for a long season. Dined by a swamp on bread and a pomegranate, near which growed much canna indica.

When we came to the river the soil was very sandy near the surface and the timber poor for about a mile from the low land, which is often overflowed with the river (to the great loss of the inhabitants), which sometimes riseth twelve or fifteen foot perpendicular. We missed our way and fell four miles below Fort Barrington, where we lodged this night. This day we found several very curious shrubs, one bearing beautiful good fruit.[1]

[*A monument was unveiled by the Long County (Ga.) Garden Club on the 176th anniversary of the discovery of this plant. It is on the south side of the main highway between Jessup and Ludowici, one mile east of the bridge spanning the Altamaha River. William Bartram's narrative is now resumed. Ed.*]

After my* return from the Creek nation, I employed myself during the spring and fore part of summer in revisiting the several districts in Georgia and the east borders of Florida, where I had noted the most curious subjects; collecting them together, and shipping them off to England. In the course of these excursions and researches, I had the opportunity of observing the new flowering shrubs, resembling the Gordonia,†

---

* William Bartram's. [Ed.]

† On first observing the fructification and habit of this tree, I was inclined to believe it a species of Gordonia; but afterwards, upon stricter examination, and comparing its flowers and fruit with those of the Gordonia lasianthus, I presently found striking characteristics abundantly sufficient to separate it from that genus, and to establish it the head of a new tribe, which we have honored with the name of the illustrious Dr. Benjamin Franklin: Franklinia Alatamaha.

Franklinia Alatamaha

in perfect bloom, as well as bearing ripe fruit. It is a flowering tree, of the first order for beauty and fragrance of blossoms: the tree grows fifteen or twenty feet high, branching alternately; the leaves are oblong, broadest towards their extremities, and terminate with an acute point, which is generally a little reflexed; they are lightly serrated, attenuate downwards, and sessile, or have very short petioles; they are placed in alternate order, and towards the extremities of the twigs are crowded together, but stand more sparsely below; the flowers are very large, expand themselves perfectly, are of a snow-white color and ornamented with a crown or tassel of gold-colored refulgent staminæ in their center. The inferior petal or segment of the corolla is hollow, formed like a cap or helmet, and entirely includes the other four, until the moment of expansion; its exterior surface is covered with a short silky hair; the borders of the petals are crisped or plicated. These large white flowers stand single and sessile in the bosom of the leaves, and being near together towards the extremities of the twigs and usually many expanded at the same time, make a gay appearance. The fruit is a large, round, dry, woody apple or pericarp, opening at each end oppositely by five alternate fissures containing ten cells, each replete with dry, woody, cuneiform seed. This very curious tree was first taken notice of about ten or twelve years ago at this place when I attended my father (John Bartram) on a botanical excursion; but, it being then late in the autumn, we could form no opinion to what class or tribe it belonged.

We never saw it grow in any other place, nor have I ever since seen it growing wild, in all my travels, from Pennsylvania to Point Coupé, on the banks of the Mississippi, which must be allowed a very singular and unaccountable circumstance; at this place there are two or three acres of ground where it grows plentifully.

Cypress Forests and Carolina Paroquets, near Palatka

[Few stands of great cypress forests remain along the St. John's, or in all Florida, for that matter. It is generally believed that not a single Carolina paroquet remains alive today. Ed.]

The high forests on this coast now wore a grand and sublime appearance; the earth rising gradually from the river westward, by easy swelling ridges, behind one another, lifting the distant groves up into the skies. The trees are of the lofty kind, as the grand laurel magnolia, palma elata, liquidambar styraciflua, fagus sylvatica, querci, juglans hickory, fraxinus, and others.

On my doubling a long point of land, the river appeared surprisingly widened, forming a large bay of an oval form and several miles in extent. On the west side it was bordered round with low marshes and invested with a swamp of cypress, the trees so lofty as to preclude the sight of the highland forests beyond them; and these trees, having flat tops, and all of equal height, seemed to be a green plain, lifted up and supported upon columns in the air, round the west side of the bay.

The Cupressus disticha stands in the first order of North American trees. Its majestic stature is surprising; and on approaching it, we are struck with a kind of awe at beholding the stateliness of the trunk, lifting its cumbrous top towards the skies and casting a wide shade upon the ground, as a dark intervening cloud, which for a time excludes the rays of the sun. The delicacy of its color and texture of its leaves exceed everything in vegetation. It generally grows in the water, or in low flat lands, near the banks of great rivers and lakes, that are covered, great part of the year, with two or three feet depth of water; and that part of the trunk which is subject to be under water, and four or five feet higher up, is greatly enlarged by prodigious buttresses, or pilasters which, in full-grown trees, project out on every side to such a distance that several men might easily hide themselves in the hollows between. Each pilaster terminates under ground in a very large, strong, serpentine root which strikes off and branches every way, just under the surface of the earth. From these roots grow woody cones, called cypress knees, four, five, and six inches high, and from six to eighteen inches and two feet in diameter at their bases. The large ones are hollow and serve very well for beehives; a small space of the tree itself is hollow, nearly as high as the buttresses already mentioned. From this place, the tree, as it were, takes another beginning, forming a grand straight column eighty or ninety feet high, when it divides every way around into an extensive flat horizontal top, like an umbrella, where eagles have their secure nests, and cranes and storks their temporary resting places; and what adds to the magnificence of their appearance is the streamers of long moss that hang from the lofty limbs and float in the winds. This is their majestic appearance when standing alone in large rice plantations or thinly planted on the banks of great rivers.

Paroquets are commonly seen hovering and fluttering on their tops: they delight to shell the balls, its seed being their favorite food. The trunks of these trees, when hollowed out, make large and durable pettiaugers* and canoes and afford

* Pirogue, a canoe made of a hollowed tree trunk. [Ed.]

Carolina Paroquets and Spanish Moss

excellent shingles, boards, and other timber adapted to every purpose in frame buildings. When the planters fell these mighty trees, they raise a stage round them, as high as to reach above the buttresses; on this stage, eight or ten Negroes ascend with their axes and fall to work round its trunk. I have seen trunks of these trees that would measure eight, ten, and twelve feet in diameter, and forty and fifty feet straight shaft.

The Magnolia

[*Though* Laurel magnolia *today refers to* Magnolia glauca, *here Bartram used that name for* Magnolia grandiflora, *or Southern magnolia. Ed.*]

Behold yon promontory projecting far into the great river, beyond the still lagoon, half a mile distant from me: what a magnificent grove arises on its banks! . . . How majestically stands the laurel, its head forming a perfect cone! Its dark green foliage seems silvered over with milk-white flowers. They are so large as to be distinctly visible at the distance of a mile or more. The laurel magnolias, which grow on this river, are the most beautiful and tall that I have anywhere seen, unless we except those which stand on the banks of the Mississippi; yet even these must yield to those of St. Juan in neatness of form, beauty of foliage and, I think, in largeness and fragrance of flower. Their usual height is about one hundred feet, and some greatly exceed that. The trunk is perfectly erect, rising in the form of a beautiful column and supporting a head like an obtuse cone. The flowers are on the extremities of the subdivisions of the branches, in the center of a coronet of dark green, shining, ovate-pointed entire leaves: they are large, perfectly white, and expanded like a full-blown rose. They are polypetalous, consisting of fifteen, twenty, or twenty-five petals: these are of a thick coriaceous texture and deeply concave, their edges being somewhat reflex when mature. In the center stands the young cone; which is large, of a flesh color, and elegantly studded with a gold-colored stigma that by the end of summer is greatly enlarged and in the autumn ripens to a large crimson cone or strobile, disclosing multitudes of large, coral-red berries, which for a time hang down from them, suspended by a fine, white, silky thread four, six, or even nine inches in length. The flowers of this tree are the largest and most complete of any yet known. When fully expanded, they are of six, eight, and nine inches diameter. The pericarpium and berries possess an agreeable spicy scent and an aromatic bitter taste. The wood, when seasoned, is of a straw color, compact, and harder and firmer than that of the poplar.

The Papaya

[*At the same time that they brought the orange to North America, the Spaniards brought the papaya. Like the orange, it naturalized itself in many areas. Ed.*]

I passed along several miles by those rich swamps: the channels of the river which encircle the several fertile islands I had passed, now uniting, formed one deep channel near three hundred yards over. The banks of the river on each side began to rise and present shelly bluffs adorned by beautiful orange groves, laurels, and live oaks. And now appeared in sight a tree that claimed my whole attention: it was the Carica papaya, both male and female, which were in flower; and the latter both in flower and fruit, some of which were ripe, as large, and of the form of a pear, and of a most charming appearance.

This admirable tree is certainly the most beautiful of any vegetable production I know of. The towering laurel Magnolia and exalted palm indeed exceed it in grandeur and magnificence, but not in elegance, delicacy, and gracefulness. It rises erect to the height of fifteen or twenty feet, with a perfectly straight, tapering stem, which is smooth and polished, of a bright ash color, resembling leaf silver, curiously inscribed with the footsteps of the fallen leaves; and these vestiges are placed in a very regular uniform imbricated order, which has a fine effect, as if the little column were elegantly carved all over. Its perfectly spherical top is formed of very large lobe-sinuate leaves, supported on very long footstalks; the lower leaves are the largest as well as their petioles the longest, and make a graceful sweep or flourish, like the long *f,* or the branches of a sconce candlestick. The ripe and green fruit are placed round about the stem or trunk, from the lowermost leaves, where the ripe fruit are, and upwards almost to the top; the heart or inmost pithy part of the trunk is in a manner hollow, or at best consists of very thin, porous medullæ or membranes. The tree very seldom branches or divides into limbs; I believe never, unless the top is by accident broke off when very young. I saw one which had two tops, or heads, the stem of which divided near the earth. It is always green, ornamented at the same time with flowers and fruit, which like figs come out singly from the trunk or stem.

Discovery of the Royal Palm (Roystonea Regia)

[*On St. John's River somewhere between Lake George and Lake Dexter. Ed.*]

The palm trees here seem to be of a different species from the cabbage tree; their straight trunks are sixty, eighty, or ninety feet high, with a beautiful taper, of a bright ash color until within six or seven feet of the top, where it is a fine green color, crowned with an orb of rich green plumed leaves. I have measured the stem of these plumes fifteen feet in length, besides the plume, which is nearly of the same length.[2]

Discovery of a Sacred Shrub

[*The oil nut, or buffalo nut, discovered by William Bartram near Broad River in the Georgia Piedmont, was named* Pyrularia pubera *by Michaux in 1803. Ed.*]

. . . . Mounting the hill, [we] gained the summit, from whence I had very agreeable prospect of the plains below. Observed . . . a very curious shrub [which] grows about two feet high, olive-shaped leaves growing opposite on slender branches bearing very large oval fruit or berries rather larger than an olive or plum, yellow when ripe, as I was informed by the Indians. They grew single in the bosom of the leaf, having a short pedical. Could find none ripe, neither could I see any flowers.

The Indian hunters carry the root with them, believing it

to have a fascinating power to bring deer to them. This the Indian doctors or conjurers make their people believe, and for which end they hold it in high esteem and make them pay dear enough for it. This was the account I had by an interpreter present. They do not eat the fruit, though it has a great pulp and seemed to have no disagreeable taste, but the root very strong and disagreeable, both smell and taste. It has also a large kernel, and possibly very oily when ripe. In fine, it is a pretty new shrub, well worth notice, and may possess qualities (yet undiscovered to us) of great use to mankind. It grows in large patches on high, dry, stony, and rather barren land.

The Discovery of Yellowroot

[*On the way from Wrightsborough to Buffalo Lick. Named* Xanthorrhiza apiifolia *by L'Hériter in 1784, now called* Xanthorrhiza simplicissima. *A common garden shrub of today. Ed.*]

This evening I discovered a very curious little shrub growing at the bottoms of these hills and on the steep banks of the creek. The foliage and form of growth a little resembled Aralia, but what was the most remarkable in it, the root affording a strong yellow tincture, near as fine as that of gum boge. It has long, slender, branching roots that run and spread about just under the surface of the earth, filling a large patch of ground with a numerous offspring. The shrub rises about two feet high, sending up a slender, bending, knotty stalk covered with a white, smooth bark which, on being rubbed off, discovers a perfectly lucid yellow wood which dyes as well as the root. It is, in my opinion, a very valuable shrub on this account where a fine yellow dye is wanted.[3]

Spanish Moss

[*Not a moss but a true flowering plant belonging to the Pineapple family. Much the same methods described here are used today in preparing the "moss" for stuffing furniture. Ed.*]

The long moss, so called (Tillandsea usneaoides), is a singular and surprising vegetable production. It grows from the limbs and twigs of all trees in these southern regions, from north latitude 35 down as far as 28, and I believe everywhere within the tropics. Wherever it fixes itself on a limb or branch it spreads into short and intricate divarications; these in time collect dust, wafted by the wind, which, probably by the moisture it absorbs, softens the bark and sappy part of the tree, about the roots of the plant, and renders it more fit for it to establish itself. From this small beginning, it increases, by sending downwards and obliquely on all sides long, pendant branches, which divide and subdivide themselves *ad infinitum*. It is common to find the spaces betwixt the limbs of large trees almost occupied by this plant. It also hangs waving in the wind, like streamers, from the lower limbs, to the length of fifteen or twenty feet, and of bulk and weight more than several men together could carry. In some places cartloads of it are lying on the ground, torn off by the violence of the wind. Any part of the living plant, torn off and caught in the limbs of a tree, will presently take root, grow, and increase in the same degree of perfection as if it had sprung up from the seed. When fresh, cattle and deer will eat it in the winter season. It seems particularly adapted to the purpose of stuffing mattresses, chairs, saddles, collars, etc., and for these purposes nothing yet known equals it. The Spaniards in South America and the West Indies work it into cables that are said to be very strong and durable. But, in order to render it useful, it ought to be thrown into shallow ponds of water and exposed to the sun, where it soon rots and the outside furry substance is dissolved. It is then taken out of the water and spread to dry; when, after a little beating and shaking, it is sufficiently clean, nothing remaining but the interior, hard, black, elastic filament, entangled together and greatly resembling horsehair.

Islands of Water Lettuce on St. John's River

It being a fine cool morning, and fair wind, I set sail early and saw, this day, vast quantities of the Pistia stratiotes, a very singular aquatic plant. It associates in large communities, or floating islands, some of them a quarter of a mile in extent, which are impelled to and fro, as the wind and current may direct. They are first produced on, or close to, the shore, in eddy water, where they gradually spread themselves into the river, forming most delightful green plains, several miles in length and in some places a quarter of a mile in breadth. These plants are nourished and kept in their proper horizontal situation by means of long fibrous roots, which descend from the nether center, downwards, towards the muddy bottom. Each plant, when full grown, bears a general resemblance to a well-grown plant of garden lettuce, though the leaves are more nervous, of a firmer contexture, and of a full green color, inclining to yellow. It vegetates on the surface of the still, stagnant water and in its natural situation is propagated from seed only. In great storms of wind and rain, when the river is suddenly raised, large masses of these floating plains are broken loose and driven from the shores into the wide water, where they have the appearance of islets and float about until broken to pieces by the winds and waves, or driven again to shore on some distant coast of the river, where they again find footing and there, forming new colonies, spread and extend themselves again, until again broken up and dispersed as before. These floating islands present a very entertaining prospect, for although we behold an assemblage of the primary productions of nature only, yet the imagination seems to remain in suspense and doubt; as, in order to enliven the delusion and form a most picturesque appearance, we see not only flowery plants, clumps of shrubs, old weather-beaten trees, hoary and barbed, with the long moss waving from their snags, but we also see them completely inhabited and alive with crocodiles, serpents, frogs, otters, crows, herons, curlews, jackdaws, etc. There seems, in short, nothing wanted but the appearance of a wigwam and a canoe to complete the scene.

Discovery of the Oak-Leaf Hydrangea

[*Crawford County, Georgia. Ed.*]

I observed here a very singular and beautiful shrub which I suppose is a species of hydrangea (H. quercifolia). It grows in coppices or clumps near or on the banks of rivers and creeks. Many stems usually arise from a root spreading itself greatly on all sides by suckers or offsets. The stems grow five or six feet high, declining or diverging from each other, and are covered with several barks or rinds, the last of which, being of a cinereous dirt color and very thin at a certain age of the stems or shoots, cracks through to the next bark and is peeled off by the winds, discovering the under, smooth, dark reddish-brown bark. [This] also cracks and peels off the next year in like manner as the former, thus every year forming a new bark. The stems divide regularly or oppositely, though the branches are crooked or wreathe about horizontally, and these again divide, forming others which terminate with large, heavy panicles or thyrsi of flowers; but these flowers are of two kinds: the numerous partial spikes which compose the panicles and consist of a multitude of very small fruitful flowers, terminate with one or more very large, expansive, neutral or mock flowers, standing on a long, slender, stiff peduncle; these flowers are composed of four broad oval petals or segments, of a dark rose or crimson color at first, but as they become older acquire a deeper red or purplish hue, and lastly are of a brown or ferruginous color. These have no perfect parts of generation of either sex, but discover in their center two, three, or four papillæ or rudiments. These neutral flowers, with the whole panicle, are truly permanent, remaining on the plant for years, until they dry and decay: the leaves which clothe the plants are very large, pinnatifid or palmated, and serrated or toothed, very much resembling the leaves of some of our oaks. They sit opposite, supported by slender petioles, and are of a fine, full green color.

"Insectivorous" Plants

[*Few plants so capture the imagination as do the pitcher plants, sundews, and Venus's-flytrap. John Bartram called the last-named plant by the enchanting name of "tipitiwichit" and considered it the most wonderful plant in the world. Ed.*]

How greatly the flowers of the yellow Sarracenia [pitcher plant] represent a silken canopy. The yellow, pendant petals are the curtains, and the hollow leaves are not unlike the cornucopia or Amalthea's horn. What a quantity of water a leaf is capable of containing: about a pint! Taste of it — how cool and animating — limpid as the morning dew. Nature seems to have furnished them with this cordated appendage, or lid, which turns over to prevent a too sudden and copious supply of water from heavy showers of rain, which would bend down the leaves, never to rise again. Because their straight, parallel nerves, which extend and support them, are so rigid and fragile, the leaf would inevitably break when bent down to a right angle. Therefore, I suppose the waters which contribute to their supply are the rebounding drops or horizontal streams wafted by the winds, which adventitiously find their way into them when a blast of wind shifts the lid. See these short stiff hairs. They all point downwards, which direct the condensed vapors down into the funiculum. These stiff hairs also prevent the varieties of insects which are caught from returning, being invited down to sip the mellifluous exudation from the interior surface of the tube, where they inevitably perish. What quantities there are of them! These latent waters undoubtedly contribute to the support and refreshment of the plant, perhaps designed as a reservoir in case of long-continued droughts or other casual-

Pitcher Plant

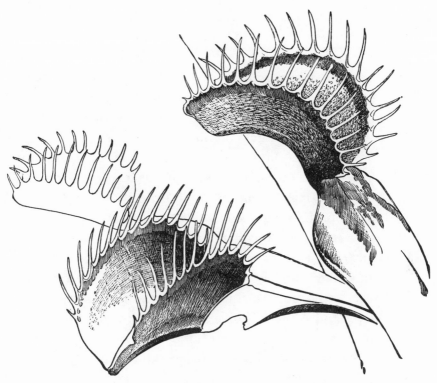

Venus's-Flytrap

ties, since these plants naturally dwell in low savannahs
liable to overflows from rain water. Although I am not of the
opinion that vegetables receive their nourishment only
through the ascending part of the plant, as the stem,
branches, leaves, etc., and that their descending parts, as the
roots and fibers, only serve to hold and retain them in their
places, yet I believe they imbibe rain and dews through
their leaves, stems, and branches by extremely minute
pores, which open on both surfaces of the leaves and on the
branches, which may communicate to little auxiliary ducts or
vessels. Or, perhaps, the cool dews and showers, by con-
stricting these pores and thereby preventing a too-free per-
spiration, may recover and again invigorate the languid
nerves of those which seem to suffer for want of water in
great heats and droughts. But, whether the insects caught in
their leaves and which dissolve and mix with the fluid serve
for aliment or support to these kind of plants, is doubtful.
All the Sarracenias are insect catchers, and so is the Drossea
rotundifolia [sundew].

But admirable are the properties of the extraordinary
Dionea muscipula [Venus's-flytrap]! A great extent on each
side of that serpentine rivulet is occupied by those sportive
vegetables — let us advance to the spot in which nature has
seated them. Astonishing production! See the incarnate lobes
expanding, how gay and sportive they appear! Ready on the
spring to entrap incautious, deluded insects! What artifice!
There, behold, one of the leaves just closed upon a struggling
fly; another has gotten a worm; its hold is sure, its prey can
never escape — carnivorous vegetable! Can we, after viewing
this object, hesitate a moment to confess that vegetable
beings are endued with some sensible faculties or attributes,
familiar to those that dignify animal nature? They are organ-

ical, living, and self-moving bodies, for we see here, in this plant, motion and volition.

The Golden Primrose (Oenothera Grandiflora)

[*Discovered at Taensa Bluff (probably near Stockton, Alabama) on the Tensaw River. Ed.*]

Early one morning, passing along by some old, uncultivated fields a few miles above Taensa, I was struck with surprise at the appearance of a blooming plant, gilded with the richest golden-yellow. Stepping on shore, I discovered it to be a new species of Oenothera, perhaps the most pompous and brilliant herbaceous plant yet known to exist. It is an annual or biennial, rising erect seven or eight feet, branching on all sides from near the earth upwards, the lower branches extensive, and the succeeding gradually shorter to the top of the plant, forming a pyramid in figure. The leaves are of a broad, lanceolate shape, dentated or deeply serrated, terminating with a slender point, and of a deep, full, green color. The large expanded flowers that so ornament this plant are of a splendid, perfect yellow color, but when they contract again, before they drop off, the underside of the petals next the calyx becomes of a reddish flesh color, inclining to vermilion. The flowers begin to open in the evening, are fully expanded during the night, and are in their beauty next morning, but close and wither before noon. There is a daily profuse succession for many weeks, and one single plant at the same instant presents to view many hundred flowers. I have measured these flowers above five inches in diameter. They have an agreeable scent.[4]

Fossil Oysters of Shell Bluff, Georgia

[*By John Bartram. This was the first scientific description of the giant fossil oysters. Nearly seventy years later they were named* Ostrea georgiana. *Ed.*]

September 10, 1765. . . . Took five or six hands and two battoes and provisions down the river [Savannah] twelve miles to the great oystershell bank, above 150 foot high, at the bottom of which issued out the loveliest spring of clear water I saw in all this journey. It came out in a body, about as much as would run through the bunghole of a hogshead, very sweet and just cold enough to drink heartily of, about six foot above the surface of the river. This perpendicular bank is formed of oystershells all broke to small particles like coarse sand . . . about as hard as the bermudous rocks used for building and just such a consistency. One may cut it very easily with a knife. It reacheth down to the water. Under the rock is a coarse yellow sand, as I found by undermining it. This perpendicular bluff continueth above 200 yards, at each end of which the hill gradually falls back from the river for several miles, until a large rich bottom is formed between the hill and the river.

The bank or middling steep, rich hill is about four, five, or six foot of vegetable mold, through which the neighboring inhabitants for many miles dig, when they come to a prodigious mass of very large oystershells, most of which is in clusters but the vacancies close filled with smaller and single ones forced in all directions. To what extent this prodigious mass is extended is yet unknown, but about thirty miles below, a bluff appears of still larger ones. Perhaps there may be an unknown continuation between them.

Bald Eagle, Vultures, and Wolves

There is a great extent of rich low land all the way from this bluff to Mr. Golphin's, except the Silver Bluff about a mile below, where the Spaniards formerly made some attempt to obtain some silver, but it being chiefly in the bed of the river, they made no hand of it. They made some attempt to turn the river by cutting through a point below, but whether the Indians drove them off or they thought it would not quit cost, they did not go forward with it. They made a pretty large entrenchment a mile above it. . . .⁵

Wolves on the Alachua Savannah in Florida

Observing a company of wolves under a few trees, about a quarter of a mile from shore, we rode up towards them. They, observing our approach, sat on their hinder parts until we came nearly within shot of them, when they trotted off towards the forests, but stopped again and looked at us, at about two hundred yards distance. We then whooped, and made a feint to pursue them, when they separated from each other, some stretching off into the plains and others seeking covert in the groves on shore. When we got to the trees, we observed they had been feeding on the carcass of a horse. The wolves of Florida are larger than a dog and are perfectly black, except the females, which have a white spot on the breast; but they are not so large as the wolves of Canada and Pennsylvania, which are of a yellowish brown color. There were a number of vultures on the trees over the carcass who, as soon as the wolves ran off, immediately settled down upon it. They were, however, held in restraint and subordination by the bald eagle.⁶

7. William Bartram Explores from Charleston, South Carolina, to Augusta, Georgia, 1774

[*In November 1774 William Bartram sailed from Spalding's Lower Store on St. John's River. Arriving in Charleston with his collection of seeds, plants, notes, and drawings, he had time to explore the surrounding country while leisurely making plans to follow Dr. John Fothergill's instructions to travel into the lands of the Cherokees and the Muscogulges. This journey took him into the mountains west of Keowe and finally south and westward to Mobile, Pensacola, and the Mississippi River.*

[*Silver Bluff, on which Fort Moore was located, lay about twelve miles south of Augusta on the Carolina shore of the Savannah. This place had been a base for Mark Catesby, who preceded the Bartrams in this area. Shell Bluff lies on the Georgia shore of the Savannah across the river from today's U.S. Atomic Energy Commission Savannah River Plant Reservation. John Bartram (see page 116) was apparently the first scientist to note the giant oystershells in the ancient fossil mound. Ed.*]

William Bartram to His Father

Charleston, March 27, 1775

Honored and Benevolent Father:

I am happy, by the blessings of the Almighty God by whose care I have been protected and led safe through a pilgrimage these three and twenty months till my return to

Charleston two days since. I am now lodged most kindly in the family of your deceased friend Lambol. His daughter, Mrs. Thomas, excellent in goodness beyond her sex, with expressions of the same affable and cordial friendship so particular in the character of her ancient, excellent parent, asked me to her house while I stay in this province, which [I] believe will be but a few days.

I wrote to my father soon after my return to Savannah from Tugaloo River, which letter gives an account of my proceedings there in that journey, which I traveled upwards of 300 miles. I collected a large number of specimens I sent to Doctor Fothergill with some drawings, in answer to which the doctor was pleased to send me a list of the new and non-described, which I was glad to find were many, and here he was pleased to express his satisfaction with the success of my labors and his willingness that I should continue my researches. This packet I received in East Florida soon after my return to Savannah, in order to forward my collections to Doctor Fothergill.

I intended to go back into the Cherokee and Creek countries, when the alarm from the frontiers of hostilities commencing between the Indians and the whites put a stop to that scheme. I then turned my views towards East Florida and prepared for it. I put my baggage on board a vessel bound from Savannah to Mr. Spalding's Store on the St. John's, intending to go by land there and set off accordingly. Got safe to the Altamaha, where I was taken ill of a fever of which I did not recover so as to be able to travel for near two months, when I set off again but was turned back again by expresses from East Florida that the Indians were up in arms against us in that province, having killed and captured several white people, and the inhabitants were flying in to

Augustine, and all the Indian stores except one were robbed and broken up. So I stayed in the south part of Georgia, waiting for a favorable turn, and here I discovered and collected many valuable and new vegetables.

Hearing that the Lower Creeks were dealing with the governor of St. Augustine for peace, I resolved to make the second attempt. I left my horse in Georgia and went down the Altamaha to Frederica on the Island St. Simon. Waited on Mr. Spalding, who was pleased to give me letters to his agent in East Florida, and in a few days went on board his vessel bound to his store on St. John's. Two days after we left Frederica we met another of his vessels. We came too, went on board. This vessel was returned from the Store, having on board numbers of traders returning from the Indian country, being drove away by the Indians. They brought very bad tales and had on board the vessel all the goods of the trading houses except a few which the governor of Florida purchased of Mr. Spalding's agent, at the request of the Seminole Indians, they being desirous to have the Lower Store kept up. These goods were landed on an island a few miles below the Store in the river St. John's, where my chest and baggage was with them. The vessel returned back to Frederica and I prevailed on them to set me on Amelia Island near the mouth of St. Mary's, being determined to pursue my journey into Florida at all events, and having some papers and books in my chest which I stood in need of; I walked the beach until I came to a plantation where I was friendly received by Lord Egmont's agent.

I stayed with him three or four days on his promising me a passage to St. John's in a boat. He going to St. Augustine, [we] went on board a boat rowed by five Negroes and in about thirty hours arrived at St. John's near the Cowford, and here I was again put to my shift, being once more left alone. However, this gentleman sent me to a plantation, in his boat, higher up the river where I purchased a small canoe. I, having furnished myself with a sail and paddle, set off on my voyage up the river St. John's and got safe to the island, where I found my chest. Went to the Store, where I heard much more favorable accounts of the Indian affairs, and on conferring with Mr. Spalding's agent, he encouraged me to stay a while until the Indians were quiet. A short time after this, some of the traders thought fit to risk a journey out to Alachua in quest of horses which they had amongst the Indians. I, having an inclination to see the Seminole Indian town of Cuscoela on the great Alachua savannah, went with them.

The savannah is vast and beautiful beyond description. The chief of the town received us most friendly, assured us of his protection, and gave the traders liberty to hunt up their horses. I rode with them near fifty miles round the green verge of this beautiful savannah and went to the sink, or vortex, where the waters are discharged. The savannah is surrounded by hammocks of rich land planted with orange groves, palm trees, Morus, Magnolia grandiflora, Tilia, Laurus ocra, Laurus coeasus and a variety of other trees and shrubs.

After a week or ten days, returned from Alachua to the Store. Continued my excursions about the country. Took a trip in my canoe up the St. John's about 100 miles above the Store to the uppermost plantation. Returned down to the Store and after some time an opportunity offered to an Indian town on Little St. Juan's River at the Bay of Apalache, about 100 miles west from the Store across the isthmus. This was a pleasant journey and afforded me many curiosities. The face and condition of this country is Indian, new and pleasing.

The Indians of the town received us with the complaisance and good breeding peculiar to them, treated us with the best they had, and offered us their protection whilst with them.

Returned to the Store and took another voyage up the St. John's. Returned with some fine roots and seeds which, together with my former collections, made up three large boxes of roots and one of seeds, which I carried up with me to Sunbury in Georgia; there I put them on board a vessel to London for Doctor Fothergill, having collected a number of curious roots in Georgia.

Dear Father, it is the greatest pleasure that I hear by my worthy Doctor Chalmers that you are alive and well, with my dear Mother, which I pray may continue. I beg leave to acquaint my benevolent parents that I am resolved, with the concurrence of Doctor Chalmers, to continue my travels another year; intend to go through the Cherokee countries to Pensacola, where I shall send my necessary baggage, and if it please God to spare my life and health, I may go to the Mississippi River. I have been often with the Doctor concerning it, and he promises to assist me with proper recommendatory letters through the Nations. Please to excuse this long, tedious letter.

I am ever your faithful son,

William Bartram

I have not had the favor of a line from my Father or Mother, whom God ever preserve.[1]

A Journey from Charleston to Augusta

April 22nd, 1775. I set off from Charleston for the Chero-kee nations and after riding this day about twenty-five miles, arrived in the evening at Jacksonburg, a village on the Pon-pon River. The next day's journey was about the same dis-tance, to a public house, or inn, on the road.

The next day, early in the morning, I set off again, and about noon stopped at a public house to dine. After the meridian heats were abated, proceeding on till evening, I obtained good quarters at a private house, having rode this day about thirty miles. At this plantation I observed a large orchard of the European mulberry tree (Morus alba), some of which were grafted on stocks of the native mulberry (Morus rubra); these trees were cultivated for the purpose of feeding silkworms (Phalaena bombyx). Having break-fasted, I set forward again.

I soon entered a high forest, continuing the space of fifteen miles to the Three Sisters, a public ferry on the Savannah River: the country generally very level; the soil a dark, loose, fertile mold, on a stratum of cinereous-colored clay; the ground shaded with its native forests, consisting of the great black oak, Quercus tinctoria, Q. rubra, Q. phellos, Q. prinos, Q. hemispherica, Juglans nigra, J. rustica, J. exaltata, Mag-nolia grandiflora, Fraxinus excelsior, Acer rubrum, Nyssa sylvatica, Platanus occidentalis, Tilia, Ulmus campestris, U. subifer, Laurus sassafras, L. Borbonia, Ilex aquifolium, Fagus sylvatica, Cornus florida, Halesia, Aesculus pavia, Sambucus, Callicarpa, and Stewartia malachodendron, with a variety of other trees and shrubs. This ancient, sublime forest, fre-quently intersected with extensive avenues, vistas, and green lawns, opening to extensive savannahs and far-distant rice plantations, agreeably employs the imagination and captivates the senses by scenes of magnificence and grandeur.

The gay mock-bird, vocal and joyous, mounts aloft on silvered wings, rolls over and over, then gently descends, and presides in the choir of the tuneful tribes.

Having dined at the ferry, I crossed the river into Georgia. On landing and ascending the bank, which was here a north prospect, I observed the Dirca palustris, growing six or seven feet high. I rode about twelve miles further through pine forests and savannahs. In the evening I took up my quarters at a delightful habitation, though not a common tavern. Having ordered my horse a stable and provender, and refreshed my spirits with a draught of cooling liquor, I betook myself to contemplation in the groves and lawns. Directing my steps towards the river, I observed in a high pine forest on the border of a savannah a great number of cattle herded together, and on my nearer approach discovered it to be a cow pen. On my coming up I was kindly saluted by my host and his wife, who I found were superintending a number of slaves, women, boys, and girls, that were milking the cows. Here were about forty milch cows and as many young calves, for in these southern countries the calves run with the cows a whole year, the people milking them at the same time. The pen, including two or three acres of ground, more or less, according to the stock, adjoining a rivulet or run of water, is enclosed by a fence. In this enclosure the calves are kept while the cows are out at range. A small part of this pen is partitioned off to receive the cows, when they come up at evening. Here are several stakes drove into the ground, and there is a gate in the partition fence for a communication between the two pens. When the milkmaid has taken her

share of milk, she looses the calf, who strips the cow, which
is next morning turned out again to range.

I found these people, contrary to what a traveler might
think, perhaps reasonably expect, from their occupation and
remote situation from the capital or any commercial town,
to be civil and courteous: and though educated as it were in
the woods, no strangers to sensibility and those moral virtues
which grace and ornament the most approved and admired
characters in civil society.

After the vessels were filled with milk, the daily and liberal supply of the friendly kine, and the good wife with her
maids and servants were returning with it to the dairy, the
gentleman was at leisure to attend to my enquiries and
observations, which he did with complaisance and apparent
pleasure. On my observing to him that his stock of horned
cattle must be very considerable to afford so many milch
cows at one time, he answered that he had about fifteen
hundred head. "My stock is but young; having lately removed from some distance to this place, I found it convenient
to part with most of my old stock and begin here anew.
Heaven is pleased to bless my endeavors and industry with
success even beyond my own expectations."

Yet continuing my interrogatories on this subject: "Your
stock, I apprehend, must be very profitable, being so convenient to the capital and seaport, in affording a vast quantity of
beef, butter, and cheese for the market, and must thereby contribute greatly towards your emolument."

"Yes, I find my stock of cattle very profitable, and I constantly contribute towards supplying the markets with beef;
but as to the articles of butter and cheese, I make no more
than what is expended in my own household, and I have a
considerable family of black people, who, though they are

slaves, must be fed and cared for. Those I have were either chosen for their good qualities or born in the family, and I find from long experience and observation that the better they are fed, clothed, and treated the more service and profit we may expect to derive from their labor. In short, I find my flock produces no more milk or any article of food or nourishment than what is expended to the best advantage amongst my family and slaves."

He added, "Come along with me towards the river bank, where I have some men at work squaring pine and cypress timber for the West India market. I will show you their day's work, when you will readily grant that I have reason to acknowledge myself sufficiently gratified for the little attention bestowed towards them. At yonder little new habitation near the bluff on the banks of the river, I have settled my eldest son; it is but a few days since he was married to a deserving young woman."

Having at length arrived near the high banks of the majestic savannah, we stood at the timber landing. Almost every object in our progress contributed to demonstrate this good man's system of economy to be not only practicable but eligible; and the slaves appeared on all sides as a crowd of witnesses to justify his industry, humanity, and liberal spirit.

The slaves, comparatively of a gigantic stature, fat and muscular, were mounted on the massive timber logs; the regular heavy strokes of their gleaming axes re-echoed in the deep forests; at the same time, contented and joyful, the sooty sons of Afric, forgetting their bondage, in chorus sung the virtues and beneficence of their master in songs of their own composition.

The log or timber landing is a capacious open area, the lofty pines having been felled and cleared away for a considerable distance round about, near an almost perpendicular bluff or steep bank of the river rising up immediately from the water to the height of sixty or seventy feet. The logs being dragged by timber wheels to this yard, and landed as near the brink of this high bank as possible with safety, and laid by the side of each other, are rolled off and precipitated down the bank into the river where, being formed into rafts, they are conducted by slaves down to Savannah, about fifty miles below this place.

Having contemplated these scenes of art and industry, my venerable host, in company with his son, conducted me to the neat habitation which is situated in a spacious airy forest a little distance from the river bank, commanding a comprehensive and varied prospect: an extensive reach of the river in front; on the right hand a spacious lawn or savannah; on the left the timber yard; the vast, fertile, low lands and forests on the river upwards, and the plantations adjoining. A cool evening arrived after a sultry day. As we approached the door, conducted by the young man, his lovely bride, arrayed in native innocence and becoming modesty, with an air and smile of grace and benignity, met and saluted us! "What a Venus! What an Adonis!" said I in silent transport. Every action and feature seemed to reveal the celestial endowments of the mind. Though a native sprightliness and sensibility appear, yet virtue and discretion direct and rule. The dress of this beauteous sylvan queen was plain but clean, neat and elegant, all of cotton, and of her own spinning and weaving.

Next morning early I set forward, prosecuting my tour. I pursued the high road leading from Savannah to Augusta for the distance of one hundred miles or more, and then recrossed the river at Silver Bluff, a pleasant villa, the property and seat of G. Golphin, esquire, a gentleman of very distinguished talents and great liberality, who possessed the most extensive trade, connections, and influence among the south and southwest Indian tribes, particularly with the Creeks and Choctaws: of whom I fortunately obtained letters of recommendation and credit to the principal traders residing in the Indian towns.

Silver Bluff is a very celebrated place. It is a considerable height upon the Carolina shore of the Savannah River, perhaps thirty feet higher than the low lands on the opposite shore, which are subject to be overflowed in the spring and fall. This steep bank rises perpendicularly out of the river, discovering various strata of earth. The surface, for a considerable depth, is a loose sandy loam with a mixture of sea shells, especially ostreæ;* the next stratum is clay, then sand; next marl; then clays again of various colors and qualities, which last insensibly mix or unite with a deep stratum of blackish or dark slate-colored saline and sulphureous earth, which seems to be of an aluminous or vitriolic quality, and lies in nearly horizontal laminæ or strata of various thickness. We discovered belemnites, pyrites, marcasites, and sulphureous nodules, shining like brass, some single of various forms, and others conglomerated, lying in this black slaty-like micaceous earth; as also, sticks, limbs, and trunks of trees, leaves, acorns, and their cups, all transmuted or changed black, hard and shining as charcoal. We also saw animal substances, as if petrified, or what are called shark's teeth; but these heterogeneous substances or petrifactions are the most abundant and conspicuous where there is a looser kind of earth, either immediately upon this vast stratum of black earth or in the divisions of the laminæ. The surface of the

* Oyster. [Ed.]

ground upon this bluff extends a mile and a half or two
miles on the river and is from a half mile to a mile in breadth,
nearly level, and a good fertile soil; as is evident from the
vast oaks, hickory, mulberry, black walnut and other trees
and shrubs which are left standing in the old fields which
are spread abroad to a great distance; and discovers various
monuments and vestiges of the residence of the ancients, as
Indian conical mounts, terraces, areas, etc., as well as remains or traces of fortresses of regular formation, as if constructed after the modes of European military architects,
which are supposed to be ancient camps of the Spaniards who
formerly fixed themselves at this place in hopes of finding
silver.

But perhaps Mr. Golphin's buildings and improvements
will prove to be the foundation of monuments of infinitely
greater celebrity and permanency than either of the preceding establishments.

The place, which at this day is called Fort Moore, is a stupendous bluff or high perpendicular bank of earth rising out
of the river on the Carolina shore, perhaps ninety or one
hundred feet above the common surface of the water. It
exhibits a singular and pleasing spectacle to a stranger, especially from the opposite shore or, as we pass up or down
the river, presents a view of prodigious walls of particolored
earths, chiefly clays and marl of various colors, as brown,
red, yellow, blue, purple, white, etc., in horizontal strata, one
over the other.

Waiting for the ferry boat to carry me over, I walked almost round the under side of the bluff, betwixt its steep wall
and the water of the river, which glided rapidly under my
feet. I came to the carcass of a calf, which the people told me
had fallen down from the edge of the precipice above, being

invited too far by grass and sweet herbs, which they say frequently happens at this place. In early times, the Carolinians had a fort and kept a good garrison here as a frontier and Indian trading post; but Augusta superseding it, this place was dismantled. Since that time, which probably cannot exceed thirty years, the river hath so much encroached upon the Carolina shore that its bed now lies where the site of the fort then was. Indeed some told me that the opposite Georgia shore, where there is now a fine house and corn field, occupies the place.

The site of Augusta is perhaps the most delightful and eligible of any in Georgia for a city: an extensive level plain on the banks of a fine navigable river, which has its numerous sources in the Cherokee mountains, a fruitful and temperate region, whence, after roving and winding about those fertile heights, they meander through a fertile hilly country, and one after another combine in forming the Tugilo and Broad Rivers, and then the famous Savannah River. Thence they continue near a hundred miles more, following its meanders and falls over the cataracts at Augusta, which cross the river at the upper end of the town. These falls are four or five feet perpendicular height in the summer season when the river is low. From these cataracts upwards, this river with all its tributaries, as Broad River, Little River, Tugilo, etc. is one continued rapid with some short intervals of still water, navigable for canoes. But from Augusta downwards to the ocean, a distance of near three hundred miles by water, the Savannah uninterruptedly flows with a gentle meandering course, and is navigable for vessels of twenty or thirty tons burthen to Savannah, where ships of three hundred tons lie in a capacious and secure harbor.

Augusta, thus seated at the head of navigation and just

below the conflux of several of its most considerable branches, without a competitor, commands the trade and commerce of vast, fruitful regions above it and from every side to a great distance; and I do not hesitate to pronounce as my opinion, will very soon become the metropolis of Georgia.

I chose to take this route up the Savannah River in preference to the straight and shorter road from Charleston to the Cherokee country by Fort Ninety-Six because, by keeping near this great river, I had frequent opportunities of visiting its steep banks, vast swamps, and low grounds; and had the advantage, without great delay or deviating from the main high road, of observing the various soils and situations of the countries through which this famous river pursues its course, and of examining their various productions, mineral, vegetable, and animal. Had I pursued the great trading path by Ninety-Six, I should have been led over a high, dry, sandy, and gravelly ridge, and a great part of the distance an old settled or resorted part of the country and consequently void of the varieties of original or novel productions of nature.

Before I leave Augusta, I shall recite a curious phenomenon, which may furnish ample matter for philosophical discussion to the curious naturalists. On the Georgia side of the river, about fifteen miles below Silver Bluff, the high road crosses a ridge of high, swelling hills of uncommon elevation, and perhaps seventy feet higher than the surface of the river. These hills, from three feet below the common vegetative surface to the depth of twenty or thirty feet, are composed entirely of fossil oystershells, internally of the color and consistency of clear, white marble. The shells are of incredible magnitude, generally fifteen or twenty inches in length, from six to eight wide, and two to four in thickness, and their hollows sufficient to receive an ordinary man's foot. They appear all to have been opened before the period of petrifaction, a transmutation they seem evidently to have suffered. They are undoubtedly very ancient or perhaps antediluvian. The adjacent inhabitants burn them to lime for building, for which purpose they serve very well and would undoubtedly afford an excellent manure when their lands require it, these hills being now remarkably fertile. The heaps of shells lie upon a stratum of a yellowish sandy mold, of several feet in depth, upon a foundation of soft white rocks that has the outward appearance of freestone but on strict examination is really a testaceous concrete or composition of sand and pulverized sea shells. In short, this testaceous rock approaches near in quality and appearance to the Bahama or Bermudian white rock.[2]

8. A Journey from Fort Prince George to the Valley of the Little Tennessee River, and the Great Trail Across Alabama

[William Bartram was the first naturalist to explore the Old Charleston-Cherokee Trail from Fort Prince George on the Keowe River to Cowee (now West's Mill, North Carolina), beyond Franklin on the Little Tennessee. Leaving Prince George, he crossed the Keowe at a ford just below the fort, followed Oconee Creek to its head, climbed Oconee Mountain, then descended to the Chattooga River. Crossing that river, he made his way up the narrow, very rugged valley of War Woman Creek (which he called Falling Creek). At the head of this creek, he turned due north, passing Rabun Gap, and entered the valley of the Little Tennessee. In the wealth of plant life he saw along the trail were many old friends, but he discovered many others new to science. Ed.]

[*May 1776.*] I waited two or three days at this post, expecting the return of an Indian who was out hunting. This man was recommended to me as a suitable person for a protector and guide to the Indian settlements over the hills, but upon information that he would not be in shortly, and there being no other person suitable for the purpose, rather than be detained, and perhaps thereby frustrated in my purposes, I determined to set off alone and run all risks.

I crossed the river at a good ford just below the old fort. The river here is just one hundred yards over. After an agreeable progress for about two miles over delightful strawberry plains and gently swelling green hills, I began to ascend more steep and rocky ridges. Having gained a very considerable elevation, looking round, I enjoyed a very comprehensive and delightful view. Keowe, which I had but just lost sight of, appeared again, and the serpentine river speeding through the lucid green plain apparently just under my feet. After observing this delightful landscape, I continued on again three or four miles, keeping the trading path, which led me over uneven rocky land, crossing rivulets and brooks, and rapidly descending over rocky precipices, when I came into a charming vale, embellished with a delightful glittering river which meandered through it and crossed my road. On my left hand, upon the grassy bases of the rising hills, appeared the remains of a town of the ancients, as the tumuli, terraces, posts or pillars, old peach and plum orchards, etc. sufficiently testify. These vales and swelling bases of the surrounding hills afford vast crops of excellent grass and herbage fit for pasturage and hay. . . .

Ginseng now appears plentifully on the north exposure of the hill, growing out of the rich, mellow, humid earth amongst the stones or fragments of rocks.

Having crossed the vales, I began to ascend again the more lofty ridges of hills, then continued about eight miles over more gentle pyramidal hills, narrow vales and lawns, the soil exceedingly fertile, producing lofty forests and odoriferous groves of Calycanthus, near the banks of rivers, with Halesia, Philadelphus inodorus, Rhododendron ferrugineum, Azalea, Stewartia montana* . . . all in full bloom and decorated with the following sweet roving climbers, Bignonia sempervirens, Big. crucigera, Lonicera sempervirens, Rosa paniculata, etc. . . . At once the mounts divided and dis-

* This was a new species of Stewartia, unknown to the European botanists and not mentioned in any catalogue. [Ed.]

closed to view the ample Oconee vale, encircled by a wreath of uniform hills, their swelling bases clad in cheerful verdure over which, issuing from between the mountains, plays along a glittering river, meandering through the meadows. Crossing these at the upper end of the vale, I began to ascend the Oconee Mountain. On the foot of the hills were ruins of the ancient Oconee town. The first step after leaving the verdant beds of the hills was a very high, rocky chain of pointed hills, extremely well timbered with the following trees: Quercus tinctoria, Querc. alba, Querc. rubra, Fraxinus excelsior, Juglans hickory various species, Ulmus, Tilia, Acer saccharinum, Morus, Juglans nigra, Juglans alba, Annona glabra, Robinia pseudacacia, Magnolia acuminata, Aesculus sylvatica, with many more, particularly a species of Robinia new to me, though perhaps the same as figured and slightly described by Catesby in his *Nat. Hist. Carol.* This beautiful flowering tree grows twenty and thirty feet high, with a crooked leaning trunk. The branches spread greatly and wreath about, some almost touching the ground. However, there appears a singular pleasing wildness and freedom in its manner of growth; the slender subdivisions of the branches terminate with heavy compound panicles of rose or pink-colored flowers, amidst a wreath of beautiful pinnated leaves.

My next flight was up a very high peak, to the top of the Oconee Mountain, where I rested; and turning about, found that I was now in a very elevated situation, from whence I enjoyed a view inexpressibly magnificent and comprehensive. The mountainous wilderness which I had lately traversed, down to the region of Augusta, appearing regularly undulated as the great ocean after a tempest; the undulations gradually depressing, yet perfectly regular, as the squamæ of fish or imbrications of tile on a roof. The nearest ground to me [was] of a perfect full green, next more glaucous, and lastly almost blue as the ether with which the most distant curve of the horizon seemed to be blended.

My imagination thus wholly engaged in the contemplation of this magnificent landscape, infinitely varied and without bound, I was almost insensible or regardless of the charming objects more within my reach: a new species of rhododendron, foremost in the assembly of mountain beauties; next the flaming azalea, Kalmia latifolia, Robinia, snowy mantled Philadelphus inodorus, perfumed Calycanthus, etc.

This species of rhododendron grows six or seven feet high; many nearly erect stems arise together from the root, forming a group or coppice. The leaves are three or four inches in length, of an oblong figure, broadest toward the extremity and terminating with an obtuse point. Their upper surface is of a deep green and polished, but the nether surface of a rusty iron color, which seems to be effected by innumerable minute reddish vesicles, beneath a fine short, downy pubescence. The numerous flexible branches terminate with a loose, spiked raceme, or cluster of large, deep-rose-colored flowers, each flower being affixed in the diffused cluster of a long peduncle which, with the whole plant, possesses an agreeable perfume.

After being recovered of the fatigue and labor in ascending the mountain, I began again to prosecute my task. Proceeding through a shady forest, I soon after gained the most elevated crest of the Oconee Mountain and then began to descend the other side. The winding, rough road carried me over rocky hills and levels shaded by incomparable forests, the soil exceedingly rich and of an excellent quality for the production of every vegetable suited to the climate. It seemed peculiarly adapted for the cultivation of vines, olives,

the almond tree, fig, and perhaps the pomegranate, as well as
peaches. . . . I passed again steep, rocky ascents and then
rich levels, where grew many trees and plants common in
Pennsylvania, New York, and even Canada, as Pinus strobus,
Pin. sylvestris, Pin. abies, Acer saccharinum, Acer striatum,
s. Pennsylvanicum, Populus tremula, Betula nigra, Juglans
alba, and so on; but what seems remarkable, the yellow Jessamine, which is killed by a very slight frost in Pennsylvania,
here on the summit of the Cherokee Mountains associates
with the Canadian vegetables and appears roving with them
in perfect bloom and gaiety; as likewise Halesia diptera, and
Hal. tetraptera, mountain Stewartia, Styrax, Ptelea, Aesculus
pavia; but all these bear our hardest frosts in Pennsylvania.
Then I entered a charming narrow vale through which flows
a rapid large creek, on whose banks are happily associated
the shrubs already recited, together with the following:
Staphylea, Euonymus Americana, Hamamelis, Azalea (various species), Aristolochia frutescens, s. odoratissima, which
rambles over the trees and shrubs on the prolific banks of
these mountain brooks. Passed through magnificent high forests and then came upon the borders of an ample meadow
on the left, embroidered by the shade of a high circular am-
phitheater of hills, the circular ridges rising magnificently
one over the other. On the green turfy bases of these ascents
appear the ruins of a town of the ancients. The upper end of
this spacious green plain is divided by a promontory or spur
of the ridges before me, which projects into it. My road led
me up into an opening of the ascents through which the glittering brook which watered the meadows ran rapidly down,
dashing and roaring over high rocky steps. Continued, yet
ascending, until I gained the top of an elevated rocky ridge,
when appeared before me a gap or opening between other

yet more lofty ascents, through which [I] continued as the
rough rocky road led me, close by the winding banks of a
large rapid brook which, at length turning to the left, pouring down rocky precipices, glided off through dark groves and
high forests, conveying streams of fertility and pleasure to
the fields below.

The surface of the land now for three or four miles was
level, yet uneven, occasioned by natural mounds or rocky
knobs, but covered with a good staple of rich earth, which affords forests of timber trees and shrubs. After this, gently descending again, I traveled some miles over a varied situation
of ground, exhibiting views of grand forests, dark detached
groves, vales, and meadows, as heretofore, and producing the
like vegetable and other works of nature. The meadows afforded exuberant pasturage for cattle, and the bases of the
encircling hills, flowering plants, and fruitful strawberry
beds. I observed frequently ruins of the habitations or villages of the ancients. Crossed a delightful river, the main
branch of Tugilo, when I began to ascend again, first over
swelling turfy ridges, varied with groves of stately forest
trees; then ascending again more steep, grassy hillsides,
rested on the top of Mount Magnolia, which appeared to me
to be the highest ridge of the Cherokee Mountains, which
separate the waters of Savannah River from those of the
Tanase or greater main branch of the Cherokee River. This,
running rapidly a northwest course through the mountains,
is joined from the northeast by the Holstein. Thence taking a
west course yet amongst the mountains, receiving into it
from either hand many large rivers, [it] leaves the mountains, immediately after being joined by a large river from
the east, becomes a mighty river by the name of Hogehege,
thence meanders many hundred miles through a vast country

consisting of forests, meadows, groves, expansive savannahs, fields, and swelling hills, most fertile and delightful, flows into the beautiful Ohio, and in conjunction with its transparent waters becomes tributary to the sovereign .Mississippi.

This exalted peak I named Mount Magnolia, from a new and beautiful species of that celebrated family of flowering trees which here, at the cascades of Falling Creek, grows in a high degree of perfection. I had, indeed, noticed this curious tree several times before, particularly on the high ridges betwixt Sinica and Keowe and on ascending the first mountain after leaving Keowe, when I observed it in flower, but here it flourishes and commands our attention.

This tree,* or perhaps rather shrub, rises eighteen to thirty feet in height; there are usually many stems from a root or source, which lean a little, or slightly diverge from each other. In this respect imitating the Magnolia tripetala. The crooked wreathing branches arise and subdivide from the main stem without order or uniformity. Their extremities turn upwards, producing a very large rosaceous, perfectly white, double or polypetalous flower, which is of a most fragrant scent. This fine flower sits in the center of a radius of very large leaves which are of a singular figure, somewhat lanceolate but broad towards their extremities, terminated with an acuminated point. Backwards they attenuate and become very narrow towards their bases, terminating that way with two long narrow ears or lappets, one on each side of the insertion of the petiole. The leaves have only short footstalks sitting very near each other at the extremities of the floriferous branches, from whence they spread themselves after a regular order, like the spokes of a wheel. Their margins,

---

* Magnolia auriculata.

touching or lightly lapping upon each other, form an expansive umbrella superbly crowned or crested with the fragrant flower, representing a white plume. The blossom is succeeded by a very large crimson cone or strobile containing a great number of scarlet berries which, when ripe, spring from their cells and are for a time suspended by a white silky web or thread. The leaves of those trees which grow in a rich, light humid soil, when fully expanded and at maturity, are frequently above two feet in length and six or eight inches where broadest. I discovered in the maritime parts of Georgia, particularly on the banks of the Altamaha, another new species of Magnolia, whose leaves were nearly of the figure of those of this tree, but they were much less in size, not more than six or seven inches in length, and the strobile very small, oblong, sharp-pointed, and of a fine deep crimson color; but I never saw the flower. These trees grow straight and erect, thirty feet or more in height and of a sharp conical form much resembling the cucumber tree (Mag. acuminata) in figure.

The day being remarkably warm and sultry, together with the labor and fatigue of ascending the mountains, made me very thirsty and in some degree sunk my spirits. Past midday, I sought a cool, shaded retreat where was water for refreshment and grazing for my horse — my faithful slave and only companion. After proceeding a little farther, descending the other side of the mountain, I perceived at some distance before me, on my right hand, a level plain supporting a grand high forest and groves. The nearer I approached, my steps were the more accelerated from the flattering prospect opening to view. I now entered upon the verge of the dark forest, charming solitude! As I advanced through the animating shades, I observed on the farther grassy verge a shady grove;

thither I directed my steps. On approaching these shades, between the stately columns of the superb forest trees, [there was] presented to view, rushing from rocky precipices under the shade of the pensile hills, the unparalleled cascade of Falling Creek, rolling and leaping off the rocks. The waters, uniting below, spread a broad glittering sheet over a vast convex elevation of plain smooth rocks and are immediately received by a spacious basin where, trembling in the center through hurry and agitation, they gently subside, encircling the painted still verge; from whence gliding swiftly, they soon form a delightful little river which, continuing to flow more moderately, is restrained for a moment, gently undulating in a little lake: they then pass on rapidly to a high perpendicular steep of rocks, from whence these delightful waters are hurried down with irresistible rapidity. I here seated myself on the moss-clad rocks, under the shade of spreading trees and floriferous fragrant shrubs, in full view of the cascades.

At this rural retirement were assembled a charming circle of mountain vegetable beauties: Magnolia auriculata, Rhododendron ferrugineum, Kalmia latifolia, Robinia montana, Azalea flammula, Rosa paniculata, Calycanthus floridus, Philadelphus inodorus, perfumed Convalaria majalis, Anemone thalictroides, Triilium sessile, Trillium cessnum, Cypripedium, Arethusa, Ophrys, Sanguinaria, Viola uvularia, Epigea, Mitchella repens, Stewartia, Halesia, Styrax, Lonicera, etc. Some of these roving beauties stroll over the mossy, shelving, humid rocks or from off the expansive wavy boughs of trees, bending over the floods, salute their delusive shade, playing on the surface. Some plunge their perfumed heads and bathe their flexile limbs in the silver stream, whilst others by the mountain breezes are tossed about, their blooming tufts bespangled with pearly and crystalline dewdrops collected from the falling mists, glistening in the rainbow arch. Having collected some valuable specimens at this friendly retreat, I continued my lonesome pilgrimage. My road for a considerable time led me winding and turning about the steep rocky hills, the descent of some of which were very rough and troublesome because of fragments of rocks, slippery clay and talc. After this I entered a spacious forest, the land having gradually acquired a more level surface. A pretty grassy vale appeared on my right, through which my wandering path led me, close by the banks of a delightful creek which, sometimes falling over steps of rocks, glided gently with serpentine meanders through the meadows.

After crossing this delightful brook and mead, the land rises again with sublime magnificence, and I am led over hills and vales, groves and high forests, vocal with the melody of the feathered songsters, the snow-white cascades glittering on the sides of the distant hills.

It is now afternoon. I approach a charming vale, amidst sublimely high forests, awful shades! Darkness gathers around; far-distant thunder rolls over the trembling hills. The black clouds with august majesty and power move slowly forwards, shading regions of towering hills and threatening all the destruction of a thunderstorm. All around is now still as death. Not a whisper is heard, but a total inactivity and silence seem to pervade the earth. The birds, afraid to utter a chirrup, in low tremulous voices take leave of each other, seeking covert and safety. Every insect is silenced, and nothing heard but the roaring of the approaching hurricane. The mighty cloud now expands its sable wings, extending from north to south, and is driven irresistibly on by the tumultuous winds, spreading its livid wings around the gloomy concave, armed with terrors of thunder and fiery shafts of lightning. Now the lofty forests bend low beneath its fury; their limbs and wavy boughs are tossed about and catch hold of each other; the mountains tremble and seem to reel about, and the ancient hills to be shaken to their foundations. The furious storm sweeps along, smoking through the vale and over the resounding hills. The face of the earth is obscured by the deluge descending from the firmament, and I am deafened by the din of the thunder. The tempestuous scene damps my spirits, and my horse sinks under me at the tremendous peals, as I hasten on for the plain.

The storm abating, I saw an Indian hunting cabin on the side of a hill, a very agreeable prospect, especially in my present condition. I made up to it and took quiet possession, there being no one to dispute it with me except a few bats and whip-poor-wills, who had repaired thither for shelter from the violence of the hurricane.

Having turned out my horse in the sweet meadows adjoining, I found some dry wood under shelter of the old cabin. I struck up a fire, dried my clothes, and comforted myself with a frugal repast of biscuit and dried beef, which was all the food my viaticum afforded me by this time, excepting a small piece of cheese which I had furnished myself with at Charleston and kept till this time.

The night was clear, calm and cool, and I rested quietly. Next morning at daybreak I was awakened and summoned to resume my daily task by the shrill cries of the social night hawk and active merry mock-bird. By the time the rising sun had gilded the tops of the towering hills, the mountains and vales rang with the harmonious shouts of the pious and cheerful tenants of the groves and meads. . . .

After passing through the meadow, the road led me over

the bases of a ridge of hills which, as a bold promontory dividing the fields I had just passed, form [these into] expansive green lawns. On these towering hills appeared the ruins of the ancient famous town of Sticoe. Here was a vast Indian mount or tumulus and great terrace, on which stood the council house, with banks encompassing their circus. There were also old peach and plumb orchards; some of the trees appeared yet thriving and fruitful. Presently, after leaving these ruins, the vale and fields were divided by means of a spur of the mountains pushing forward. Here, likewise, the road forked; the left-hand path continued up the mountains to the Overhill towns. I followed the vale to the right hand and soon began to ascend the hills, riding several miles over very rough, stony land, yielding the like vegetable productions as heretofore, and descending again gradually, by a dubious winding path, leading into a narrow vale and lawn through which rolled on before me a delightful brook, water of the Tanase. I crossed it and continued a mile or two down the meadows, when the high mountains on each side, suddenly receding, discovered the opening of the extensive and fruitful vale of Cowe, through which meanders the head branch of the Tanase, almost from its source, sixty miles, following its course down to Cowe.

I left for a little while the stream which passed swiftly and foaming over its rocky bed, lashing the steep craggy banks, and then suddenly sank from my sight, murmuring hollow and deep under the rocky surface of the ground. On my right hand the vale expands, receiving a pretty, silvery brook of water which came hastily down from the adjacent hills and entered the river a little distance before me. I then turned from the heights on my left, the road leading into the level lawns, to avoid the hollow rocky grounds, full of holes and cavities, arching over the river through which the waters are seen gliding along. But the river is soon liberated from these solitary and gloomy recesses and appears waving through the green plain before me. I continued for several miles, pursuing my serpentine path through and over the meadows and green fields. I crossed the river, which is here incredibly increased in size by the continual accession of brooks flowing in from the hills on each side, dividing their green turfy beds, forming them into parterres, vistas, and verdant swelling knolls, profusely productive of flowers and fragrant strawberries, their rich juice dyeing my horse's feet and ankles.

These swelling hills, the prolific beds on which the towering mountains repose, seem to have been the common situations of the towns of the ancients, as appears from the remaining ruins of them yet to be seen, and the level rich vale and meadows in front, their planting grounds.

[I] continue yet ten or twelve miles down the vale, my road leading at times close to the banks of the river. The azalea, kalmia, rhododendron, Philadelphus, etc. beautify this now-elevated shore and paint the coves with a rich and cheerful scenery, continually unfolding new prospects as I traverse the shores. Towering mountains seem continually in motion as I pass along, pompously raising their superb crests towards the lofty skies, traversing the far-distant horizon.

The Tanase is now greatly increased with the conflux of the multitude of rivulets and brooks descending from the hills on either side, generously contributing to establish its future fame, already a copious river.

The mountains recede, the vale expands. Two beautiful rivulets stream down through lateral vales, gliding in serpentine mazes over the green turfy knolls, and enter the Tanase nearly opposite to each other. Straight forwards, the expansive green vale seems yet infinite. Now on the right hand a lofty pyramidal hill terminates a spur of the adjacent mountain and advances almost into the river; but immediately after doubling this promontory, an expanded wing of the vale spreads on my right, down which comes precipitately a very beautiful creek, which flows into the river just before me. But now, behold, high upon the side of a distant mountain, overlooking the vale, the fountain of this brisk-flowing creek. The unparalleled waterfall* appears as a vast edifice with crystal front, or a field of ice lying on the bosom of the hill.

I now approached the river at the fording place which, greatly swollen by the floods of rain that fell the day before, ran with foaming rapidity; but observing that it had fallen several feet perpendicular, and perceiving the bottom or bed of the river to be level and covered evenly with pebbles, I ventured to cross over. However, I was obliged to swim two or three yards at the deepest channel of it and landed safely on the banks of a fine meadow which lay on the opposite shore, where I immediately alighted and spread abroad on the turf my linen, books, and specimens of plants, etc. to dry. I turned my steed to graze and then advanced into the strawberry plains to regale on the fragrant, delicious fruit, welcomed by communities of the splendid meleagris (turkey), the capricious roebuck (deer), and all the free and happy tribes which possess and inhabit those prolific fields, who appeared to invite and joined with me in the participation of the bountiful repast presented to us from the lap of nature. . . .

My winding path now led me again over the green fields into the meadows, sometimes visiting the decorated banks of

* Estatoah Falls. [Ed.]

the river, as it meandered through the meadows, boldly swept along the bases of the mountains, its surface receiving images reflected from the flowery banks above.

Thus was my agreeable progress for about fifteen miles since I came upon the sources of the Tanase at the head of this charming vale. In the evening, espying a human habitation at the foot of the sloping green hills, beneath lofty forests of the mountains on the left hand, and at the same time observing a man crossing towards me, I waited his approach. He hailed me and I answered I was for Cowe. He entreated me very civilly to call at his house, adding that he would presently come with me.

I was received and entertained here until next day with the most perfect civility. After I had dined, towards evening, a company of Indian girls, inhabitants of a village in the hills at a small distance, called, having baskets of strawberries; and this man, who kept here a trading house, being married to a Cherokee woman of family, was indulged to keep a stock of cattle, and his helpmate being an excellent housewife, and a very agreeable good woman, treated us with cream and strawberries.

Next morning, after breakfasting on excellent coffee, relished with buccaned venison, hot corn cakes, excellent butter and cheese, [I] set forwards again for Cowe, which was about fifteen miles' distance, keeping the trading path which coursed through the low lands between the hills and the river, now spacious and well beaten by travelers but somewhat intricate to a stranger, from the frequent collateral roads falling into it from villages or towns over the hills. After riding about four miles, mostly through fields and plantations, the soil incredibly fertile, I arrived at the town of Echoe, consisting of many good houses, well inhabited. I passed through and continued three miles farther to Nucasse, and three miles more brought me to Whatoga. Riding through this large town, the road carried me winding through their little plantations to young corn, beans, etc., divided from each other by narrow strips or borders of grass, which marked the bounds of each one's property, their habitation standing in the midst. Finding no common high road to lead me through the town, I was now at a stand how to proceed farther; when, observing an Indian man at the door of his habitation, three or four hundred yards' distance from me, beckoning me to come to him, I ventured to ride through their lots, being careful to do no injury to the young plants, the rising hopes of their labor and industry. I crossed a little grassy vale, watered by a silver stream which gently undulated through; then I ascended a green hill to the house, where I was cheerfully welcomed at the door and led in by the chief, giving the care of my horse to two handsome youths, his sons. During my continuance here, about half an hour, I experienced the most perfect and agreeable hospitality conferred on me by these happy people; I mean happy in their disposition, in their apprehension of rectitude with regard to our social or moral conduct. O divine simplicity and truth, friendship without fallacy or guile, hospitality disinterested, native, undefiled, unmodified by artificial refinement!

My venerable host gracefully and with an air of respect led me into an airy, cool apartment; where, being seated on cabins, his women brought a refreshing repast, consisting of sodden venison, hot corn cakes, etc., with a pleasant cooling liquor made of hominy well boiled, mixed afterwards with milk; this is served up, either before or after eating, in a large bowl, with a very large spoon or ladle to sup it with.

After partaking of this simple but healthy and liberal collation, and the dishes cleared off, tobacco and pipes were brought. The chief, filling one of them, whose stem, about four feet long, was sheathed in a beautiful speckled snake skin and adorned with feathers and strings of wampum, lit it, smoked a few whiffs, puffing the smoke first towards the sun, then to the four cardinal points, and lastly over my breast, and handed it towards me, which I cheerfully received from him and smoked; when we fell into conversation. He first inquired if I came from Charleston. If I knew John Stewart, Esq. How long since I left Charleston. . . . Having satisfied him in my answers in the best manner I could, he was greatly pleased, which I was convinced of by his attention to me, his cheerful manners, and his ordering my horse a plentiful bait of corn, which last instance of respect is conferred on those only to whom they manifest the highest esteem, saying that corn was given by the Great Spirit only for food to man.

I acquainted this ancient prince and patriarch with the nature and design of my peregrinations, and that I was now for Cowe, but having lost my road in the town, requested that I might be informed. He cheerfully replied that he was pleased I was come in their country, where I should meet with friendship and protection, and that he would himself lead me into the right path.

After ordering my horse to the door, we went forth together, he on foot, and I leading my horse by the bridle; thus walking together near two miles, we shook hands and parted, he returning home, and I continuing my journey to Cowe.

This prince is the chief of Whatoga, a man universally beloved and particularly esteemed by the whites for his pacific and equitable disposition, and revered by all for his exemplary virtues, just, moderate, magnanimous, and intrepid.

He was tall and perfectly formed; his countenance cheerful and lofty, and at the same time truly characteristic of the red men, that is, the brow ferocious, and the eye active, piercing or fiery as an eagle. He appeared to be about sixty years of age, yet upright and muscular and his limbs active as youth.

After leaving my princely friend, I traveled about five miles through old plantations, now under grass, but each appeared to have been planted last season; the soil exceedingly fertile, loose, black, deep, and fat. I arrived at Cowe about noon. This settlement is esteemed the capital town; it is situated on the bases of the hills on both sides of the river, near to its bank, and here terminates the great vale of Cowe, exhibiting one of the most charming natural mountainous landscapes perhaps anywhere to be seen; ridges of hills rising grand and sublimely one above and beyond another, some boldly and majestically advancing into the verdant plain, their feet bathed with the silver flood of the Tanase, whilst others far distant, veiled in blue mists, sublimely mounting aloft with yet greater majesty, lift up their pompous crests and overlook vast regions.

The vale is closed at Cowe by a ridge of mighty hills, called the Jore Mountain,* said to be the highest land in the Cherokee country, which crosses the Tanase here.

On my arrival at this town I waited on the gentlemen to whom I was recommended by letter and was received with respect and every demonstration of hospitality and friendship. . . .

* Now Wesser Bald. [Ed.]

The town of Cowe consists of about one hundred dwellings, near the banks of the Tanase, on both sides of the river.

The Cherokees construct their habitations on a different plan from the Creeks; that is, but one oblong four-square building, of one story high. The materials consist of logs or trunks of trees, stripped of their bark, notched at their ends, fixed one upon another, and afterwards plastered well, both inside and out, with clay well tempered with dry grass. The whole is covered or roofed with the bark of the chestnut tree or long broad shingles. This building is, however, partitioned transversely, forming three apartments, which communicate with each other by inside doors. Each house or habitation also has a little conical house covered with dirt, which is called the winter or hothouse; this stands a few yards distant from the mansion house, opposite the front door.

The council or town house is a large rotunda, capable of accommodating several hundred people. It stands on the top of an ancient artificial mount of earth about twenty feet perpendicular, and the rotunda on the top of it, being above thirty feet more, gives the whole fabric an elevation of about sixty feet from the common surface of the ground. But it may be proper to observe that this mount, on which the rotunda stands, is of a much ancienter date than the building, and perhaps was raised for another purpose. The Cherokees themselves are as ignorant as we are, by what people or for what purpose these artificial hills were raised. They have various stories concerning them, the best of which amount to no more than mere conjecture and leave us entirely in the dark; but they have a tradition in common with the other nations of Indians that they found them in much the same condition as they now appear when their forefathers arrived from the west and possessed themselves of the country, after vanquishing the nations of red men who then inhabited it, who themselves found these mounts when they took possession of the country. The former possessors delivered the same story concerning them. Perhaps they were designed and appropriated by the people who constructed them to some religious purpose, as great altars and temples similar to the high places and sacred groves amongst the Canaanites and other nations of Palestine and Judea.

The rotunda is constructed after the following manner. They first fix in the ground a circular range of posts or trunks of trees, about six feet high, at equal distances, which are notched in like manner at top, to receive another range of beams or wall plates. Within this is another circular order of very large and strong pillars, above twelve feet high, notched in like manner at top, to receive another range of wall plates, and within this is yet another or third range of stronger and higher pillars, but fewer in number and standing at a greater distance from each other. Lastly, in the center stands a very strong pillar which forms the pinnacle of the building and to which the rafters center at top. These rafters are strengthened and bound together by crossbeams and laths which sustain the roof or covering, which is a layer of bark neatly placed and tight enough to exclude the rain, and sometimes they cast a thin superficies of earth over all. There is but one large door, which serves at the same time to admit light from without and the smoke to escape when a fire is kindled. But, as there is but a small fire kept, sufficient to give light at night, and that fed with dry, small, sound wood divested of its bark, there is but little smoke. All around the inside of the building, betwixt the second range of pillars and the wall, is a range of cabins or sofas, consisting of two or three steps, one above or behind the other, in theatrical order, where the assembly sit or lean down. These sofas are covered with mats or carpets, very curiously made of thin splints of ash or oak, woven or plaited together. Near the great pillar in the center the fire is kindled for light, near which the musicians seat themselves, and round about this the performers exhibit their dances and other shows at public festivals, which happen almost every night throughout the year.

About the close of the evening I accompanied Mr. Galahan and other white traders to the rotunda, where was a grand festival, music and dancing. This assembly was held principally to rehearse the ball-play dance, this town being challenged to play against another the next day.

The people being assembled and seated in order, and the musicians having taken their station, the ball opens, first with a long harangue or oration spoken by an aged chief in commendation of the manly exercise of the ball-play, recounting the many and brilliant victories which the town of Cowe had gained over the other towns in the nation, not forgetting or neglecting to recite his own exploits, together with those of other aged men now present, coadjutors in the performance of these athletic games in their youthful days.

This oration was delivered with great spirit and eloquence and was meant to influence the passions of the young men present, excite them to emulation, and inspire them with ambition.

This prologue being at an end, the musicians began, both vocal and instrumental; when presently a company of girls, hand in hand, dressed in clean white robes and ornamented with beads, bracelets, and a profusion of gay ribands, entering the door, immediately began to sing their responses in a gentle, low, and sweet voice, and formed themselves in a semicircular file or line, in two ranks, back to back, facing the spectators and musicians, moving slowly round and round. This continued about a quarter of an hour, when we were surprised by a sudden very loud and shrill whoop, uttered at once by a company of young fellows who came in briskly after one another, with rackets or hurls in one hand. These champions likewise were well dressed, painted, and ornamented with silver bracelets, gorgets, and wampum, neatly ornamented with moccasins and high waving plumes in their diadems. They immediately formed themselves in a semicircular rank also, in front of the girls, when these changed their order and formed a single rank parallel to the men, raising their voices in responses to the tunes of the young champions, the semicircles continually moving round. There was something singular and diverting in their step and motions, and I imagine not to be learned to exactness but with great attention and perseverance. The step, if it can be so termed, was performed after the following manner. First, the motion began at one end of the semicircle, gently rising up and down upon their toes and heels alternately; when the first was up on tip-toe, the next began to raise the heel, and by the time the first rested again on the heel, the second was on tip-toe, thus from one end of the rank to the other, so that some were always up and some down, alternately and regularly, without the least balk or confusion; and they at the same time, and in the same motion, moved on obliquely or sideways, so that the circle performed a double or complex motion in its progression, and at stated times exhibited a grand or universal movement, instantly and unexpectedly to the spectators, by each rank turning to right and left, taking each other's places: the movements were managed with incon-

ceivable alertness and address and accompanied with an in-
stantaneous and universal elevation of the voice, and shrill
whoop.

The Cherokees, besides the ball-play dance, have a variety
of others equally entertaining. The men especially exercise
themselves with a variety of gesticulations and capers, some
of which are ludicrous and diverting enough; and they have
others which are of the martial order, and others of the
chase; these seem to be somewhat of a tragical nature,
wherein they exhibit astonishing feats of military prowess,
masculine strength, and activity. Indeed all their dances and
musical entertainments seem to be theatrical exhibitions or
plays, varied with comic and sometimes lascivious interludes.
The women, however, conduct themselves with a very becoming grace and decency, insomuch that, in amorous interludes,
when their responses and gestures seem consenting to natural liberties, they veil themselves, just discovering a glance
of their sparkling eyes and blushing faces, expressive of sensibility.

Next morning early I set off on my return and, meeting
with no material occurrences on the road, in two days arrived safe at Keowe.

The Great Trail Across Alabama, 1777

[*The Indians being dangerously aroused, William Bartram gave
up his plan to visit the Overhill towns in the Nantahala Valley
(Jore) and returned to Fort James Dartmouth on the peninsula
formed by the junction of the Broad and Savannah Rivers. Crossing the Savannah River to Fort Charlotte on the Carolina side,
about a mile below Dartmouth, he joined some traders who were
assembling for a journey to the Creek Nations.*]

[*On June 22nd they set off. One night they camped at Flat Rock, probably beside one of the branches of Brier Creek between Dearing and Warren (Ga.). They followed the Lower Creek trading path and Old Horse trail, pausing at the Ocmulgee fields, now in the Ocmulgee National Monument just east of Macon, and arrived at Uche Town in July 1777. Uche lay on the west bank of the Chattahoochee near the north base of the "peninsula" formed by that river where it pushes most deeply into Georgia south of Columbus. Apalachucla was a little south of Uche Town, while Coweta lay north of it, about two and one half miles northeast of Fort Mitchell.*

[*Leaving Apalachucla, they followed the Great Trail to the Tallapoosa River. Bartram visited towns in the general locality of Tallassee, followed the east bank of the Tallapoosa to Coolome on the south bank of the river, about twelve miles east of Montgomery, continued through the present town of Snowdoun and across Route 31, close to Fort Deposit. The trail followed the county line between Conecuh and Monroe, then branched at Burnt Corn Springs. Bartram crossed Little River at Mount Pleasant, going on to the Tensaw River. Somewhere near Stockton, he boarded a boat for Mobile.*

[*The following account concerns his journey from the Indian town of Coolome on the Tallapoosa River to the Mobile River. The trail followed the higher ridges through forests of great beauty, of which there now is scarcely a remnant. Along this trail, Bartram discovered several new plants. Ed.*]

Being now recruited and refitted, having obtained a guide to set us in the great trading path for West Florida, early in the morning we set off for Mobile. Our progress for about eighteen miles was through a magnificent forest, just without or skirting on the Indian plantations, frequently having a view of their distant towns, over plains or old fields; and at evening we came to camp under shelter of a grove of venerable spreading oaks, on the verge of the great plains; their enormous limbs loaded with Tillandsia usneaoides, waving in the winds. These oaks were some shelter to us from the violence of an extraordinary shower of rain, which suddenly came down in such floods as to inundate the earth and keep us standing on our feet the whole night, for the surface of the ground was under water almost till morning. Early next morning our guide, having performed his duty, took leave, returning home, and we continued on our journey, entering on the great plains. We had not proceeded far before our people roused a litter of young wolves, to which giving chase, we soon caught one of them, it being entangled in high grass; one of our people caught it by the hind legs, and another beat out its brains with the butt of his gun — barbarous sport! — This creature was about half the size of a small cur dog, and quite black.

We continued over these expansive illumined grassy plains, or native fields, about twenty miles in length and in width eight or nine, lying parallel to the river, which was about ten miles' distance. They are invested by high forests, extensive points, or promontories, which project into the plains on each side, dividing them into many vast fields opening on either hand as we passed along, which presents a magnificent and pleasing sylvan landscape of primitive, uncultivated nature. Crossed several very considerable creeks, their serpentine courses being directed across the plain by gently swelling knolls perceptible at a distance, but which seemed to vanish and disappear as we came upon them; the creeks were waters of the Alabama, the name of the east arm of the Mobile below the confluence of the Tallapoosa. These rivulets were ornamented by groves of various trees and shrubs which do not spread far from their banks. I observed amongst them the wild crab and wild plumb, and on the grassy turf adjoining grew an abundance of strawberry vines. The surface of the plains or fields is clad with tall grass, intermixed with a variety of herbage. The most conspicuous, both for beauty and novelty, is a tall species of Silphium; the radical leaves are large, long and lightly sinuated, but those which garnish the stem are few and less sinuated. These leaves, with the whole plant, except the flowers, appear of a whitish-green color, which is owing to a fine soft, silky down or pubescence. The flower stem, which is eight or ten feet in length when standing erect, terminates upwards with a long heavy spike of large golden-yellow radiated flowers; the stem is usually seen bowing on one side or other, occasioned by the weight of the flowers, and many of them are broken, just under the panicle or spike, by their own weight after storms and heavy rains, which often crack or split the stem, from whence exudes a gummy or resinous substance, which the sun and air harden into semipellucid drops or tears of a pale amber color. This resin possesses a very agreeable fragrance and bitterish taste, somewhat like frankincense or turpentine; it is chewed by the Indians and traders, to cleanse their teeth and mouth and sweeten their breath.

The upper stratum or vegetable mold of these plains is perfectly black, soapy, and rich, especially after rains, and renders the road very slippery. It lies on a deep bed of white, testaceous limestone rocks, which in some places resemble chalk and in other places are strata or subterrene banks of various kinds of sea shells, as ostrea (oyster) and so on; these, dissolving near the surface of the earth and mixing with the superficial mold, render it extremely productive.

Immediately after leaving the plains we entered the grand high forests. There were stately trees of the Robinea pseudacacia, Tilia, Morus, Ulmus, Juglans exalta, Juglans nigra,

Pyrus coronaria, Cornus florida, Cercis, and so on. Our road now for several miles led us near the Alabama, within two or three miles of its banks. The surface of the land was broken into hills and vales, some of considerable elevation, covered with forests of stately trees such as already mentioned, but they are of much larger growth than those of the same kind which grow in the southern or inhabited parts of Georgia and Carolina. We now left the river at a good distance, the Alabama bearing away southerly, and entered a vast open forest which continued above seventy miles, east and west, without any considerable variation, generally on a level plain, except near the banks of creeks that course through. The soil on the surface was dusky brownish mold or sandy loam, on a foundation of stiff clay; and the surface, pebbles or gravel mixed with clay on the summits of the ridges. The forests consisted chiefly of oak, hickory, ash, sour gum (Nyssa sylvatica), sweet gum (Liquidambar styraciflua), beech, mulberry, scarlet maple, black walnut, dogwood (Cornus florida), Aesculus pavia, Prunus indica, Ptelea, and an abundance of chestnut (Fag. castanea) on the hills, with Pinus taeda and Pinus lutea. During our progress over this vast high forest, we crossed extensive open plains, the soil gravelly, producing a few trees and shrubs or undergrowth, which were entangled with grape vines of a peculiar species. The bunches (racemes) of fruit were very large, as were the grapes that composed them, though yet green and not fully grown, but when ripe they are of various colors, and their juice sweet and rich. The Indians gather great quantities of them, which they prepare for keeping by first sweating them on hurdles over a gentle fire and afterwards drying them on their bunches in the sun and air, and store them up for provision. These grape vines do not climb into high trees but creep along from one low shrub to another, extending their branches to a great distance horizontally round about; and it is very pleasing to behold the clusters pendant from the vines, almost touching the earth; indeed, some of them lie upon the ground.

We now entered a very remarkable grove of dogwood trees, which continued nine or ten miles unalterable, except here and there a towering magnolia. The land on which they stand is an exact level: the surface a shallow, loose, black mold, on a stratum of stiff, yellowish clay. These trees were about twelve feet high, spreading horizontally. Their limbs, meeting and interlocking with each other, formed one vast, shady, cool grove, so dense and humid as to exclude the sunbeams and prevent the intrusion of almost every other vegetable, affording us a most desirable shelter from the fervid sunbeams at noonday. This admirable grove by way of eminence has acquired the name of The Dogwoods.

During a progress of near seventy miles through this high forest, there constantly presented to view on one hand or the other spacious groves of this fine flowering tree which must, in the spring season, when covered with blossoms, present a most pleasing scene; when at the same time a variety of other sweet shrubs display their beauty, adorned in their gay apparel, as the Halesia, Stewartia, Aesculus pavia, Aesc. alba, Aesc. florida . . . Azalea, and so on, entangled with garlands of Bignonia crucigera, Big. sempervirens, Glycine frutescens, Lonicera sempervirens, and so on, at the same time the superb Magnolia grandiflora, standing in front of the dark groves, towering above the common level.

The evening cool, we encamped on the banks of a glittering rivulet amidst a spicy grove of the Illicium floridanum.

Early next morning we arose, hunted up our horses, and proceeded on, continuing about twenty miles over a district which presented to view another landscape: expansive plains of cane meadows and detached groves, contrasted by swelling ridges and vales supporting grand forests of the trees already noted, embellished with delightful creeks and brooks, the low grounds producing very tall canes, and the higher banks groves of the Illicium, callicanthus, and others, particularly Magnolia auriculata. In the evening we forded the river Schambe about fifty yards over, the stream active but shallow, which carries its waters into the bay of Pensacola. Came to camp on the banks of a beautiful creek, by a charming grove of the Illicium floridanum. From this we traveled over a level country above fifty miles, very gently but perceptibly descending southeastward before us. This district exhibited a landscape very different from what had presented to view since we left the Nation, and not much unlike the low countries of Carolina. It is, in fact, one vast, flat, grassy savannah and cane meadows, intersected or variously scrolled over with narrow forests and groves, on the banks of creeks and rivulets, or hummocks and swamps at their sources; with long-leaved pines, scatteringly planted, amongst the grass; and on the high sandy knolls and swelling ridges, Quercus nigra, Quercus flammula, Quercus incana, with various other trees and shrubs as already noted inhabiting such situations. The rivulets, however, exhibited a different appearance. They are shallower, course more swiftly over gravelly beds, and their banks are adorned with illicium groves, magnolias, azaleas, halesia, andromedas, etc. The highest hills near large creeks afford high forests with abundance of chestnut trees.[1]

9. The Mississippi River Region in William Bartram's Day: August 1777

The Mississippi River

[*Manchac, or Fort Manchac, was on the north side of Manchac Bayou (or Iberville River), about forty miles south of Baton Rouge. Ed.*]

AT EVENING arrived at Manchac, when I directed my steps to the banks of the Mississippi, where I stood for a time as it were fascinated by the magnificence of the great sire* of rivers.

The depth of the river here, even in this season, at its lowest ebb is astonishing. It is not less than forty fathoms and the width about a mile or somewhat less, but it is not expansion of surface alone that strikes us with ideas of magnificence. The altitude and theatrical ascents of its pensile banks, the steady course of the mighty flood, the trees, high forests, even every particular object, as well as societies, bear the stamp of superiority and excellence; all unite or combine in exhibiting a prospect of the grand sublime. The banks of the river at Manchac, though frequently overflowed by the vernal inundations, are about fifty feet perpendicular height above the surface of the water (by which the channel at those times must be about two hundred and ninety feet

---

* Which is the meaning of the word Mississippi.

163

deep); and these precipices, being an accumulation of the sediment of muddy waters annually brought down with the floods, of a light loamy consistence, continually cracking and parting, present to view deep yawning chasms; in time [they] split off, as the active perpetual current undermines, and the mighty masses of earth tumble headlong into the river, whose impetuous current sweeps away and lodges them elsewhere. There are yet visible some remains of a high artificial bank in front of the buildings of the town, formerly cast up by the French to resist the inundations, but found to be ineffectual and now in part tumbled down the precipice. As the river daily encroaches on the bluff, some of the habitations are in danger and must be very soon removed or swallowed up in the deep gulf of waters. A few of the buildings that have been established by the English, since taking possession of the colony, are large and commodious, particularly the warehouses of Messrs. Swanson & Co., Indian traders and merchants.

The Spaniards have a small fortress and garrison on the point of land below the Iberville, close by the banks of the river, which has a communication with Manchac by a slender, narrow wooden bridge across the channel of Iberville, supported on wooden pillars and not a bow shot from the habitations of Manchac. The Iberville in the summer season is dry, and its bed twelve or fifteen feet above the surface of the Mississippi; but in the winter and spring has a great depth of water and a very rapid stream which flows into the Amite, thence down through the lakes into the Bay of Pearls to the ocean.

Having recommendations to the inhabitants of Baton Rouge, now called New Richmond, more than forty miles higher up the river, one of these gentlemen being present at Manchac gave me a friendly and polite invitation to accompany him on his return home. A pleasant morning; we set off after breakfast, well accommodated in a handsome convenient boat rowed by three blacks. Two miles above Manchac we put into shore at Alabama. This Indian village is delightfully situated on several swelling green hills, gradually ascending from the verge of the river. The people are a remnant of the ancient Alabama nation, who inhabited the east arm of the great Mobile River, which bears their name to this day, now possessed by the Creeks or Muscogulges, who conquered the former.

My friend having purchased some baskets and earthenware, the manufactures of the people, we left the village and, proceeding twelve miles higher up the river, landed again at a very large and well-cultivated plantation, where we lodged all night. Observed growing in a spacious garden adjacent to the house many useful as well as curious exotics, particularly the delicate and sweet tuberose. It grows here in the open garden; the flowers were very large and abundant on the stems, which were five, six, or seven feet high, but I saw none

Whooping Cranes by the Mississippi River

here having double flowers. In one corner of the garden was a pond, or marsh, round about which grew luxuriantly the Scotch grass. The people introduced this valuable grass from the West India islands. They mow or reap it at any time and feed it green to cows or horses; it is nourishing food for all cattle. The Humble plant (Mimosa pudica) grows here five or six feet high, rambling like brier vines over the fences and shrubs, all about the garden. The people here say it is an indigenous plant, but this I doubt, as it is not seen growing wild in the forests and fields, and it differs in no respect from that which we protect in greenhouses and stoves, except in the extent and luxuriancy of its branches, which may be owing to the productive virgin mold and temperature of the climate. They, however, pay no attention to its culture, but rather condemn it as a noxious, troublesome weed, for wherever it gets footing it spreads itself by its seed in so great abundance as to oppress and even extirpate more useful vegetables.

Next day we likewise visited several delightful and spacious plantations on the banks of the river, during our progress upwards. In the evening we arrived at my friend's habitation, a very delightful villa with extensive plantations of corn, indigo, cotton, and some rice.

A day or two after our arrival, we agreed upon a visit to Point Coupé, a flourishing French settlement on the Spanish shore of the Mississippi.

Early next morning we set off in a neat cypress boat with three oars, proceeded up the river, and by night got to a large plantation near the White Cliffs, now called Brown's Cliffs in honor of the late governor of West Florida, now of the Bahama Islands, who is proprietor of a large district of country lying on and adjacent to the Cliffs. At the time of my residence with Mr. Rumsey at Pearl Island, Governor Brown, then on his passage to his government of the Bahamas, paid Mr. Rumsey a visit, who politely introduced me to his excellency, acquainting him with my character and pursuits. He desired me to explore his territory and give him my opinion of the quality of the White Plains.

Having in readiness horses well equipt, early in the morning of August the 27th we set off for the plains. About a mile from the river we crossed a deep gully and small rivulet, then immediately entered the cane forests, following a straight avenue cut through them, off from the river, which continued about eight miles, the ground gradually but imperceptibly rising before us. When at once expansive plains opened to view which are a range of native grassy fields of many miles' extent, lying parallel with the river, surrounded and intersected with cane brakes and high forests of stately trees; the soil black, extremely rich and productive, but the virgin mold becomes thinner and less fertile as it verges on to the plains, which are so barren as scarcely to produce a bush or even grass in the middle or highest parts. The upper stratum or surface of the earth is a whitish clay or chalk, with veins of sea shells, chiefly of those little clams called *les coquilles,* or interspersed with the white earth or clay, so tenacious and hard as to render it quite sterile. Scarcely any vegetable growth to be seen, except short grass or crustaceous mosses, and some places quite bare where it is on the surface; but where it lies from eighteen inches to two or three feet below, it has the virtue of fertilizing the virgin mold above, rendering it black, humid, soapy, and incredibly productive.

I observed two or three scrubby pine trees, or rather dwarf bushes upon the highest ridge of these plains which are viewed here as a curiosity, there being no pine forests

within several leagues' distance from the banks of this great
river but, on the contrary, seemingly an endless wilderness
of canes and the most magnificent forests of the trees already
noted, but particularly Platanus, Liriodendron, Magnolia
grandiflora, Liquidambar, Juglans, Tilea, Morus, Gleditsia,
Laurus borbonia, and sassafras; this last grows here to a vast
tree, forty or fifty feet straight trunk; its timber is found to be
useful, sawn into boards and scantling or hewn into posts for
building and fencing.

On the more fertile borders of the plains adjoining the
surrounding forests are Sideroxylon, Pyrus coronaria, and
strawberry vines, but no fruit on them. The inhabitants
assured me they bore fruit in their season, very large, of a
fine red color, delicious and fragrant.

Having made our tour and observations on the White
Plains, we returned to the river at the close of the day and
next morning set off for Point Coupé, passed under the high
painted cliffs, and then set our course across the Mississippi,
which is here near two miles over; touched at a large island
near the middle of the river, being led there, a little out of
our way, in pursuit of a bear crossing from the main, but he
outswam us, reached the island, and made a safe retreat in
the forests entangled with vines; we, however, pursued him
on shore, but to no purpose. After resting a while, we reembarked and continued on our voyage, coasting the east
shore of the island to the upper end. Here we landed again,
on an extended projecting point of clean sand and pebbles
where were to be seen pieces of coal sticking in the gravel
and sand, together with other fragments of the fossil kingdom, brought down by inundations and lodged there. We
observed a large kind of mussel in the sand; the shell of an
oval form, having horns or protuberances near half an inch

in length and as thick as a crow quill, which I suppose serve the purpose of grapnels to hold their ground against the violence of the current. Here were great numbers of wild fowl wading in the shoal water that covers the sandy points to a vast distance from the shores. They were geese, brant, gannet, and the great and beautiful whooping crane (grus alber). Embarked again, doubled the point of the island, and arrived at Point Coupé in the evening.

We made our visit to a French gentleman, an ancient man and wealthy planter who, according to the history he favored us with of his own life and adventures, must have been very aged. His hair was of a silky white, yet his complexion was florid and constitution athletic. He said that soon after he came to America with many families of his countrymen, they ascended the river to the Cliffs of the Natches, where they sat down, being entertained by the natives, and under cover of a strong fortress and garrison, established a settlement; and by cultivating the land and forming plantations, in league and friendship with the Indians, in a few years they became a populous, rich, and growing colony. Then, through the imprudent and tyrannical conduct of the commandant towards the Natches, the ancients of the country, a very powerful and civilized nation of red men, who were sovereigns of the soil and possessed the country round about them, they became tired of these comers and, exasperated at their cruelty and licentiousness and at length determined to revenge themselves of such inhumanity and ingratitude, secretly conspired their destruction. Their measures were so well concerted with other Indian tribes that if it had not been for the treachery of one of their princesses, with whom the commander was in favor (for by her influence her nation attempted the destruction of the settlement, before their auxiliaries joined them, which afforded an opportunity for some few of the settlers to escape), they would have fully accomplished their purpose. However, the settlement was entirely broken up, most of the inhabitants being slaughtered in one night, and the few who escaped betook themselves to their canoes, descending the river until they arrived at this place, where they established themselves again. This gentleman had only time and opportunity to take into his boat one heifer calf, which he assured us was the mother of the numerous herds he now possesses, consisting of many hundred head. Here is now a very respectable village, defended by a strong fortress and garrison of Spaniards, the commander being governor of the district.

The French here are able, ingenious, and industrious planters. They live easy and plentifully and are far more regular and commendable in the enjoyment of their earnings than their neighbors the English. Their dress is of their own manufactures, well wrought and neatly made up, yet not extravagant or foppish; manners and conversation easy, moral, and entertaining.

Next morning we set off again on our return home and called by the way at the Cliffs, which is a perpendicular bank or bluff rising up out of the river near one hundred feet above the present surface of the water, whose active current sweeps along by it. From eight or nine feet below the loamy vegetative mold at top, to within four or five feet of the water, these cliffs present to view strata of clay, marl, and chalk of all colors, as brown, red, yellow, white, blue, and purple. There are separate strata of these various colors, as well as mixed or particolored. The lowest stratum next the water is exactly of the same black mud or rich soil as the adjacent low cypress swamps above and below the bluff. Here in the cliffs we saw vast stumps of cypress and other trees, which at this day grow in these low, wet swamps and which range on a level with them. These stumps are sound, stand upright, and seem to be rotted off about two or three feet above the spread of their roots; their trunks, limbs, etc. lie in all directions about them. But when these swampy forests were growing, and by what cause they were cut off and over-whelmed by the various strata of earth, which now rise near one hundred feet above, at the brink of the cliffs, and two or three times that height but a few hundred yards back, are inquiries perhaps not easily answered. . . .

The severe disorder in my eyes subverted the plan of my peregrinations and contracted the span of my pilgrimage southwestward. This disappointment affected me very sensibly, but resignation and reason resuming their empire over my mind, I submitted, and determined to return to Carolina.[1]

10. Frontier Types in the 18th Century

A Refuge During a Georgia Storm

I SET OFF for the settlements on the Altamaha, still pursuing the high road for Fort Barrington till towards noon, when I turned off to the left, following the road to Darian, a settlement on the river twenty miles lower down and near the coast. The fore part of this day's journey was pleasant, the plantations frequent, and the roads in tolerable good repair, but the country being now less cultivated, the roads became bad. I pursued my journey almost continually through swamps and creeks, waters of Newport and Sapello, till night, when I lost my way. But, coming up to a fence, I saw a glimmering light which conducted me to a house, where I stayed all night and met with very civil entertainment. Early next morning I set off again, in company with the overseer of the farm, who piloted me through a large and difficult swamp, when we parted; he in chase of deer, and I towards Darian. I rode several miles through a high forest of pines, thinly growing on a level plain, which admitted an ample view and a free circulation of air, to another swamp. Crossing a considerable branch of the Sapello River, I then came to a small plantation by the side of another swamp, where the people were remarkably civil and hospitable. The man's name was M'Intosh, a family of the first colony established in Georgia, under the conduct of general Oglethorpe. Was there ever such a scene of primitive simplicity, as was here exhibited, since the days of the good king Tammany!

The venerable gray-headed Caledonian smilingly meets me coming up to his house. "Welcome, stranger; come in and rest; the air is now very sultry; it is a very hot day."

I was treated with some excellent venison, and here found friendly shelter from a tremendous thunderstorm which came up from the northwest and soon after my arrival began to discharge its fury all around. Stepping to the door to observe the progress and direction of the tempest, the fulgor and rapidity of the streams of lightning passing from cloud to cloud and from the clouds to the earth exhibited a very awful scene; when instantly the lightning, as it were, opening a fiery chasm in the black cloud, darted with inconceivable rapidity on the trunk of a large pine tree that stood thirty or forty yards from me and set it in a blaze. The flame instantly ascended upwards of ten or twelve feet and continued flaming about fifteen minutes, when it was gradually extinguished by the deluges of rain that fell upon it.

I saw here a remarkably large turkey of the native wild breed. His head was above three feet from the ground when he stood erect. He was a stately, beautiful bird, of a very dark dusky-brown color, the tips of the feathers of his neck, breast, back, and shoulders edged with a copper color which in a certain exposure looked like burnished gold, and he seemed not insensible of the splendid appearance he made. He was reared from an egg found in the forest and hatched by a hen of the common domestic fowl.

Our turkey of America is a very different species from the meleagris of Asia and Europe, being nearly thrice their size and weight. I have seen several that have weighed between twenty and thirty pounds, and some have been killed that weighed near forty. They are taller and have a much longer neck proportionally, and likewise longer legs, and stand more erect; they are also very different in color. Ours are all, male and female, of a dark-brown color, not having a black feather on them; but the male exceedingly splendid, with changeable colors. In other particulars they differ not.

The tempest being over, I waited till the floods of rain had run off the ground, then took leave of my friends and departed.

Amelia Island, off the North Florida Coast, 1774

As we ran by Cumberland Isle, keeping the channel through the sound, we saw a sail ahead coming up towards us. Our captain knew it to be the trading schooner from the stores on St. John's and immediately predicted bad news, as she was not to sail until our arrival there. As she approached us, his apprehensions were more and more confirmed, from the appearance of a number of passengers on deck. We laid to until she came up, when we hailed her, "What news?"

"Bad; the Indians have plundered the Upper Store, and the traders have escaped only with their lives." Upon this, both vessels came to anchor very near each other when, learning the particulars, it appeared that a large party of Indians had surprised and plundered two trading houses in the isthmus beyond the river St. John's; and a third, being timely apprised of their hostile intentions by a faithful runner, had time to carry off part of the effects, which they secreted in a swamp at some distance from it, covering them with skins.

The Upper Store had saved their goods in like manner; and the Lower Store, to which we were bound, had removed the chief of theirs and deposited them on a small island, in the river, about five miles below the store. With these effects was my chest, which I had forwarded in this vessel from Savannah, not being at that time determined whether to make this journey by land or water. The captain of our vessel resolved to put about and return to Frederica for fresh instructions how to proceed; but for my part, I was determined to proceed for the island up St. John's, where my chest was lodged, there being some valuable books and papers in it which I could not do well without. I accordingly desired our captain to put me on shore on Little St. Simon's, which was not far distant, intending to walk a few miles to a fort at the south end of that island, where some fishermen resided who, as I expected, would set me over on Amelia Island; a large plantation was there, the property of Lord Egmont, a British nobleman whose agent, while I was at Frederica, gave me an invitation to call on him as I passed toward East Florida; and here I had expectations of getting a boat to carry me to St. John's. Agreeably to my desire, the captain put me on shore with a young man, a passenger for East Florida, who promised to continue with me and share my adventures. We landed safely; the captain, wishing us a prosperous journey, returned on board his vessel, and we proceeded for the fort, encountering some harsh treatment from thorny thickets and prickly vines. However, we reached the fort in the evening.

The commander was out in the forest, hunting. My companion being tired, or indolent, betook himself to rest while I made a tour round the south point of the island, walking the shelly paved sea beach, picking up novelties. I had not gone about a mile before I came up to a roebuck, lying slain on the sands. Hearing the report of a gun, not far off, and supposing it to be from the captain of the fort, whom I expected soon to return to take up his game, I retired to a little distance, mounted the sand hills, and sat down, enjoying a fine prospect of the rolling billows and foaming breakers beating on the bar, and the north promontory of Amelia Isle opposite to me. The captain of the fort soon came up with a slain buck on his shoulders. We hailed each other and returned together to the fort, where we were well treated.

Next morning, at my request, the captain obligingly set us over, landing us safely on Amelia. After walking through a spacious forest of live oaks and palms and crossing a creek that ran through a narrow salt marsh, I and my fellow traveler arrived safe at the plantation, where the agent, Mr. Egan, received us very politely and hospitably. This gentleman is a very intelligent and able planter, having already greatly improved the estate, particularly in the cultivation of indigo. Great part of this island consists of excellent hummocky land, which is the soil this plant delights in, as well as cotton, corn, batatas, and almost every other esculent vegetable. Mr. Egan politely rode with me over a great part of the island. On Egmont estate are several very large Indian tumuli, which are called Ogeechee mounts, so named from that nation of Indians who took shelter here after being driven from their native settlements on the main near Ogeechee River. Here they were constantly harassed by the Carolinians and Creeks and at length slain by their conquerors, and their bones entombed in these heaps of earth and shells. I observed here the ravages of the common gray caterpillar, so destructive to forest and fruit trees in Pennsylvania and through the northern states by stripping them of their leaves in the spring, while young and tender.

Mr. Egan, having business of importance to transact in St. Augustine, pressed me to continue with him a few days, when he would accompany me to that place, and, if I chose, I should have a passage as far as the Cowford, on St. John's, where he would procure me a boat to prosecute my voyage.

It may be a subject worthy of some inquiry why those fine islands on the coast of Georgia are so thinly inhabited; though perhaps Amelia may in some degree plead an exemption, as it is a very fertile island on the north border of East Florida and at the capes of St. Mary, the finest harbor in this new colony. If I should give my opinion, the following seem to be the most probable reasons. The greatest part of these are as yet the property of a few wealthy planters who have their residence on the continent, where lands on the large rivers, as Savannah, Ogeechee, Altamaha, St. Ille, and others, are of a nature and quality adapted to the growth of rice, which the planters chiefly rely upon for obtaining ready cash and purchasing family articles. They settle a few poor families on their insular estates who rear stocks of horned cattle, horses, swine, and poultry and protect the game for their proprietors. The inhabitants of these islands also lie open to the invasion and ravages of pirates and, in case of a war, to incursions from their enemies' armed vessels; in which case they must either remove with their families and effects to the main or be stripped of all their movables and their houses laid in ruins.

The soil of these islands appears to be particularly favorable to the culture of indigo and cotton, and there are on them some few large plantations for the cultivation and manufacture of those valuable articles. The cotton is planted only by the poorer class of people, just enough for their family consumption. They plant two species of it, the annual and West Indian; the former is low, and planted every year; the balls of this are very large and the phlox long, strong, and perfectly white; the West Indian is a tall perennial plant, the stalk somewhat shrubby, several of which rise up from the root for several years successively; the stems of the former year being killed by the winter frosts. The balls of this latter species are not quite so large as those of the herbaceous cotton; but the phlox, or wool, is long, extremely fine, silky, and white. A plantation of this kind will last several years, with moderate labor and care, whereas the annual sort is planted every year.

The coasts, sounds, and inlets environing these islands abound with a variety of excellent fish. . . . The shark and great black stingray are insatiable cannibals and very troublesome to the fishermen. The bays and lagoons are stored with oysters and a variety of other shellfish: crabs, shrimp, etc. The clams, in particular, are large, their meat white, tender, and delicate.

There is a large space betwixt this chain of seacoast islands and the mainland, perhaps generally near three leagues in breadth; but all this space is not covered with water. I estimate nearly two thirds of it to consist of low salt plains, which produce barilla, sedge, rushes, etc. and which border on the mainland and the western coasts of the islands. The east sides of these islands are, for the most part, clean, hard, sandy beaches, exposed to the wash of the ocean. Between these islands are the mouths or entrance of some rivers, which run down from the continent winding about through these low salt marshes and delivering their waters into the sounds, which are very extensive, capacious harbors from three to five and six to eight miles over and communicate with each other by parallel salt rivers, or passes, that flow into the sound. They afford an extensive and secure inland navigation for most craft, such as large schooners, sloops, pettiaugers, boats, and canoes; and this inland communication of waters extends along the seacoast with but few and short interruptions from the bay of Chesapeake, in Virginia, to the Mississippi, and how much further I know not, perhaps as far as Vera Cruz. Whether this chain of seacoast islands is a step, or advance, which this part of our continent is now making on the Atlantic Ocean, we must leave to future ages to determine. But it seems evident, even to demonstration, that those salt marshes adjoining the coast of the main, and the reedy and grassy islands and marshes in the rivers, which are now overflowed at every tide, were formerly high swamps of firm land, affording forests of cypress, tupelo, Magnolia grandiflora, oak, ash, sweet bay, and other timber trees, the same as are now growing on the river swamps, whose surface is two feet or more above the spring tides that flow at this day. It is plainly to be seen by every planter along the coast of Carolina, Georgia, and Florida, to the Mississippi, when they bank in these grassy tide marshes for cultivation, that they cannot sink their drains above three or four feet below the surface before they come to strata of cypress stumps and other trees, as close together as they now grow in the swamps.

The White Trader of Spalding's Upper Store

[*The Upper Store was located near the bridge at Astor, a few miles south of the upper end of Lake George. Ed.*]

On our arrival at the Upper Store, we found it occupied by a white trader who had for a companion a very handsome Seminole young woman. Her father, who was a prince by the name of White Captain, was an old chief of the Seminoles, and with part of his family, to the number of ten or twelve, was encamped in an orange grove near the stores, having lately come in from a hunt.

This white trader, soon after our arrival, delivered up the goods and storehouses to my companion and joined his father-in-law's camp, and soon after went away into the forests on hunting and trading amongst the flying camps of Seminoles.

He is at this time unhappy in his connections with his beautiful savage. It is but a few years since he came here, I think from North Carolina, a stout, genteel, well-bred man, active and of a heroic and amiable disposition; and by his industry, honesty, and engaging manners had gained the affections of the Indians and soon made a little fortune by traffic with the Seminoles. When he unfortunately met with this little charmer, they were married in the Indian manner. He loves her sincerely, as she possesses every perfection in her person to render a man happy. Her features are beautiful and manners engaging. Innocence, modesty, and love appear to a stranger in every action and movement, and these powerful graces she has so artfully played upon her beguiled and vanquished lover and unhappy slave as to have already drained him of all his possessions, which she dishonestly distributes amongst her savage relations. He is now poor, emaciated, and half distracted, often threatening to shoot her and afterwards put an end to his own life; yet he has not resolution even to leave her, but now endeavors to drown and forget his sorrows in deep draughts of brandy. Her father condemns her dishonesty and cruel conduct.

These particulars were related to me by my old friend the trader, directly after a long conference which he had with the White Captain on the subject, his son-in-law being present. The scene was affecting; they both shed tears plentifully. My reasons for mentioning this affair, so foreign to my business, was to exhibit an instance of the power of beauty in a savage and her art and finesse in improving it to her private ends. It is, however, but doing justice to the virtue and moral conduct of the Seminoles, and American aborigines in general, to observe that the character of this woman is condemned and detested by her own people of both sexes. If her husband should turn her away, according to the customs and usages of these people, she would not get a husband again, as a divorce seldom takes place but in consequence of a deliberate, impartial trial and public condemnation, and then she would be looked upon as a harlot.

Such is the virtue of these untutored savages; but I am afraid this is a common-phrase epithet, having no meaning or at least improperly applied; for these people are both well tutored and civil. It is apparent to an impartial observer, who resides but a little time amongst them, that it is from the most delicate sense of the honor and reputation of their tribes and families that their laws and customs receive their force and energy. This is the divine principle which influences their moral conduct and solely preserves their constitution and civil government in that purity in which they are found to prevail amongst them.

Pack-Train Caravan Across Alabama

Our caravan consisted of between twenty and thirty horses, sixteen of which were loaded, two pack-horse men, and myself, under the direction of the chief trader. One of our young men was a Mustee Creek, his mother being a Choctaw slave, and his father a half breed, betwixt a Creek and a white man. I loaded one horse with my effects, some presents to the Indians to enable me to purchase a fresh horse in case of necessity; for my old trusty slave, which had served me faithfully almost three years, having carried me on his back at least six thousand miles, was by this time almost worn out, and I expected every hour he would give up, especially after I found the manner of these traders' traveling. They seldom decamp until the sun is high and hot. Each one having a whip made of the toughest cow skin, they start all at once, the horses having ranged themselves in regular Indian file, the veteran in the van and the younger in the rear. Then the chief drives, with the crack of his whip and a whoop or shriek which rings through the forests and plains; he speaks in Indian, commanding them to proceed, which is repeated by all the company. Then we start at once, keeping up a brisk and constant trot which is incessantly urged and continued as long as the miserable creatures are able to move forward. We then come to camp, though frequently in the middle of the afternoon, which is the pleasantest time of the day for traveling. Every horse has a bell on which, being stopped when we start in the morning with a twist of grass or leaves, soon shakes out, and they are never stopped again during the day. The constant ringing and clattering of the bells, smacking of the whips, whooping and too-frequent cursing these miserable quadrupeds cause an incessant uproar and confusion, inexpressibly disagreeable.

After three days traveling in this mad manner, my old servant was on the point of giving out, and several of the company's horses were tired, but were relieved of their burthens by the led horses which attended for that purpose. I was now driven to disagreeable extremities and had no other alternative but either to leave my horse in the woods, pay a very extravagant hire for a doubtful passage to the Nation, or separate myself from my companions and wait the recovery of my horse alone. The chief gave me no other comfortable advice in this dilemma than that there was a company of traders on the road ahead of us from the Nation, to Mobile, who had a large gang of led horses with them for sale when they should arrive. He expected, from the advice which he had received at Mobile before we set off from thence, that this company must be very near to us and probably would be up tomorrow, or at least in two or three days, and this man condescended so far as to moderate a little his mode of traveling, that I might have a chance of keeping up with them until the evening of next day; besides, I had the comfort of observing that the traders and pack-horse men carried themselves towards me with evident signs of humanity and friendship, often expressing sentiments of sympathy and saying I must not be left alone to perish in the wilderness.

Although my apprehensions on this occasion were somewhat tumultuous, since there was little hope, on the principle of reason, should I be left alone, of escaping cruel captivity and perhaps being murdered by the Choctaws (for the company of traders was my only security, as the Indians never attack the traders on the road, though they be trading with nations at enmity with them), yet I had secret hopes of relief and deliverance that cheered me and inspired confidence and peace of mind. . . .

About the middle of the afternoon we were joyfully surprised at the distant prospect of the trading company coming up, and we soon met, saluting each other several times with a general Indian whoop, or shout of friendship. Then each company came to camp within a few paces of each other, and before night I struck up a bargain with them for a handsome strong young horse, which cost me about ten pounds sterling. I was now constrained to leave my old slave behind, to feed in rich cane pastures, where he was to remain and recruit until the return of his new master from Mobile; from whom I extorted a promise to use him gently and, if possible, not to make a pack horse of him. . . .

A few days before we arrived at the Nation, we met a company of emigrants from Georgia, a man, his wife, a young woman, several young children, and three stout young men, with about a dozen horses loaded with their property. They informed us their design was to settle on the Alabama, a few miles above the confluence of the Tombigbe.

Being now near the Nation, the chief trader with another of our company set off ahead for his town to give notice to the Nation, as he said, of his approach with the merchandise, each of them taking the best horse they could pick out of the gang, leaving the goods to the conduct and care of the young Mustee and myself. Early in the evening we came to the banks of a large, deep creek, a considerable branch of the Alabama. The waters ran furiously, being overcharged with

the floods of rain which had fallen the day before. We discovered immediately that there was no possibility of crossing
it by fording; its depth and rapidity would have swept our
horses, loads and all, instantly from our sight. My companion, after consideration, said we must make a raft to ferry
over our goods, which we immediately set about, after un-
loading our horses and turning them out to range. I undertook to collect dry canes, and my companion dry timber or
logs and vines to bind them together. Having gathered the
necessary materials and laid them in order on the brinks of
the river, ready to work upon, we betook ourselves to repose,
and early next morning set about building our raft. This was
a novel scene to me and I could not, until finished and put to
practice, well comprehend how it could possibly answer the
effect desired. In the first place we laid, parallel to each
other, dry, sound trunks of trees, about nine feet in length
and eight or nine inches in diameter; which binding fast together with grape vines and withes until we had formed this
first floor about twelve or fourteen feet in length, we then
bound the dry canes in bundles, each near as thick as a man's
body, with which we formed the upper stratum, laying them
close by the side of each other and binding them fast. After
this manner our raft was constructed. Then, having two strong
grape vines, each long enough to cross the river, we fastened
one to each end of the raft, which was now completed. Loading on as much as it would safely carry, the Indian took
the end of one of the vines in his mouth, plunged into the
river, and swam over with it, and the vine fixed to the other
end was committed to my charge, to steady the raft and haul
it back again after being unloaded. As soon as he had safe
landed and hauled taut his vine, I pushed off the raft,
which he drew over as quick as possible, I steadying it with

my vine. In this manner, though with inexpressible danger
of losing our effects, we ferried all safe over. The last load,
with other articles, contained my property, with all my
clothes, which I stripped off, except my breeches, for they
contained matters of more value and consequence than all
the rest of my property put together. Besides, I did not
choose to expose myself entirely naked to the alligators and
serpents in crossing the flood. Now seeing all the goods safe
over, and the horses at a landing place on the banks of the
river about fifty yards above, I drove them all in together,
when, seeing them safe landed, I plunged in after them and,
being a tolerable swimmer, soon reached the opposite shore.
But my difficulties at this place were not yet at an end, for
our horses all landed just below the mouth of a considerable
branch of this river, of fifteen or twenty feet width, and its
perpendicular banks almost as many feet in height above its
swift waters, over which we were obliged to carry every
article of our effects, and this by no other bridge than a
sapling felled across it, which is called a raccoon bridge.
Over this my Indian friend would trip as quick and light as
that quadruped, with one hundred weight of leather on his
back, when I was scarcely able to shuffle myself along over it
astride. At last having repacked and set off again, without
any material occurrence intervening, in the evening we arrived at the banks of the great Tallapoosa River and came to
camp under shelter of some Indian cabins, in expansive fields
close to the river bank, opposite the town of Savannuca. Late
in the evening a young white man, in great haste and seeming confusion, joined our camp. He immediately related that,
being on his journey from Pensacola, it happened that the
very night after we had passed the company of emigrants he
met them and joined their camp in the evening; when, just

at dark, the Choctaws surrounding them, plundered their camp, and carried all the people off captive, except himself, he having the good fortune to escape with his horse, though closely pursued.*

Next morning very early, though very cold and the surface of the earth as hoary as if covered with a fall of snow, the trader stood on the opposite shore entirely naked, except for a breechclout. Encircled by a company of red men in the like habit, he hailed us and presently, with canoes, brought us all over with the merchandise and conducted us safe to the town of Mucclassee, a mile or two distant.

Intrigue at Mucclassee

[*On the Tallapoosa River. Ed.*]

On my arrival I was not a little surprised at a tragical revolution in the family of my friend the trader, his stores shut up and guarded by a party of Indians. In a few minutes, however, the whole affair was related to me. It appeared that this son of Adonis had been detected in an amorous intrigue with the wife of a young chief the day after his arrival. The chief was out on a hunt but arrived next day, and upon information of the affair, the fact being confirmed, he with his friends and kindred resolved to exact legal satisfaction, which in this case is cutting off both ears of the deliquent, close to the head, which is called cropping. This being determined upon, he took the most secret and effectual methods to effect his purpose. About a dozen young Indian fellows conducted by their chief (the injured husband), having

* The young emigrants from Georgia so recently encountered by Bartram. [Ed.]

provided and armed themselves with knotty cudgels of green hickory which they concealed under their mantles, in the dusk of the evening paid a pretended friendly visit to the trader at his own house. When the chief, feigning a private matter of business, took him aside in the yard he whistled through his fingers (the signal preconcerted) and he was instantly surrounded, knocked down, and then stripped to his skin and beaten with their knotty bludgeons. However, he had the subtilty to feign himself speechless before they really killed him, which he supposed was their intention. When he had now lain for dead, the executioner drew out his knife with an intention of taking off his ears. This small respite gave him time to reflect a little, and he instantly sprang up, ran off, leaped the fence, and had the good fortune to get into a dark swamp, overgrown with vines and thickets, where he miraculously eluded the earnest researches of his enemies. He finally made a safe retreat to the house of his father-in-law, the chief of the town, throwing himself under his protection, who gave his word that he would do him all the favor that lay in his power. This account I had from his own mouth, for hearing of my return the next morning after my arrival, he sent a trusty messenger, by whom I found means of access to him. He farther informed me that there had been a council of the chiefs of the town convened to deliberate on the affair, and their final determination was that he must lose his ears, or forfeit all his goods, which amounted to upwards of one thousand pounds sterling, and even that forfeiture would not save his ears unless Mr. Golphin interposed in his behalf; and, after all, the injured Indian declares that he will have his life. He entreated me with tears to make what speed I could to Silver Bluff to represent his dangerous situation to Mr. Golphin and solicit that gentleman's most speedy and effectual interference; which I assured him I would undertake. . . .

On my way down I also called at Silver Bluff and waited on the honorable G. Golphin, Esq., to acknowledge my obligations to him and likewise to fulfil my engagements on the part of Mr. T——y, trader of Mucclassee. Mr. Golphin assured me that he was in a disagreeable predicament and that he feared the worst, but said he would do all in his power to save him.

A Bear and Cub Are Shot

When traveling on the east coast of the isthmus of Florida, ascending the South Mosquito River in a canoe, we observed numbers of deer and bears near the banks and on the islands of the river. The bears were feeding on the fruit of the dwarf creeping Chamærops (this fruit is of the form and size of dates, and is delicious and nourishing food). We saw eleven bears in the course of the day; they seemed no way surprised or affrighted at the sight of us. In the evening my hunter, who was an excellent marksman, said that he would shoot one of them for the sake of the skin and oil, for we had plenty and variety of provisions in our bark. We accordingly, on sight of two of them, planned our approaches as artfully as possible by crossing over to the opposite shore in order to get under cover of a small island. This we cautiously coasted round to a point which we apprehended would take us within shot of the bears; but here, finding ourselves at too great a distance from them and discovering that we must openly show ourselves, we had no other alternative to effect our purpose but to make oblique approaches. We gained gradually on our prey by this artifice without their noticing us. Finding ourselves near enough, the hunter fired and laid the target dead on the spot where she stood; when presently the other, not seeming the least moved at the report of our piece, approached the dead body, smelled and pawed it, and, appearing in agony, fell to weeping and looking upwards, then towards us, and cried out like a child. Whilst our boat approached very near, the hunter was loading his rifle in order to shoot the survivor, which was a young cub, and the slain supposed to be the dam. The continual cries of this afflicted child, bereft of its parent, affected me very sensibly. I was moved with compassion and, charging myself as if accessory to what now appeared to be a cruel murder, endeavored to prevail on the hunter to save its life, but to no effect! By habit he had become insensible to compassion towards the brute creation. Being within a few yards of the harmless, devoted victim, he fired and laid it dead upon the body of the dam.

Deer Hunt on the Alachua Savannah

We soon came to the verge of the groves, when a vast, verdant bay of the savannahs presented itself to view. We discovered a herd of deer feeding at a small distance. Upon the sight of us they ran off, taking shelter in the groves on the opposite point or cape of this spacious meadow. My companions, being old expert hunters, quickly concerted a plan for their destruction. One of our company immediately struck off, obliquely crossing the meadow for the opposite groves, in order to intercept them if they should continue their course up the forest to the main, and we crossed

Virginia Deer

straight over to the point, if possible to keep them in sight and watch their motions, knowing that they would make a stand thereabouts before they would attempt their last escape. On drawing near the point, we slackened our pace and cautiously entered the groves, when we beheld them, thoughtless and secure, flouncing in a sparkling pond in a green meadow or cove beyond the point. Some were lying down on their sides in the cool waters, whilst others were prancing like young kids, the young bucks in playsome sport, with their sharp horns hooking and spurring the others, urging them to splash the water.

I endeavored to plead for their lives, but my old friend,

though he was a sensible, rational and good sort of man, would not yield to my philosophy. He requested me to mind our horses while he made his approaches, cautiously gaining ground on them from tree to tree, when they all suddenly sprang up and herded together. A princely buck, who headed the party, whistled and bounded off; his retinue followed, but unfortunately for their chief, he led them with prodigious speed out towards the savannah very near us, and when passing by, the lucky old hunter fired and laid him prostrate upon the green turf but a few yards from us. His affrighted followers at the instant sprang off in every direction, streaming away like meteors or phantoms, and we quickly lost sight of them. My friend opened his body, took out the entrails, and placed the carcass in the fork of a tree, casting his frock or hunting shirt over it to protect it from the vultures and crows who follow the hunter as regularly as his own shade.[1]

11. Camping Along the Trail

A Camp on the Altamaha

[*While delayed on his journey to Florida by Indian troubles, Bartram explored several Georgia areas. Here he was camped beside the Altamaha, fifty miles above the last English settlement. Ed.*]

MY BARQUE being securely moored, and having reconnoitered the surrounding groves and collected firewood, I spread my skins and blanket by my cheerful fire under the protecting shade of the hospitable live oak and reclined my head on my hard but healthy couch. I listened, undisturbed, to the divine hymns of the feathered songsters of the groves, whilst the softly whispering breezes faintly died away.

The sun now below the western horizon, the moon majestically rising in the east, again the tuneful birds became inspired. How melodious is the social mock-bird! The groves resound the unceasing cries of the whip-poor-will. The moon about an hour above the horizon; lo! a dark eclipse* of her glorious brightness came slowly on. At length, a silver thread alone encircled her temples: at this boding change, a universal silence prevailed.

---

* The air at this time being serene, and not a cloud to be seen, I saw this annual, almost total autumnal eclipse in its highest degree of perfection.

Nature now weary, I resigned myself to rest. The night passed over; the cool dews of the morning awoke me; my fire burnt low, the blue smoke scarce rose above the moistened embers. All was gloomy: the late starry skies, now overcast by thick clouds, warned me to rise and be going. The livid purple clouds thickened on the frowning brows of the morning; the tumultuous winds from the east now exerted their power. O peaceful Altamaha! Gentle by nature! How thou wert ruffled! Thy wavy surface disfigured every object, presenting them obscurely to the sight, and they at length totally disappeared, whilst the furious winds and sweeping rains bent the lofty groves and prostrated the quaking grass, driving the affrighted creatures to their dens and caverns.

The tempest now relaxed, its impetus being spent, and a calm serenity gradually took place. By noon the clouds broke away, the blue sky appeared, the fulgid sunbeams spread abroad their animating light, and the steady western wind resumed his peaceful reign. The waters were purified, the waves subsided, and the beautiful river regained its native calmness. So it is with the varied and mutable scenes of human events on the stream of life. The higher powers and affections of the soul are so blended and connected with the inferior passions that the most painful feelings are excited in the mind when the latter are crossed. Thus, in the moral system, which we have planned for our conduct, as a ladder whereby to mount to the summit of terrestrial glory and happiness, and from whence we perhaps meditated our flight to heaven itself at the very moment when we vainly imagine ourselves to have attained its point, some unforeseen accident intervenes and surprises us. The chain is violently shaken, we quit our hold and fall. The well-contrived system at once becomes a chaos; every idea of happiness recedes; the splendor of glory darkens and at length totally disappears; every pleasing object is defaced, all is deranged, and the flattering scene passes quite away; a gloomy cloud pervades the understanding, and when we see our progress retarded and our best intentions frustrated, we are apt to deviate from the admonitions and convictions of virtue, to shut our eyes upon our guide and protector, doubt of his power, and despair of his assistance. But let us wait and rely on our God, who in due time will shine forth in brightness, dissipate the envious cloud, and reveal to us how finite and circumscribed is human power when assuming to itself independent wisdom.

The Enchanting Little Isle of Palms and a Camp Beside Lake George

I was induced to deviate a little from my intended course and touch at the enchanting little Isle of Palms. This delightful spot, planted by nature, is almost an entire grove of palms, with a few pyramidal magnolias, live oaks, golden orange, and the animating Zanthoxylon. What a beautiful retreat is here! Blessed, unviolated spot of earth, rising from the limpid waters of the lake: its fragrant groves and blooming lawns invested and protected by encircling ranks of the Yucca gloriosa. A fascinating atmosphere surrounds this blissful garden; the balmy Lantana, ambrosial Citra, perfumed Crinum, perspiring their mingled odors, wafted through Zanthoxylon groves. I at last broke away from the enchanting spot and stepped on board my boat, hoisted sail, and soon approached the coast of the main, at the cool eve of day. Then, traversing a capacious semicircular cove of the lake, verged by low, extensive grassy meadows, I at length by dusk made a safe harbor in a little lagoon, on the seashore or strand of a bold sandy point which descended from the surf of the lake. This was a clean, sandy beach, hard and firm by the beating surf when the wind sets from the east coast. I drew up my light vessel on the sloping shore, that she might be safe from the beating waves in case of a sudden storm of wind in the night. A few yards back the land was a little elevated and overgrown with thickets of shrubs and low trees, consisting chiefly of Zanthoxylon, Olea americana, Rhamnus fragula, Sideroxylon, Morus, Ptelea, Halesia, Querci, Myrica cerifera, and others. These groves were but low, yet sufficiently high to shelter me from the chilling dews; and being but a few yards' distance from my vessel, here I fixed my encampment. A brisk wind arising from the lake drove away the clouds of mosquitoes into the thickets. I now, with difficulty and industry, collected a sufficiency of dry wood to keep up a light during the night and to roast some trout which I had caught when descending the river. Their heads I stewed in the juice of oranges, which, with boiled rice, afforded me a wholesome and delicious supper. I hung the remainder of my broiled fish on the snags of some shrubs over my head. I at last, after reconnoitering my habitation, returned, spread abroad my skins and blanket upon the clean sands by my fireside, and betook myself to repose.

How glorious the powerful sun, minister of the Most High in the rule and government of this earth, leaves our hemisphere, retiring from our sight beyond the western forests! I behold with gratitude his departing smiles, tinging the fleecy roseate clouds, now riding far away on the eastern horizon; behold, they vanished from sight in the azure skies!

All now silent and peaceable, I suddenly fall asleep. At

midnight I awake; when, raising my head erect, I find myself alone in the wilderness of Florida, on the shores of Lake George. Alone indeed, but under the care of the Almighty, and protected by the invisible hand of my guardian angel.

When quite awake, I start at the heavy tread of some animal; the dry limbs of trees upon the ground crack under his feet; the close, shrubby thickets part and bend under him as he rushes off.

I rekindle my sleepy fire; lay in contact the exfoliated smoking brands, damp with the dew of heaven.

The bright flame ascends and illuminates the ground and groves around me.

Looking up, I found my fish carried off, though I had thought them safe on the shrubs, just over my head; but their scent, carried to a great distance by the damp nocturnal breezes, I suppose were too-powerful attractions to resist.

Camping on an Indian Burying Ground

[*On St. John's River, between Lake Dexter and Lake Beresford. Ed.*]

All this day's voyage, the banks of the river on both shores were middling high, perpendicular, and washed by the brisk current. The shores were not lined with the great lawns of floating aquatics, and consequently not very commodious resorts or harbors for crocodiles. . . . I, however, did not like to lodge on those narrow ridges infested by dreary swamps and, evening approaching, I began to be anxious for high land for a camping place. It was quite dark before I came up to a bluff which I had in view a long time, over a very extensive point of meadows. I landed, however, at last, in the best manner I could, at a magnificent forest of orange groves, oaks, and palms. I here, with little labor or difficulty, soon collected a sufficient quantity of dry wood. There was a pleasant vista of grass betwixt the grove and the edge of the river bank which afforded a very convenient, open, airy encamping place under the protection of some spreading oaks. . . .

As I have already observed, when I landed it was quite dark, and in collecting wood for my fire, strolling in the dark about the groves, I found the surface of the ground very uneven, by means of little mounts and ridges. In the morning I found I had taken up my lodging on the border of an ancient burying ground containing sepulchers or tumuli of the Yamasees, who were here slain by the Creeks in the last decisive battle, the Creeks having driven them into this point between the doubling of the river, where few of them escaped the fury of the conquerors. These graves occupied the whole grove, consisting of two or three acres of ground. There were near thirty of these cemeteries of the dead, nearly of an equal size and form, being oblong, twenty feet in length, ten or twelve feet in width, and three or four feet high, now overgrown with orange trees, live oaks, laurel magnolias, red bays, and other trees and shrubs, composing dark and solemn shades.

I here, for the first time since I left the trading house, enjoyed a night of peaceful repose.

A Camp on the Southern Shore of Lake George

At the approach of day the dread voice of the alligators shook the isle and resounded along the neighboring coasts, proclaiming the appearance of the glorious sun. I arose and prepared to accomplish my daily task. A gentle favorable gale led us out of the harbor. We sailed across the lake, and towards evening entered the river on the opposite south coast, where we made a pleasant and safe harbor at a shelly promontory, the east cape of the river on that side of the lake. It is a most desirable situation, commanding a full view of the lake. The cape opposite to us was a vast cypress swamp, environed by a border of grassy marshes, which were projected farther into the lake by floating fields of the bright green Pistia stratoites, which rose and fell alternately with the waters. Just to leeward of this point, and about half a mile in the lake, is the little round island already mentioned. But let us take notice of our harbor and its environs. It is a beautiful little cove, just within the sandy point, which defends it from the beating surf of the lake. From a shelly bank, ten or twelve feet perpendicular from the water, we entered a grove of live oaks, palm, magnolia, and orange trees, which grow amongst shelly hills and low ridges, occupying about three acres of ground, comprehending the isthmus and a part of the peninsula which joins it to the grassy plains. This enchanting little forest is partly encircled by a deep creek, a branch of the river that has its source in the high forests of the main, southeast from us; and winds through the extensive grassy plains which surround this peninsula to an almost infinite distance, and then unites its waters with those of the river in this little bay which formed our harbor. This bay, about the mouth of the creek, is almost covered with the leaves of the Nymphæa nelumbo. Its large sweet-scented yellow flowers are lifted up two or three feet above the surface of the water, each upon a green starol, representing the cap of liberty.

The evening drawing on and there being no convenient landing place for several miles higher up the river, we concluded to remain here all night. Whilst my fellow travelers were employing themselves in collecting firewood and fixing our camp, I improved the opportunity in reconnoitering our ground. Taking my fusee with me, I penetrated the grove and afterwards entered some almost unlimited savannahs and plains, which were absolutely enchanting. They had been lately burnt by the Indian hunters and had just now recovered their vernal verdure and gaiety.

How happily situated is this retired spot of earth! What an elysium it is! where the wandering Seminole, the naked red warrior, roams at large and after the vigorous chase retires from the scorching heat of the meridian sun. Here he reclines and reposes under the odoriferous shades of Zanthoxylon, his verdant couch guarded by the Deity; Liberty and the Muses inspiring him with wisdom and valor, whilst the balmy zephyrs fan him to sleep.

Seduced by these sublime, enchanting scenes of primitive nature and these visions of terrestrial happiness, I had roved far away from Cedar Point but, awakening to my cares, I turned about and in the evening regained our camp.

My companion, the trader, was desirous of crossing the river to the opposite shore in hopes of getting a turkey; I chose to accompany him, as it offered a good opportunity to observe the natural productions of those rich swamps and islands of the river. Having crossed the river, which is here five or six hundred yards wide, we entered a narrow channel

Turkeys and Live Oak Tree

which, after a serpentine course for some miles, rejoins the main river again, above; forming a large fertile island of rich low land. We landed on this island and soon saw a fine roebuck at some distance from us, who appeared leader of a company of deer that were feeding near him on the verge of a green meadow. My companion parted from me in pursuit of the deer, one way; and I, observing a flock of turkeys at some distance, on the other, directed my steps towards them, and with great caution got near them. When, singling out a large cock, and being just on the point of firing, I observed that several young cocks were affrighted and in their language warned the rest to be on their guard against an enemy, who I plainly perceived was industriously making his subtile approaches towards them, behind the fallen trunk of a tree, about twenty yards from me. This cunning fellow hunter was a large, fat, wild cat. He saw me and at times seemed to watch my motions as if determined to seize the delicious prey before me. Upon which I changed my object, and leveled my piece at him. At that instant, my companion, at a distance, also discharged his piece at the deer. The report of which alarmed the flock of turkeys; and my fellow hunter, the cat, sprang over the log and trotted off. The trader also missed his deer: thus we foiled each other. By this time, it being near night, we returned to camp where, having a delicious meal ready prepared for our hungry stomachs, we sat down in a circle round our wholesome repast.

How supremely blessed were our hours at this time! Plenty of delicious and healthful food, our stomachs keen, with contented minds; under no control, but what reason and ordinate passions dictated, far removed from the seats of strife.

Our situation was like that of the primitive state of man,

Mico Chlucco (Long Warrior), king of the Seminoles. (All drawings in this picture section are by William Bartram.)

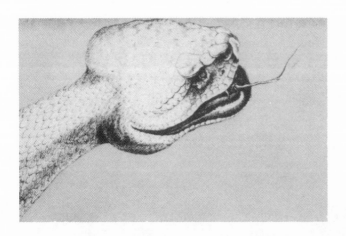

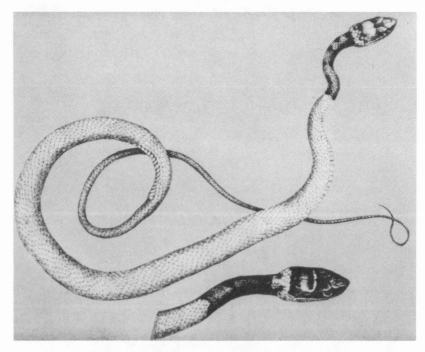

top: Rattlesnake head. *bottom:* Eastern coachwhip snake. (Originals in British Museum; from photostats, Historical Society of Pennsylvania.)

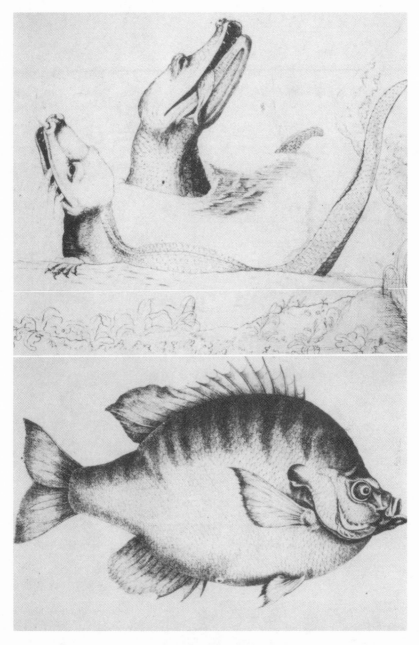

top: American alligator, East Florida. *bottom:* Bream, East Florida. (Originals in British Museum; from photostats, Historical Society of Pennsylvania.)

top. Yellow-root. *bottom:* Golden canna, gastropod mollusk, cow-killer ant, and stone pipe bowl. (Original drawing of latter in British Museum; from photostat, Historical Society of Pennsylvania.)

Hydrangea Quercifolia.

top: Black vulture, Bartram's "carrion crow." *bottom:* Cardinal, Bartram's "crested redbird of Florida." (Originals in British Museum; from photostats, Historical Society of Pennsylvania.)

Florida sandhill crane. (Original in British Museum; from photostat, Historical Society of Pennsylvania.)

Certhia, or brown creeper.

peaceable, contented and sociable. The simple and necessary calls of nature being satisfied, we were altogether as brethren of one family, strangers to envy, malice, and rapine.

A Camp in the Vale of Keowe

[*A valley of the Keowe River lying north of Clemson, South Carolina. In early colonial days, Fort Prince George was an important point on the trade route from Charleston to the Little Tennessee. Ed.*]

Keowe is a most charming situation, and the adjacent heights are naturally so formed and disposed as with little expense of military architecture to be rendered almost impregnable. It lies in a fertile vale, at this season enameled with the incarnate fragrant strawberries and blooming plants, through which the beautiful river meanders, sometimes gently flowing but more frequently agitated, gliding swiftly between the fruitful strawberry banks, environed at various distances by high hills and mountains, some rising boldly almost upright upon the verge of the expansive lawn, so as to overlook and shadow it, whilst others more lofty, superb, misty, and blue majestically mount far above.

The evening still and calm, all silent and peaceable, a vivifying gentle breeze continually wafted from the fragrant strawberry fields and aromatic calycanthean groves on the surrounding heights; the wary moor fowl thundering in the distant-echoing hills: how the groves and hills ring with the shrill perpetual voice of the whip-poor-will!

Abandoned as my situation now was, yet thank heaven many objects met together at this time and conspired to conciliate and in some degree compose my mind, heretofore

somewhat dejected and unharmonized: all alone in a wild Indian country, a thousand miles from my native land, and a
vast distance from any settlements of white people. It is
true, here were some of my own color, yet they were strangers; and though friendly and hospitable, their manners and
customs of living so different from what I had been accustomed to, administered but little to my consolation: some
hundred miles yet to travel; the savage, vindictive inhabitants lately ill-treated by the frontier Virginians; blood being
spilt between them, and the injury not yet wiped away by
formal treaty: the Cherokees extremely jealous of white people traveling about their mountains, especially if they should
be seen peeping in amongst the rocks or digging up their
earth.

The vale of Keowe is seven or eight miles in extent, that is,
from the little town of Kulsage about a mile above, thence
down the river six or seven miles, where a high ridge of hills
on each side of the river almost terminates the vale but
opens again below the narrow ridge and continues ten or
twelve miles down to Sinica, and in width one and two miles.
This fertile vale, within the remembrance of some old traders
with whom I conversed, was one continued settlement. The
swelling sides of the adjoining hills were then covered with
habitations, and the rich level grounds beneath, lying on the
river, were cultivated and planted, which now exhibit a very
different spectacle, humiliating indeed to the present generation, the posterity and feeble remains of the once potent
and renowned Cherokees: the vestiges of the ancient Indian
dwellings are yet visible on the feet of the hills bordering
and fronting on the vale, such as posts or pillars of their habitations.

There are several Indian mounts or tumuli, and terraces,

monuments of the ancients, at the old site of Keowe, near Fort Prince George, but no Indian habitations at present; and here are several dwellings inhabited by white people concerned in the Indian trade.

The old fort, Prince George, now bears no marks of a fortress but serves for a trading house.

The Flat Rock Camp

[*Several flat rocks in Georgia were used by the Indians and early traders as camp sites. This one was probably close to the eastern boundary of Warren County directly south of Mesena, where the Upper Creek trading path crossed one of the small tributaries of Brier Creek. Ed.*]

Early in the evening we arrived at the Flat Rock, where we lodged. This is a common rendezvous or camping place for traders and Indians. It is an expansive, clean, flat or horizontal rock but a little above the surface of the ground and near the banks of a delightful rivulet of excellent water, which is one of the head branches of Great Ogeechee. In the loose, rich soil verging round this rock grew several very curious herbaceous plants, particularly one of singular elegance and beauty, which I take to be a species of Ipomea. . . . It grows erect, three feet high, with a strong stem which is decorated with plumed or pinnatifid linear leaves, somewhat resembling those of the Delphinium. From about one half of its length upwards, it sends out on all sides ascendant branches which divide again and again. These terminate with large tubular or funnel-formed flowers; their limbs equally divided into five segments; these beautiful flowers are of a perfect rose color, elegantly besprinkled on the inside of their petals with crimson specks; the flowers are in great abundance and, together with the branches and delicately fine-cut leaves, compose a conical spike or compound panicle. I saw a species of this plant, if not the very same, growing on the seacoast islands near St. Augustine. The blue-flowered malva and delphinium were its associates about the Flat Rock.

There are extensive cane brakes or cane meadows spread abroad round about, which afford the most acceptable and nourishing food for cattle.

This evening two companies of Indian traders from Augusta arrived and encamped near us; and as they were bound to the Nation, we concluded to unite in company with them, they generously offering us their assistance, having many spare horses and others lightly loaded, several of ours by this time being jaded: this was a favorable opportunity of relief in case of necessity.

Next morning, as soon as the horses were packed and in readiness, we decamped and set forward together.

I thought it worthy of taking notice of a singular method the traders make use of to reduce the wild young horses to their hard duty. When any one persists in refusing to receive his load, if threats, the discipline of the whip, and other common abuse prove insufficient, after being haltered, a pack-horse man catches the tip end of one of his ears betwixt his teeth and pinches it, when instantly the furious strong creature, trembling, stands perfectly still until he is loaded.[1]

12. Earthquakes, Hurricane, Crystal Springs, & Flood

Earthquakes

[*By John Bartram. Ed.*]

WE HAVE HAD, within these thirty years, four earthquakes. One of them, about twelve years ago, was felt about eleven o'clock at night. It shook our houses, so as to rock the chairs, tables, and chests of drawers, and affrighted some of our women. The others seemed like thunder at a distance, or a hollow rumbling in the ground. If the observations of some people hold good, we may expect another soon; for we now have the driest season that, I believe, ever was known. The ground near us has not been wet plough-deep since the beginning of March. Our spring was extremely dry, windy, and cold; and since June, the weather has been very hot and dry. Our fields have no more grass in them than in the midst of winter, and the meadow ground, that used to bear two good crops, has no more grass than the middle of the street, both root and branch being scorched as with fire; and the ground is as dry as dust, two feet deep. The very briers are withering, and the fruit upon them appearing scorched and drying up. Our springs have failed and the runs dried up. Yet, not withstanding this extraordinary drought, we have rarely been without rain for five days since March; and during the winter we were not so long without snow, though we had but three snows that stayed long with us, all the winter; most of the rest would hardly cover the ground. Thus, in the summer, one week's rain every day would scarcely afford as much moisture as one common nightly dew.[1]

Hurricane at Lake Beresford

[*William Bartram's narrative is resumed. Ed.*]

About noon I got within a mile of Beresford Plantation when I was forced ashore in an open marsh by a most dreadful hurricane. Happy it was for me that I did not get up to a woody bluff which I was endeavoring for, as it might have been fatal to me. No sooner had I moored to a bush under the bank of the marsh than I beheld with astonishment and terror the strength and fury of this storm; the crash and wrenching of trees in the woods a little way off from me. Trees were twisted off by the top and others split to the ground; vast splinters flew like javelins in the air; the tops of the tough, yielding hickory bent down into the water. But what was incredible, I beheld the invincible, sturdy live oak yielding to the fury of the tempest, whose firm and almost inflexible limbs, as thick as large trees, were twisted off, as flax or dry weeds, whirled aloft, and floated in the air. This tempest showed itself first in the west by a dark bank of murmuring thunderclouds two or three hours before this terrible invasion, but as it rose, the pointed white-capped clouds shot up swiftly through the skies, spreading on each side, clashed by each other, casting a purple, glowing flame color over the sky attended with continual streams of lightning and terrible thunder. At last these clouds, from all points of the horizon, met overhead and cast a universal darkness all around. It continued to rain and blow incessantly for near two hours. The rain almost filled my canoe and thoroughly wet all my things.

After the hurricane abated, I bailed my boat and got to the plantation, where I beheld with amazement the devastation of this mighty storm. Almost every house was blown away, and near twenty of the largest live oaks I had seen, which were left about the houses for shade, were torn up by the roots, and those that stood it out had their tops almost torn to pieces and the limbs lapped to the stump. The indigo and corn were almost destroyed and the people greatly terrified, but by a providential care which seemed really miraculous, they escaped unhurt. It was two days here before I got my papers dried. I lost some valuable specimens of new plants but luckily had a duplicate left behind me at the Store.[2]

A Vast Fountain of Hot Mineral Water

[*Now called Blue Springs. About three miles west of Route 11 at Orange City, Fla. Ed.*]

My friend rode with me about four miles' distance from the house to show me a vast fountain of warm or rather hot mineral water, which issued from a high ridge or bank on the river, in a great cove or bay a few miles above the mouth of the creek which I ascended to the lake. It boils up with great force, forming immediately a vast circular basin capacious enough for several shallops to ride in, and runs with rapidity into the river three or four hundred yards' distance. This creek, which is formed instantly by this admirable fountain, is wide and deep enough for a sloop to sail up into the basin. The water is perfectly diaphanous, and here are continually a prodigious number and variety of fish. They appear as plain as though lying on a table before your eyes, although many feet deep in the water. This tepid water has a most disagreeable taste, brassy and vitriolic, and very offensive to the smell, much like bilge water or the washings of a gun barrel, and is smelt at a great distance. A pale bluish or pearl-colored coagulum covers every inanimate substance that lies in the water, as logs, limbs of trees, etc. Alligators and gar were numerous in the basin, even at the apertures where the ebullition emerges through the rocks; as also many other tribes of fish. In the winter season several kinds of fish and aquatic animals migrate to these warm fountains. The forbidding taste and smell of these waters seems to be owing to vitriolic and sulphureous fumes or vapors; and these, being condensed, form this coagulum, which represents flakes of pearly clouds in the clear cerulean waters in the basin. A charming orange grove, with magnolias, oaks, and palms, half surrounded this vast fountain. A delightful stream of cool, salubrious water issues from the ridge, meandering along and entering the creek just below the basin.

Six-Mile Springs

[*Now Salt Springs. A good road branching north from Route 40
about ten miles east of Ocala, Florida, dead-ends at the Springs.
Ed.*]

The morning being clear, I set sail with a favorable breeze,
coasting along the shores, when on a sudden the waters became transparent and discovered the sandy bottom and the
several nations of fish, passing and repassing each other. Following this course, I was led to the cape of the little river,
descending from Six-Mile Springs and meandering six miles
from its source through green meadows. I entered this pellucid stream, sailing over the heads of innumerable squadrons
of fish which, although many feet deep in the water, were distinctly to be seen. I passed by charming islets of flourishing
trees, as palm, red bay, ash, maple, nyssa, and others. As I approached the distant high forest on the main, the river widened. Floating fields of the green pistia surrounded me, the
rapid stream winding through them. What an alluring scene
was now before me! A vast basin or little lake of crystal waters, half encircled by swelling hills, clad with orange and
odoriferous illicium groves, the towering magnolia, itself a
grove, and the exalted palm, as if conscious of their transcend-
ent glories tossed about their lofty heads, painting, with mutable shades, the green, floating fields beneath. The social,
prattling coot enrobed in blue and the squealing water hen,
with wings half expanded, tripped after each other over the
watery mirror.

I put in at an ancient landing place, which is a sloping
ascent to a level grassy plain, an old Indian field. As I in-

tended to make my most considerable collections at this
place, I proceeded immediately to fix my encampment but a
few yards from my safe harbor, where I securely fastened my
boat to a live oak which overshadowed my port.

After collecting a good quantity of firewood, as it was
about the middle of the afternoon, I resolved to reconnoiter
the ground about my encampment. Having penetrated the
groves next to me, I came to the open forests, consisting of
exceedingly tall straight pines that stood at a considerable
distance from each other, through which appeared at northwest an almost unlimited plain of grassy savannahs, embellished with a chain of shallow ponds as far as the sight could
reach. Here is a species of Magnolia that associates with the
Gordonia lasianthus; it is a tall tree, sixty or eighty feet in
height; the trunk is straight; its head terminating in the form
of a sharp cone; the leaves are oblong, lanceolate, of a fine
deep green, and glaucous beneath; the flowers are large, perfectly white, and extremely fragrant: with respect to its flowers and leaves, it differs very little from the Magnolia glauca.
The silvery whiteness of the leaves of this tree had a striking
and pleasing effect on the sight, as it stood amidst the dark
green of the Quercus dentata, Nyssa sylvatica, Nys. aquatica,
Gordonia lasianthus, and many others of the same hue. The
tall aspiring Gordonia lasianthus, which now stood in my
view in all its splendor, is every way deserving of our ad-
miration. Its thick foliage, of a dark-green color, is flowered
over with large, milk-white, fragrant blossoms on long slender elastic peduncles, at the extremities of its numerous
branches, from the bosom of the leaves, and renewed every
morning; and that in such incredible profusion that the tree
appears silvered over with them and the ground beneath covered with the fallen flowers. It at the same time continually

pushes forth new twigs, with young buds on them, and in the winter and spring the third year's leaves, now partly concealed by the new and perfect ones, are gradually changing color from green to golden yellow, from that to a scarlet, from scarlet to crimson, and lastly to a brownish purple, and then fall to the ground. So that the Gordonia lasianthus may be said to change and renew its garments every morning throughout the year; and every day appears with unfading luster. And, moreover, after the general flowering is past, there is a thin succession of scattering blossoms to be seen on some parts of the tree almost every day throughout the remaining months, until the floral season returns again. Its natural situation, when growing, is on the edges of shallow ponds or low wet grounds on rivers, in a sandy soil, the nearest to the water of any other tree, so that in droughty seasons its long serpentine roots, which run near or upon the surface of the earth, may reach into the water. When the tree has arrived to the period of perfect magnitude, it is sixty, eighty, or a hundred feet high, forming a pyramidal head. The wood of old trees when sawn into plank is deservedly admired in cabinet work or furniture; it has a cinnamon-colored ground, marbled and veined with many colors: the inner bark is used for dying a reddish or sorrel color; it imparts this color to wool, cotton, linen, and dressed deer skins, and is highly esteemed by tanners.

The Cactus opuntia is very tall, erect, and large, and strong enough to bear the weight of a man: some are seven or eight feet high. The whole plant or tree seems to be formed of great oval compressed leaves or articulations; those near the earth continually increase, magnify, and indurate as the tree advances in years, and at length lose the bright-green color and glossy surface of their youth, acquiring a ligneous quality, with a whitish, scabrous cortex. Every part of the plant is nearly destitute of aculea, or those fascicles of barbed bristles which are in such plenty on the common dwarf Indian Fig.

The cochineal insects were feeding on the leaves. The female of this insect is very large and fleshy, covered with a fine white silk or cottony web, which feels always moist or dewy and seems designed by nature to protect them from the violent heat of the sun. The males are very small in comparison to the females, and but very few in number: they each have two oblong pellucid wings. The large polypetalous flowers are produced on the edges of the last year's leaves,* are of a fine, splendid yellow, and are succeeded by very large pear-shaped fruit, of a dark livid purple when ripe. Its pulp is charged with a juice of a fine, transparent crimson color and has a cool, pleasant taste, somewhat like that of a pomegranate. Soon after eating this fruit the urine becomes of the same crimson color, which very much surprises and affrights a stranger but is attended with no other ill consequence; on the contrary, it is esteemed wholesome, though powerfully diuretic.

I now directed my steps towards my encampment, in a different direction. I seated myself upon a swelling green knoll, at the head of the crystal basin. Near me, on the left, was a point or projection of an entire grove of the aromatic Illicium; on my right, and all around behind me, was a fruitful orange grove, with palms and magnolias interspersed; in front, just under my feet, was the enchanting and amazing crystal fountain, which incessantly threw up, from dark, rocky caverns below, tons of water every minute, forming a basin capacious enough for large shallops to ride in, and a creek of four or five feet depth of water and near twenty

* Branches. [Ed.]

yards over, which meanders six miles through green meadows, pouring its limpid waters into the great Lake George,
where they seem to remain pure and unmixed. About twenty
yards from the upper edge of the basin and directly opposite
to the mouth or outlet of the creek, is a continual and
amazing ebullition, where the waters are thrown up in such
abundance and amazing force as to jet and swell up two or
three feet above the common surface: white sand and small
particles of shells are thrown up with the waters, near to the
top, when they diverge from the center, subside with the expanding flood, and gently sink again, forming a large rim or
funnel round about the aperture or mouth of the fountain,
which is a vast perforation through a bed of rocks, the ragged
points of which are projected out on every side. Thus far I
know to be matter of real fact, and I have related it as near as
I could conceive or express myself. But there are yet remaining scenes inexpressibly admirable and pleasing.

Behold, for instance, a vast circular expanse before you,
the waters of which are so extremely clear as to be absolutely diaphanous or transparent as the ether; the margin of
the basin ornamented with a great variety of fruitful and
floriferous trees, shrubs, and plants, the pendant golden
orange dancing on the surface of the pellucid waters, the
balmy air vibrating with the melody of the merry birds, tenants of the encircling aromatic grove.

At the same instant, innumerable bands of fish are seen,
some clothed in the most brilliant colors; the voracious crocodile stretched along at full length, as the great trunk of
a tree in size; the devouring garfish, inimical trout, and all
the varieties of gilded, painted bream; the barbed catfish,
dreaded stingray, skate, and flounder, spotted bass, sheeps-
head and ominous drum; all in their separate bands and com-

munities, with free and unsuspicious intercourse performing their evolutions. There are no signs of enmity, no attempt to devour each other. The different bands seem peaceably and complaisantly to move a little aside, as it were, to make room for others to pass by.

But behold yet something far more admirable, see whole armies descending into an abyss, into the mouth of the bubbling fountain: they disappear! Are they gone for ever? I raise my eyes with terror and astonishment; I look down again to the fountain with anxiety, when behold them as it were emerging from the blue ether of another world, apparently at a vast distance; at their first appearance, no bigger than flies or minnows; now gradually enlarging, their brilliant colors begin to paint the fluid.

Now they come forward rapidly, and instantly emerge, with the elastic expanding column of crystalline waters into the circular basin or funnel. See now how gently they rise, some upright, others obliquely, or seem to lie as it were on their sides, suffering themselves to be gently lifted or borne up by the expanding fluid towards the surface, sailing or floating like butterflies in the cerulean ether. Then again they as gently descend, diverge and move off; when they rally, form again, and rejoin their kindred tribes.

This amazing and delightful scene, though real, appears at first but as a piece of excellent painting; there seems no medium; you imagine the picture to be within a few inches of your eyes, and that you may without the least difficulty touch any one of the fish, or put your finger upon the crocodile's eye, when it really is twenty or thirty feet under water.

And although this paradise of fish may seem to exhibit a just representation of the peaceable and happy state of nature which existed before the Fall, yet in reality it is a mere representation; for the nature of the fish is the same as if they were in Lake George or the river; but here the water or element in which they live and move is so perfectly clear and transparent, it places them all on an equality with regard to their ability to injure or escape from one another (as all river fish of prey, or such as feed upon each other, as well as the unwieldy crocodile, take their prey by surprise; secreting themselves under covert or in ambush, until an opportunity offers, when they rush suddenly upon them); but here is no covert, no ambush; here the trout freely passes by the very nose of the alligator and laughs in his face, and the bream by the trout.

But what is really surprising is that the consciousness of each other's safety, or some other latent cause, should so absolutely alter their conduct, for here is not the least attempt made to injure or disturb one another.

The sun passing below the horizon and night approaching, I arose from my seat and, proceeding on, arrived at my camp, kindled my fire, supped, and reposed peaceably. Rising early, I employed the fore part of the day in collecting specimens of growing roots and seeds. In the afternoon, I left these Elysian springs and the aromatic groves and briskly descended the pellucid little river, re-entering the great lake.

Manatee Spring

[*This spring is now a state park and may be reached by the dirt road branching from the highway just north of Chiefland, Florida. Ed.*]

About noon we approached the admirable Manatee Spring, three or four miles down the river. This charming nymphæum is the product of primitive nature, not to be imitated, much less equaled, by the united effort of human power and ingenuity! As we approach it by water, the mind of the inquiring traveler is previously entertained and gradually led on to greater discovery: first by a view of the sublime, dark grove, lifted up on shore by a range or curved chain of hills at a small distance from the lively green verge of the river, on the east banks; as we gently descend, floating fields of the Nymphæa nelumbo, intersected with vistas of the yellow-green Pistia stratiotes, which cover a bay or cove of the river opposite the circular woodland hills.

It is amazing and almost incredible, what troops and bands of fish and other watery inhabitants are now in sight, all peaceable; and in what variety of gay colors and forms, continually ascending and descending, roving and figuring amongst one another, yet every tribe associating separately. We now ascended the crystal stream. The current swift, we entered the grand fountain, the expansive circular basin, the source of which arises from under the bases of the high woodland hills, nearly half encircling it. The ebullition is astonishing and continual, though its greatest force of fury intermits, regularly, for the space of thirty seconds of time. The waters appear of a lucid sea-green color, in some measure owing to the reflection of the leaves above. The ebullition is perpendicular upwards, from a vast ragged orifice through a bed of rocks a great depth below the common surface of the basin, throwing up small particles or pieces of white shells, which subside with the waters at the moment of intermission, gently settling down round about the orifice, forming a vast funnel. At those moments, when the waters rush upwards, the surface of the basin immediately over the orifice is greatly swollen or raised a considerable height; and then it is impossible to keep the boat or any other floating vessel over the fountain; but the ebullition quickly subsides. Yet, before the surface becomes quite even, the fountain vomits up the waters again, and so on perpetually. The basin is generally circular, about fifty yards over; and the perpetual stream from it into the river is twelve or fifteen yards wide and ten or twelve feet in depth. The basin and stream are continually peopled with prodigious numbers and variety of fish and other animals; as the alligator, and the manatee or sea cow, in the winter season. Part of a skeleton of one, which the Indians had killed last winter, lay upon the banks of the spring. The grinding teeth were about an inch in diameter, the ribs eighteen inches in length and two inches and a half in thickness, bending with a gentle curve. This bone is esteemed equal to ivory. The flesh of this creature is counted wholesome and pleasant food; the Indians call them by a name which signifies the big beaver. My companion, who was a trader in Talahasochte last winter, saw three of them at one time in this spring. They feed chiefly on aquatic grass and weeds. The ground round about the head of the basin is generally level for the distance of a few yards; then gradually ascends, forming moderately high hills. The soil at top is a light, grayish, sandy mold, which continues some feet in depth, lying on a stratum of yellowish clay. Then clay and gravel, then sand, and so on, stratum upon stratum, down to the general foundation of testaceous rocks. In other places a deep stratum of whitish, chalky limestone. The vegetable productions which cover and ornament those eminences are generally live oaks, Magnolia grandiflora (in the Creek tongue, Tolo-chlucco, which signifies the Big bay); Red bay (in the Creek tongue Etomico, that is, King's tree); Olea americana and Liquidambar, with other trees, shrubs, and herbaceous plants common in East Florida.

The hills and groves environing this admirable fountain, affording amusing subjects of inquiry, occasioned my stay here a great part of the day; and towards evening we returned to the town.

The Alligator Hole

[*Blue Sink, about a mile north of Newberry, Florida, is believed to be the Alligator Hole. Eruptions of water in Florida still occur. A librarian at the State Library in Tallahassee told me about setting out by bus for Jacksonville and of the complications that occurred when they found a part of the highway washed away by an overflowing spring. Ed.*]

Early in the morning we left the town and the river in order to fix our encampment in the forests about twelve miles from the river. Our companions with the pack horses went ahead to the place of rendezvous, and our chief conducted me another way to show me a very curious place called the Alligator Hole, which was lately formed by an extraordinary eruption or jet of water. It is one of those vast circular sinks which we beheld almost everywhere about us as we traversed these forests, after we left the Alachua savannah. This remarkable one is on the verge of a spacious meadow, the surface of the ground round about uneven by means of gentle rising knolls. Some detached groups of rocks and large spreading live oaks shade it on every side. It is about sixty yards over, and the surface of the water six or seven feet below the rim of the funnel or basin. The water is transparent, cool, and pleasant to drink, and well stored with fish; a very large alligator at present is lord or chief; many have been killed here, but the throne is never long vacant, the vast neighboring ponds so abound with them.

The account that this gentleman, who was an eyewitness of the last eruption, gave me of its first appearance being very wonderful, I proceed to relate what he told me whilst we were in town. It was confirmed by the Indians and one or more of our companions who also saw its progress, as well as by my own observations after I came to the ground.

This trader, being near the place (before it had any visible existence in its present appearance) about three years ago, as he was looking for some horses which he expected to find in these parts, on a sudden was astonished by an inexpressible rushing noise, like a mighty hurricane or thunderstorm. Looking round, he saw the earth overflowed by torrents of water which came wave after wave, rushing down a vale or plain very near him, which it filled with water, and soon began to overwhelm the higher ground, attended with a terrific noise and tremor of the earth. Recovering from his first surprise, he immediately resolved to proceed for the place from whence the noise seemed to come and soon came in sight of the incomparable fountain and saw, with amazement, the floods rushing upwards many feet high and the expanding waters, which prevailed every way, spreading themselves

far and near. He at length concluded (he said) that the fountains of the deep were again broken up and that a universal
deluge had commenced. He instantly turned about and fled
to alarm the town, about nine miles' distance, but before he
could reach it, he met several of the inhabitants who, already alarmed by the unusual noise, were hurrying on towards the place; upon which he returned with the Indians,
taking their stand on an eminence to watch its progress and
the event. It continued to jet and flow in this manner for several days, forming a large, rapid creek or river, descending
and following the various courses and windings of the valley
for the distance of seven or eight miles, emptying itself into a
vast savannah, where was a lake and sink which received and
gave vent to its waters.

The fountain, however, gradually ceased to overflow and
finally withdrew itself beneath the common surface of the
earth, leaving this capacious basin of waters which, though
continually near full, hath never since overflowed. There yet
remains and will, I suppose, remain for ages the dry bed of
the river, or canal, generally four, five, and six feet below the
natural surface of the land. The perpendicular, ragged banks
on each side show the different strata of the earth, and at
places, where ridges or a swelling bank crossed and opposed
its course and fury, are vast heaps of fragments of rocks, white
chalk, stones, and pebbles, which were collected and thrown
into the lateral valley until the main stream prevailed over
and forced them aside, overflowing the levels and meadows
for some miles' distance from the principal stream on either
side. We continued down the great vale along its banks, quite
to the savannah and lake where it vented itself, while its ancient subterranean channel was gradually opening which, I
imagine, from some hidden event or cause had been choked

up and which, we may suppose, was the immediate cause of the eruption.

A Place of Many Sinks

[*A camp by Long Pond near Chiefland, Florida, was headquarters for the trading party as they went about the country in search of scattered groups of horses. Ed.*]

The ground, during our progress this morning, everywhere about us presented to view those funnels, sinks, and wells in groups of rocks, amidst the groves. . . .

Near our next encampment, one more conspicuous than I had elsewhere observed presenting itself, I took occasion from this favorable circumstance of observing them in all their variety of appearances. Its outer superficial margin was fifty or sixty yards over, which equally and uniformly on every side sloped downwards towards the center: on one side of it was a considerable pathway or road leading down to the water, worn by the frequent resort of wild creatures for drink when the waters were risen even or above the rocky bed, but at this time they were sunk many yards below the surface of the earth. We descended first to the bed of rocks, which was perforated with perpendicular tubes, exactly like a walled well, four, five, or six feet in diameter, and may be compared to cells in a honeycomb, through which appeared the water at bottom. Many of these were broken or worn one into another, forming one vast well with uneven walls consisting of projecting jambs, pilasters, or buttresses, and excavated semicircular niches, as if a piece were taken out of a honeycomb. The bed of rocks is from fifteen to twenty feet deep, or in thickness, though not of one solid mass but of many generally horizontal laminæ, or strata, of various thicknesses, from eighteen inches to two or three feet; which admit water to weep through, trickling down, drop after drop, or chasing each other in winding little rills down to the bottom. One side of the vast, cool grotto was so shattered and broken in, I thought it possible to descend down to the water at bottom. My companion, assuring me that the Indians and traders frequently go down for drink, encouraged me to make the attempt, as he agreed to accompany me.

Having provided ourselves with a long snagged sapling, called an Indian ladder . . . we both descended safely to the bottom, which we found nearly level and not quite covered over with water. On one side was a bed of gravel and fragments of rocks or stones and on the other a pool of water near two feet deep, which moved with a slow current under the walls on a bed of clay and gravel.

After our return to the surface of the earth, I again ranged about the groves and grottos, examining a multitude of them. Being on the margin of one in the open forest and observing some curious vegetable productions growing on the side of the sloping funnel towards its center, the surface of the ground covered with grass and herbage; unapprehensive of danger, I descended precipitately towards the group of shrubs. When I was surprised, and providentially stopped in my career, at the ground sounding hollow under my feet; and observing chasms through the ground, I quickly drew back. Returning again with a pole with which I beat in the earth, to my astonishment and dread appeared the mouth of a well through the rocks, and I observed the water glimmering at the bottom.

The Ocmulgee, Oconee, and Ogeechee Rivers in Flood

After leaving the [Chattahoochee] River, we met with nothing material or worth particular observation until our arrival at Ocmulgee, towards evening, where we encamped in expansive, ancient Indian fields, in view of the foaming flood of the river, now raging over its banks. Here were two companies of traders from Augusta, bound to the Nation, consisting of fifteen or twenty men, with seventy or eighty horses, most of which had their loads of merchandise. They crossed the river this morning and lost six horses in the attempt. They were drowned, being entangled in the vines under water at landing. But the river now falling again, we were in hopes that by next morning the waters would be again confined within the banks. We immediately set about rigging our portable leather boat, about eight feet long, which was of thick sole leather, folded up and carried on the top of a pack of deer skins. The people soon got her rigged, which was effected after the following manner. We, in the first place, cut down a white-oak sapling, and by notching this at each end, bent it up, which formed the keel, stem and stern post of one piece. This was placed in the bottom of the boat, and pretty strong hoop poles, being fixed in the bottom across the keel, turning up their ends, expanded the hull of the boat which, being fastened by thongs to two other poles bent round the outside of the rim, formed the gunwales. Thus, in an hour's time our bark was rigged, to which afterwards we added two little oars or sculls. Our boat being now in readiness and our horses turned out to pasture, each one retired to repose or to such exercise as most effectually contributed to divert the mind. I was at this time rather dejected and sought comfort in retirement, turning my course to the expansive fields, fragrant groves, and sublime forests. Returned to camp by dusk, where I found my companions cheerful and thoughtless rather to an extreme. It was a calm, still evening and warm; the woodcock chirruping high up in the air gently descended by a spiral circular tract, and alighted on the humid plain. This bird appears in Pennsylvania early in the spring, when the elm and maple begin to flower; and here the scarlet maple, elm, and elder began to show their flowers; the yellow jasmin was just ready to open its fragrant, golden blossoms, and the gay azalea also preparing to expand its beauties.

The morning was cool and pleasant. After reconnoitering the shores of the rivers and consulting with our brethren in distress, who had not yet decamped, resolving to stay and lend their assistance in passing over this rapid gulf, we were encouraged to proceed. Launching our bark into the raging flood, after many successful trips we ferried over all the goods, then drove in our horses altogether, and had the pleasure of seeing them all safely landed on the opposite shore. Lastly I embarked with three of our people and several packs of leather; we then put off from shore, bidding adieu to our generous friends left behind, who re-echoed our shouts upon our safe landing. We proceeded again, crossed the Oconee in the same manner and with the like success, and came to camp in the fertile fields, on the banks of that beautiful river; and proceeding thence next day, in the evening came to camp on the waters of great Ogeechee. The following day, after crossing several of its considerable branches, came to camp; and next day crossed the main branch of that famous river which, being wide and very rapid, proved difficult and dangerous fording; yet we crossed without any loss, but some of our pack horses were badly bruised, being swept off their feet and dashed against the rocks. My horse too was carried away with the current, and plunging off sunken shelving rocks into deep holes, I got very wet, but I kept my seat and landed safe: however I suffered much, it being a cold, freezing day. We came to camp early and, raising great fires with pine knots and other wood, we dried ourselves and kept warm during the long night, and after two days' more hard traveling we arrived at Augusta.[3]

13. A Terrifying Battle with Alligators, and Reports on Other Reptiles

A Terrible Battle with Alligators

[*Near the entrance of St. John's River into Lake Dexter. Today any naturalist watching the alligators from the Anhinga Trail in the Everglades National Park seldom fails to speculate as to whether the protection of those big reptiles and their consequent increase may someday result in a sight such as Bartram describes. Even in an area where the big reptiles are abundant, only a tremendous concentration of food would cause them to collect in great numbers. Ed.*]

THE EVENING was temperately cool and calm. The crocodiles began to roar and appear in uncommon numbers along the shores and in the river. I fixed my camp in an open plain near the utmost projection of the promontory, under the shelter of a large live oak which stood on the highest part of the ground but a few yards from my boat. From this open, high situation, I had a free prospect of the river, which was a matter of no trivial consideration to me, having good reason to dread the subtle attacks of the alligators who were crowding about my harbor. Having collected a good quantity of wood for the purpose of keeping up a light and smoke during the night, I began to think of preparing my supper when, upon examining my stores, I found but a scanty provision. I thereupon determined, as the most expeditious way of supplying my necessities, to take my bob and try for some trout. About one hundred yards above my harbor began a cove or bay of the river, out of which opened a large lagoon. The mouth or entrance from the river to it was narrow, but the waters soon after spread and formed a little lake, extending into the marshes. Its entrance and shores within I observed to be verged with floating lawns of pistia and nymphea and other aquatic plants; these I knew were excellent haunts for trout.

The verges and islets of the lagoon were elegantly embellished with flowering plants and shrubs; the laughing coots

Alligator Battle

with wings half spread were tripping over the little coves and hiding themselves in the tufts of grass; young broods of the painted summer teal, skimming the still surface of the waters and following the watchful parent, unconscious of danger, were frequently surprised by the voracious trout; and he, in turn, as often by the subtle, greedy alligator. Behold him rushing forth from the flags and reeds. His enormous body swells. His plaited tail, brandished high, floats upon the lake. The waters like a cataract descend from his opening jaws. Clouds of smoke issue from his dilated nostrils. The earth trembles with his thunder. When immediately from the opposite coast of the lagoon emerges from the deep his rival champion. They suddenly dart upon each other. The boiling surface of the lake marks their rapid course, and a terrific conflict commences. They now sink to the bottom folded together in horrid wreaths. The water becomes thick and discolored. Again they rise; their jaws clap together, re-echoing through the deep surrounding forests. Again they sink, when the contest ends at the muddy bottom of the lake, and the vanquished makes a hazardous escape, hiding himself in the muddy, turbulent waters and sedge on a distant shore. The proud victor, exulting, returns to the place of action. The shores and forests resound his dreadful roar, together with the triumphing shouts of the plaited tribes around, witnesses of the horrid combat.

My apprehensions were highly alarmed after being a spectator of so dreadful a battle. It was obvious that every delay would but tend to increase my dangers and difficulties, as the sun was near setting, and the alligators gathered around my harbor from all quarters. From these considerations I concluded to be expeditious in my trip to the lagoon, in order to take some fish. Not thinking it prudent to take my fusee with me, lest I might lose it overboard in case of a battle, which I had every reason to dread before my return, I therefore furnished myself with a club for my defense, went on board, and penetrated the first line of those which surrounded my harbor. They gave way; but being pursued by several very large ones, I kept strictly on the watch and paddled with all my might towards the entrance of the lagoon, hoping to be sheltered there from the multitude of my assailants. But, ere I had halfway reached the place, I was attacked on all sides, several endeavoring to overset the canoe.

My situation now became precarious to the last degree. Two very large ones attacked me closely at the same instant, rushing up with their heads and part of their bodies above the water, roaring terribly and belching floods of water over me. They struck their jaws together so close to my ears as almost to stun me, and I expected every moment to be dragged out of the boat and instantly devoured. But I applied my weapons so effectually about me, though at random, that I was so successful as to beat them off a little. When I found that they designed to renew the battle, I made for the shore as the only means left me for my preservation. By keeping close to it I should have my enemies on one side of me only, whereas, I was before surrounded by them. Now there was a probability, if pushed to the last extremity, of saving myself by jumping out of the canoe on shore, as it is easy to outwalk them on land, although comparatively as swift as lightning in the water. I found this last expedient alone could fully answer my expectations, for as soon as I gained the shore, they drew off and kept aloof. This was a happy relief, as my confidence was, in some degree, recovered by it.

On recollecting myself, I discovered that I had almost reached the entrance of the lagoon, and determined to ven-

ture in, if possible, to take a few fish and then return to my
harbor while daylight continued. I could now, with caution
and resolution, make my way with safety along shore; and indeed there was no other way to regain my camp without leaving my boat and making my retreat through the marshes and
reeds which, if I could even effect, would have been in a manner throwing myself away, for then there would have been
no hopes of ever recovering my bark and returning in safety
to any settlements of men. I accordingly proceeded and made
good my entrance into the lagoon, though not without op-
position from the alligators, who formed a line across the entrance, but did not pursue me into it, nor was I molested by
any there, though there were some very large ones in a cove
at the upper end. I soon caught more trout than I had present occasion for, and the air was too hot and sultry to admit
of their being kept for many hours, even though salted or
barbecued.

I now prepared for my return to camp, which I succeeded
in with but little trouble by keeping close to the shore; yet I
was opposed upon re-entering the river out of the lagoon and
pursued near to my landing (though not closely attacked),
particularly by an old daring one, about twelve feet in
length, who kept close after me. When I stepped on shore
and turned about in order to draw up my canoe, he rushed
up near my feet, and lay there for some time, looking me in
the face, his head and shoulders out of water. I resolved he
should pay for his temerity, and having a heavy load in my
fusee, I ran to my camp and, returning with my piece, found
him with his foot on the gunwale of the boat, in search of
fish. On my coming up he withdrew sullenly and slowly into
the water, but soon returned and placed himself in his former position, looking at me and seeming neither fearful nor

any way disturbed. I soon dispatched him by lodging the contents of my gun in his head, and then proceeded to cleanse and prepare my fish for supper. I accordingly took them out of the boat, laid them down on the sand close to the water, and began to scale them. Then, raising my head, I saw before me, through the clear water, the head and shoulders of a very large alligator moving slowly towards me. I instantly stepped back when, with a sweep of his tail, he brushed off several of my fish. It was certainly most providential that I looked up at that instant, as the monster would probably, in less than a minute, have seized and dragged me into the river.

This incredible boldness of the animal disturbed me greatly, supposing there could now be no reasonable safety for me during the night but by keeping continually on the watch. Therefore, as soon as I had prepared the fish, I proceeded to secure myself and effects in the best manner I could. In the first place, I hauled my bark upon the shore, almost clear out of the water, to prevent their oversetting or sinking her. After this, every movable was taken out and carried to my camp, which was but a few yards off. Then, ranging some dry wood in such order as was the most convenient, I cleared the ground round about it, that there might be no impediment in my way in case of an attack in the night, either from the water or the land, for I discovered by this time that this small isthmus, from its remote situation and fruitfulness, was resorted to by bears and wolves. Having prepared myself in the best manner I could, I charged my gun and proceeded to reconnoiter my camp and the adjacent grounds; when I discovered that the peninsula and grove, at the distance of about two hundred yards from my encampment, on the land side, were invested by a cypress swamp, covered with water, which below was joined to the shore of

the little lake, and above to the marshes surrounding the
lagoon; so that I was confined to an islet exceedingly circumscribed, and I found there was no other retreat for me, in
case of an attack, but by either ascending one of the large
oaks or pushing off with my boat.

It was by this time dusk, and the alligators had nearly
ceased their roar, when I was again alarmed by a tumultuous
noise that seemed to be in my harbor and therefore engaged
my immediate attention. Returning to my camp, I found it
undisturbed and then continued on to the extreme point of
the promontory, where I saw a scene, new and surprising,
which at first threw my senses into such a tumult, that it was
some time before I could comprehend what was the matter.
However, I soon accounted for the prodigious assemblage of
crocodiles at this place, which exceeded everything of the
kind I had ever heard of.

How shall I express myself so as to convey an adequate idea
of it to the reader, and at the same time avoid raising suspi-
cions of my veracity? Should I say that the river (in this
place), from shore to shore and perhaps near half a mile
above and below me, appeared to be one solid bank of fish of
various kinds, pushing through this narrow pass of St. Juan's
into the little lake on their return down the river, and that
the alligators were in such incredible numbers and so close
together from shore to shore that it would have been easy to
have walked across on their heads, had the animals been
harmless? What expressions can sufficiently declare the
shocking scene that for some minutes continued, whilst this
mighty army of fish were forcing the pass? During this attempt, thousands, I may say hundreds of thousands, of them
were caught and swallowed by the devouring alligators. I
have seen an alligator take up out of the water several great

fish at a time, and just squeeze them betwixt his jaws, while the tails of the great trout flapped about his eyes and lips, ere he had swallowed them. The horrid noise of their closing jaws, their plunging amidst the broken banks of fish and rising with their prey some feet upright above the water, the floods of water and blood rushing out of their mouths, and the clouds of vapor issuing from their wide nostrils were truly frightful. This scene continued at intervals during the night, as the fish came to the pass. After this sight, shocking and tremendous as it was, I found myself somewhat easier and more reconciled to my situation; being convinced that their extraordinary assemblage here was owing to the annual feast of fish; and that they were so well employed in their own element that I had little occasion to fear their paying me a visit.

It being now almost night, I returned to my camp, where I had left my fish broiling and my kettle of rice stewing; and having with me oil, pepper, and salt, and excellent oranges hanging in abundance over my head (a valuable substitute for vinegar), I sat down and regaled myself cheerfully. Having finished my repast, I rekindled my fire for light, and whilst I was revising the notes of my past day's journey, I was suddenly roused with a noise behind me toward the mainland. I sprang up on my feet and, listening, I distinctly heard some creature wading the water of the isthmus. I seized my gun and went cautiously from my camp, directing my steps towards the noise. When I had advanced about thirty yards, I halted behind a coppice of orange trees and soon perceived two very large bears, which had made their way through the water and had landed in the grove about one hundred yards' distance from me and were advancing towards me. I waited until they were within thirty yards of me. They there began to snuff and look towards my camp. I snapped my piece, but it flashed, on which they both turned about and galloped off, plunging through the water and swamp, never halting, as I suppose, until they reached fast land, as I could hear them leaping and plunging a long time. They did not presume to return again, nor was I molested by any other creature, except being occasionally awakened by the whooping of owls, screaming of bitterns, or the wood rats running amongst the leaves.

The wood rat is a very curious animal. It is not half the size of the domestic rat; of a dark brown or black color; its tail slender and shorter in proportion and covered thinly with short hair. It is singular with respect to its ingenuity and great labor in the construction of its habitation, which is a conical pyramid about three or four feet high, constructed with dry branches which it collects with great labor and perseverance and piles up without any apparent order; yet they are so interwoven with one another that it would take a bear or wild cat some time to pull one of these castles to pieces, and would allow the animals sufficient time to secure a retreat with their young.

The noise of the crocodiles kept me awake the greater part of the night; but when I arose in the morning, contrary to my expectations there was perfect peace; very few of them to be seen, and those were asleep on the shore. Yet I was not able to suppress my fears and apprehensions of being attacked by them in future; and indeed yesterday's combat with them, notwithstanding I came off in a manner victorious or at least made a safe retreat, had left sufficient impression on my mind to damp my courage. It seemed too much for one of my strength, being alone in a very small boat, to encounter such collected danger. To pursue my voyage up the river and be obliged every evening to pass such dangerous defiles appeared to me as perilous as running the gauntlet betwixt two rows of Indians armed with knives and firebrands. I resolved, however, to continue my voyage one day longer, if I possibly could with safety, and then return down the river, should I find the like difficulties to oppose. Accordingly, I got everything on board, charged my gun, and set sail, cautiously, along shore. As I passed by Battle Lagoon, I began to tremble and keep a good lookout. Suddenly a huge alligator rushed out of the reeds and with a tremendous roar came up and darted as swift as an arrow under my boat, emerging upright on my lee quarter with open jaws and belching water and smoke that fell upon me like rain in a hurricane. I laid soundly about his head with my club and beat him off and, after plunging and darting about my boat, he went off on a straight line through the water, seemingly with the rapidity of lightning, and entered the cape of the lagoon. I now employed my time to the very best advantage in paddling close along shore, but could not forbear looking now and then behind me, and presently perceived one of them coming up again. The water of the river hereabouts was shoal and very clear. The monster came up with the usual roar and menaces and passed close by the side of my boat, when I could distinctly see a young brood of alligators, to the number of one hundred or more, following after her in a long train. They kept close together in a column, without straggling off to the one side or the other. The young appeared to be of an equal size, about fifteen inches in length, almost black, with pale yellow transverse waved clouds or blotches, much like rattlesnakes in color. I now lost sight of my enemy again.

Still keeping close along shore, on turning a point or projection of the river bank at once I beheld a great number of hillocks or small pyramids, resembling haycocks, ranged like an encampment along the banks. They stood fifteen or twenty yards distant from the water, on a high marsh, about four feet perpendicular above the water. I knew them to be the nests of the crocodile, having had a description of them before, and now expected a furious and general attack, as I saw several large crocodiles swimming abreast of these buildings. These nests being so great a curiosity to me, I was determined at all events immediately to land and examine them. Accordingly, I ran my bark on shore at one of their landing places, which was a sort of nick or little dock, from which ascended a sloping path or road up to the edge of the meadow, where their nests were. Most of them were deserted, and the great, thick, whitish egg shells lay broken and scattered upon the ground round about them.

The nests or hillocks are of the form of an obtuse cone, four feet high and four or five feet in diameter at their bases; they are constructed with mud, grass, and herbage. At first they lay a floor of this kind of tempered mortar on the ground, upon which they deposit a layer of eggs, and upon this a stratum of mortar, seven or eight inches in thickness, and then another layer of eggs; and in this manner one stratum upon another, nearly to the top. I believe they commonly lay from one to two hundred eggs in a nest. These are hatched, I suppose, by the heat of the sun. Perhaps the vegetable substances mixed with the earth, being acted upon by the sun, may cause a small degree of fermentation and so increase the heat in those hillocks. The ground for several acres about these nests showed evident marks of a continual resort of alligators. The grass was everywhere beaten down, hardly a blade or straw was left standing; whereas, all about, at a distance, it was five or six feet high and as thick as it could grow together. The female, as I imagine, carefully watches her own nest of eggs until they are all hatched; or perhaps, while she is attending her own brood, she takes under her care and protection as many as she can get at one time, either from her own particular nest or others. Certain it is that the young are not left to shift for themselves; for I have had frequent opportunities of seeing the female alligator leading about the shores her train of young ones, just as a hen does her brood of chickens. She is equally assiduous and courageous in defending the young which are under her care and providing for their subsistence. When she is basking upon the warm banks, with her brood around her, you may hear the young ones continually whining and barking like young puppies. I believe but few of a brood live to the years of full growth and magnitude, as the old feed on the young as long as they can make prey of them.

The alligator when full grown is a very large and terrible creature and of prodigious strength, activity, and swiftness in the water. I have seen them twenty feet in length, and some are supposed to be twenty-two or twenty-three feet. Their body is as large as that of a horse; their shape exactly resembles that of a lizard, except their tail, which is flat or cuneiform, being compressed on each side, and gradually diminishing from the abdomen to the extremity, which, with the whole body, is covered with horny plates or squamæ, impenetrable when on the body of the live animal, even to a rifle ball, except about their head and just behind their forelegs or arms, where it is said they are only vulnerable. The head of a full-grown one is about three feet, and the mouth opens nearly the same length. Their eyes are small in proportion, and seem sunk deep in the head by means of the prominency of the brows. The nostrils are large, inflated and prominent on the top, so that the head in the water resembles, at a distance, a great chunk of wood floating about. Only the upper jaw moves, which they raise almost perpendicular, so as to form a right angle with the lower one. In the forepart of the upper jaw, on each side, just under the nostrils, are two very large, thick, strong teeth or tusks, not very sharp, but rather the shape of a cone. These are as white as the finest polished ivory and are not covered by any skin or lips, and always in sight, which gives the creature a frightful appearance. In the lower jaw are holes opposite to these teeth, to receive them. When they clap their jaws together it causes a surprising noise, like that which is made by forcing a heavy plank with violence upon the ground, and may be heard at a great distance.

But what is yet more surprising to a stranger is the incredible loud and terrifying roar which they are capable of making, especially in the spring season, their breeding time. It most resembles very heavy, distant thunder, not only shaking the air and waters but causing the earth to tremble; and when hundreds and thousands are roaring at the same time, you can scarcely be persuaded but that the whole globe is violently and dangerously agitated.

An old champion, who is perhaps absolute sovereign of a little lake or lagoon (when fifty less than himself are obliged to content themselves with swelling and roaring in little coves round about), darts forth from the reedy coverts all at once, on the surface of the waters, in a right line; at first seemingly as rapid as lightning, but gradually more slowly until he arrives at the center of the lake, when he stops. He now swells himself by drawing in wind and water through his mouth, which causes a loud, sonorous rattling in the throat for near a minute, but it is immediately forced out again through his mouth and nostrils, with a loud noise, brandishing his tail in the air, and the vapor ascending from his nostrils like smoke. At other times, when swollen to an extent ready to burst, his head and tail lifted up, he spins or twirls round on the surface of the water. He acts his part like an Indian chief when rehearsing his feats of war; and then retiring, the exhibition is continued by others who dare to step forth and strive to excel each other, to gain the attention of the favorite female.

Rattlesnakes and the Seminoles

I was in the forenoon busy in my apartment in the council house drawing some curious flowers, when, on a sudden, my attention was taken off by a tumult without, at the Indian camp. I stepped to the door opening to the piazza, where I met my friend the old interpreter, who informed me that there was a very large rattlesnake in the Indian camp, which had taken possession of it, having driven the men, women and children out. He heard them saying that they would send for Puc-Puggy (for that was the name which they had given me, signifying the Flower Hunter) to kill him or take him out of their camp. I answered that I desired to have nothing to do with him, apprehending some disagreeable consequences, and desired that the Indians might be acquainted that I was engaged in business that required application and quiet and was determined to avoid it if possible.

My old friend turned about to carry my answer to the Indians. I presently heard them approaching and calling for Puc-Puggy. Starting up to escape from their sight by a back door, a party consisting of three young fellows, richly dressed and ornamented, stepped in, and with a countenance and action of noble simplicity, amity, and complaisance, requested me to accompany them to their encampment. I desired them to excuse me at this time. They pleaded and entreated me to go with them, in order to free them from a great rattlesnake which had entered their camp. None of them had freedom or courage to expel him and, understanding that it was my pleasure to collect all their animals and other natural productions of their land, desired that I would come with them and take him away, that I was welcome to him. I at length consented and attended on them to their encampment, where I beheld the Indians greatly disturbed indeed; the men with sticks and tomahawks and the women and children collected together at a distance in affright and trepidation, whilst the dreaded and revered serpent leisurely traversed their camp.

The men gathered around me, exciting me to remove him. Being armed with a lightwood knot, I approached the reptile, who instantly collected himself in a vast coil (their attitude of defense). I cast my missile weapon at him which, luckily taking his head, dispatched him instantly and laid him trembling at my feet. I took out my knife, severed his head from his body; then turning about, the Indians complimented me with every demonstration of satisfaction and approbation for my heroism and friendship for them. I carried off the head of the serpent bleeding in my hand as a trophy of victory; and, taking out the mortal fangs, deposited them carefully amongst my collections.

I had not been long retired to my apartment before I was again roused from it by a tumult in the yard. Hearing Puc-Puggy called on, I started up, when instantly the old interpreter met me again and told me the Indians were approaching in order to scratch me. I asked him for what? He answered, for killing the rattlesnake within their camp. Before I could make any reply or effect my escape, three young fellows, singing arm in arm, came up to me. I observed one of the three was a young prince who had, on my first interview with him, declared himself my friend and protector, when he told me that if ever occasion should offer in his presence, he would risk his life to defend mine or my property. This young champion stood by his two associates, one on each side of him. The two, affecting a countenance and air of displeasure and importance, instantly presenting their scratching instruments, and flourishing them, spoke boldly, and said that I was too heroic and violent, that it would be good for me to lose some of my blood to make me more mild and tame, and for that purpose they were come to scratch me. They gave me no time to expostulate or reply but attempted to lay hold on me, which I resisted. My friend, the young prince, interposed and pushed them off, saying that I was a brave warrior and his friend; that they should not insult me. Instantly they altered their countenance and behavior. They all whooped in chorus, took me friendly by the hand, clapped me on the shoulder, and laid their hands on their breasts in token of sincere friendship, and laughing aloud, said I was a sincere friend to the Seminoles, a worthy and brave warrior, and that no one should hereafter attempt to injure me. They then all three joined arm in arm again and went off, shouting and proclaiming Puc-Puggy was their friend, etc. Thus it seemed that the whole was a ludicrous farce to satisfy their people and appease the manes* of the dead rattlesnake.

The next day was employed by the Indians in preparations

* These people never kill the rattlesnake or any other serpent, saying if they do so, the spirit of the killed snake will excite or influence his living kindred or relatives to revenge the injury or violence done to him when alive.

for their departure, such as taking up their goods from the trading house, collecting together their horses, making up their packs, etc., and the evening joyfully spent in songs and dances. The succeeding morning, after exhibiting the war farce, they decamped, proceeding on their expedition against their enemy. . . .

But let us again resume the subject of the rattlesnake, a wonderful creature when we consider his form, nature, and disposition. It is certain that he is capable by a puncture or scratch of one of his fangs not only to kill the largest animal in America, and that in a few minutes' time, but to turn the whole body into corruption. But such is the nature of this dreadful reptile that he cannot run or creep faster than a man or child can walk, and he is never known to strike until he is first assaulted or fears himself in danger. Even then he always gives the earliest warning by the rattles at the extremity of the tail. I have in the course of my travels in the Southern states (where they are the largest, most numerous, and supposed to be the most venomous and vindictive) stepped unknowingly so close as almost to touch one of them with my feet, and when I perceived him, he was already drawn up in circular coils ready for a blow. But, however incredible it may appear, the generous — I may say magnanimous — creature lay as still and motionless as if inanimate; his head crouched in, his eyes almost shut. I precipitately withdrew, unless when I have been so shocked with surprise and horror as to be in a manner riveted to the spot, for a short time not having strength to go away; when he often slowly extends himself and quietly moves off in a direct line, unless pursued, when he erects his tail as far as the rattles extend, and gives the warning alarm by intervals. But if you pursue and overtake him with a show of enmity, he instantly throws himself into the spiral coil; his tail by the rapidity of its motion appears like a vapor, making a quick, tremulous sound; his whole body swells through rage, continually rising and falling as a bellows; his beautiful particolored skin becomes speckled and rough by dilatation; his head and neck are flattened, his cheeks swollen and his lips constricted, discovering his mortal fangs; his eyes red as burning coals, and his brandishing forked tongue of the color of the hottest flame; he continually menaces death and destruction, yet never strikes unless sure of his mark.

The rattlesnake is the largest serpent yet known to exist in North America. I have heard of their having been seen formerly at the first settling of Georgia, seven, eight, and even ten feet in length, and six or eight inches diameter. There are none of that size now to be seen, yet I have seen them above six feet in length and above six inches in thickness, or as large as a man's leg; but their general size is four, five, and six feet in length.

Since, within the circle of my acquaintance, I am known to be an advocate or vindicator of the benevolent and peaceable disposition of animal creation in general, not only towards mankind, whom they seem to venerate, but always towards one another, except where hunger or the rational and necessary provocations of the sensual appetite interfere, I shall mention a few instances, amongst many, which I have had an opportunity of remarking during my travels, particularly with regard to the animal I have been treating of. I shall strictly confine myself to facts.

When on the seacoast of Georgia, I consented, with a few friends, to make a party of amusement at fishing and fowling on the Sapello, one of the seacoast islands. We accordingly descended the Altamaha, crossed the sound, and landed on the north end of the island, near the inlet, fixing our en-campment at a pleasant situation, under the shade of a grove of live oaks and laurels* on the high banks of a creek which we ascended, winding through a salt marsh, which had its source from a swamp and savannah in the island. Our situa-tion, elevated and open, commanded a comprehensive land-scape. The great ocean, the foaming surf breaking on the sandy beach, the snowy breakers on the bar, the endless chain of islands, checkered sound, and high continent all ap-peared before us. The diverting toils of the day were not fruitless, affording us opportunities of furnishing ourselves plentifully with a variety of game, fish, and oysters for our supper.

About two hundred yards from our camp was a cool spring, amidst a grove of the odoriferous Myrica. The winding path to this salubrious fountain led through a grassy savannah. I visited the spring several times in the night, but little did I know, or any of my careless, drowsy companions, that every time we visited the fountain we were in imminent danger, as I am going to relate. Early in the morning, excited by uncon-querable thirst, I arose and went to the spring. Having no thought of harm or danger . . . along the serpentine foot-path my hasty steps were suddenly stopped by the sight of a hideous serpent, the formidable rattlesnake, in a high spiral coil, forming a circular mound half the height of my knees, within six inches of the narrow path. As soon as I recovered my senses and strength from so sudden a surprise, I started back out of his reach, where I stood to view him. He lay quiet whilst I surveyed him, appearing no way surprised or disturbed, but kept his half-shut eyes fixed on me. My im-agination and spirits were in a tumult, almost equally di-

---

* Magnolia grandiflora, called by the inhabitants the Laurel.

vided betwixt thanksgiving to the supreme Creator and Pre-
server, and the dignified nature of the generous though terrible creature who had suffered us all to pass many times by
him during the night without injuring us in the least, although we must have touched him, or our steps guided there-
from by a supreme guardian spirit. I hastened back to acquaint my associates, but with a determination to protect the
life of the generous serpent. I presently brought my companions to the place. They were, beyond expression, surprised
and terrified at the sight of the animal, and in a moment acknowledged their escape from destruction to be miraculous.
I am proud to assert that all of us, except one person, agreed
to let him lie undisturbed, and that person was at length prevailed upon to suffer him to escape.

Again, when in my youth, attending my father on a journey to the Catskill Mountains, in the government of New
York, having nearly ascended the peak of Gilead, being
youthful and vigorous in the pursuit of botanical and novel
objects, I had gained the summit of a steep rocky precipice,
ahead of our guide; when just entering a shady vale I saw, at
the root of a small shrub, a singular and beautiful appearance, which I remember to have instantly apprehended to
be a large kind of fungus which we call Jew's-ears, and was
just drawing back my foot to kick it over when at the instant
my father, being near, cried out, "A rattlesnake, my son!"
and jerked me back, which probably saved my life. I had
never before seen one. This was of the kind which our guide
called a yellow one; it was very beautiful, speckled, and
clouded. My father pleaded for his life, but our guide was in-
exorable, saying he never spared the life of a rattlesnake,
and killed him; my father took his skin and fangs.

Some years after this, when again in company with my fa-

ther on a journey into East Florida, on the banks of St. Juan
. . . I attended him on a botanical excursion. Some time
after we had been rambling in a swamp about a quarter of a
mile from the camp, I being ahead a few paces, my father bid
me observe the rattlesnake before and just at my feet. I
stopped and saw the monster formed in a high spiral coil,
not half his length from my feet. Another step forward
would have put my life in his power, as I must have touched
if not stumbled over him. The fright and perturbation of my
spirits at once excited resentment; at that time I was entirely insensible to gratitude or mercy. I instantly cut off a
little sapling and soon dispatched him. This serpent was
about six feet in length. The encounter deterred us from
proceeding on our researches for that day. I cut off a long,
tough withe, or vine, which fastening round the neck of the
slain serpent, I dragged him after me, his scaly body sounding over the ground; and entering the camp with him in tri-
umph, I was soon surrounded by the amazed multitude, both
Indians and my countrymen.

The adventure soon reached the ears of the commander,
who sent an officer to request that, if the snake had not bit
himself, he might have him served up for his dinner. I readily delivered up the body of the snake to the cooks, and being that day invited to dine at the governor's table, saw the
snake served up in several dishes; Governor Grant being
fond of the flesh of the rattlesnake. I tasted of it, but could
not swallow it.

I, however, was sorry after killing the serpent, when coolly
recollecting every circumstance. He certainly had it in his
power to kill me almost instantly, and I make no doubt but
that he was conscious of it. I promised myself that I would
never again be accessory to the death of a rattlesnake, which

promise I have invariably kept to. This dreaded animal is easily killed; a stick no thicker than a man's thumb is sufficient to kill the largest at one stroke, if well directed, either on the head or across the back; nor can they make their escape by running off, nor indeed do they attempt it when attacked.

More Observations About Snakes

The bastard rattlesnakes, by some called ground rattlesnakes, are dangerous little creatures. Their bite is certainly mortal if present medical relief is not administered. They seem to be much of the nature of the asp or adder of the Old World.

These little vipers are in form and color much like the rattlesnake, but not so bright and uniformly marked. Their heads are broader and shorter in proportion to the other parts of their bodies. Their noses prominent and turned upwards. Their tails become suddenly small from the vent to the extremity, which terminates with three minute articulations resembling rattles. When irritated, they turn up their tails, which vibrate so quick as to appear like a mist or vapor, but cause little or no sound or noise. Yet, it is the common report of the inhabitants that they cause that remarkable vehement noise so frequently observed in forests in the heat of summer and autumn, very terrifying to strangers, which is probably caused by a very sable small insect of the genus cicadae, or which are called locusts in America. Yet it is possible I may be mistaken in this conjecture. These dangerous vipers are from eight to ten inches in length and of proportionate thickness. They are spiteful, snappish creatures and, throwing themselves into little coils, swell and flatten themselves, continually darting out their heads. They seem capable of springing beyond their length. They seem destitute of the pacific disposition and magnanimity of the rattlesnake and are unworthy of an alliance with him. No man saves their lives, yet they remain too numerous, even in the oldest parts of the country.

The riband snakes are also very beautiful, innocent serpents. They are eighteen inches in length, and about the thickness of a man's little finger; the head is very small; the ground color of a full, clear vermilion, variegated with transverse bars or zones of a dark brown, which people fancy represents a riband wound round the creature's body. They are altogether inoffensive to man and are in a manner domestic, frequenting old wooden buildings, open grounds, and plantations.

The chicken snakes are large, strong and swift serpents, six or seven feet in length but scarcely so thick as a man's wrist. They are of a cinereous, earthy color and striped longitudinally with broad lines or lists, of a dusky or blackish color. They are a domestic snake, haunting about houses and plantations, and would be useful to man if tamed and properly tutored, being great devourers of rats. But they are apt to disturb hen roosts and prey upon chickens. They are as innocent as a worm with respect to venom, are easily tamed, and soon become very familiar.

The pine or bull snakes are very large and inoffensive with respect to mankind but devour squirrels, birds, rabbits, and every other creature they can take as food. They are the largest snakes yet known in North America, except the rattlesnakes, and perhaps exceed these in length. They are pied black and white, they utter a terrible loud hissing noise, sounding very hollow and like distant thunder when irritated or at the time of incubation, when the males contend with each other for the desired female. These serpents are also called horn snakes, from their tail terminating with a hard, horny spur, which they vibrate very quick when disturbed, but they never attempt to strike with it; they have dens in the earth, whither they retreat precipitately when apprehensive of danger.

A Hawk and the Coach-Whip Snake

The high road being here open and spacious at a good distance before me, I observed a large hawk on the ground in the middle of the road. He seemed to be in distress, endeavoring to rise. Coming up near him, I found him closely bound up by a very long coach-whip snake that had wreathed himself several times round the hawk's body, who had but one of his wings at liberty. Beholding their struggles awhile, I alighted off my horse with an intention of parting them; when, on coming up, they mutually agreed to separate themselves, each one seeking his own safety, probably considering me as their common enemy. The bird rose aloft and fled away as soon as he recovered his liberty, and the snake as eagerly made off. I soon overtook him, but could not perceive that he was wounded.

I suppose the hawk had been the aggressor and fell upon the snake with an intention of making a prey of him; and that the snake dexterously and luckily threw himself in coils round his body and girded him so close as to save himself from destruction.

The coach-whip snake is a beautiful creature. When full grown it is six and seven feet in length, and the largest part of its body not so thick as a cane or common walking stick. Its head is not larger than the end of a man's finger; its neck is very slender, and from the abdomen tapers away in the manner of a small switch or coach-whip. The top of the head and neck, for three or four inches, is as black and shining as a raven; the throat and belly as white as snow; and the upper side of the body of a chocolate color, excepting the tail part, almost from the abdomen to the extremity, which is black. It may be proper to observe, however, that it varies in respect to the color of the body; some I have seen almost white or cream color, others of a pale chocolate or clay color, but in all, the head and neck are black, and the tail dark brown or black. It is extremely swift, seeming almost to fly over the surface of the ground; and, which is very singular, it can run swiftly on its tail part only, carrying the head and body upright.* One very fine one accompanied me along the roadside at a little distance, raising himself erect, now and then looking me in the face, although I proceeded on a good round trot on purpose to observe how fast he could proceed in that position. His object seemed mere curiosity or observation; with respect to venom it is as innocent as a worm, and seems to be familiar with man. It appears to be a particular inhabitant of East Florida, though I have seen some in the maritime parts of Carolina and Georgia, but in these regions it is neither so large nor beautiful.

* It is evident, from this and from the other numerous errors contained in William Bartram's reports on reptiles, that he was a better botanist than herpetologist. It is well for the reader to keep constantly in mind that the Bartrams were living in, and reporting on, the period of first recordings by American scientists. Farida A. Wiley.

The Soft-Shelled Tortoise

Here are, as well as in all the rivers, lakes, and ponds of East Florida, the great soft-shelled tortoises. They are very large when full grown, from twenty to thirty and forty pounds weight, extremely fat and delicious, but if eaten to excess, are apt to purge people not accustomed to eat their meat.

They are flat and very thin; two feet and a half in length and eighteen inches in breadth across the back; in form, appearance, and texture, very much resembling the sea turtle. The whole back shell, except the vertebra or ridge, which is not at all prominent, and ribs on each side, is soft or cartilaginous and easily reduced to a jelly when boiled. The anterior and posterior extremities of the back shell appear to be embossed with round, horny warts or tubercles. The belly or nether shell is but small and semicartilaginous, except a narrow cross bar connecting it at each end with the back shell, which is hard and osseous. The head is large and clubbed, of nearly an oval form; the upper mandible, however, is protended forward and truncated, somewhat resembling a swine's snout, at the extreme end of which the nostrils are placed. On each side of the root or base of this proboscis are the eyes, which are large. The upper beak is hooked and sharp, like a hawk's bill; the lips and corners of the mouth large, tumid, wrinkled, and barbed with long, pointed warts, which he can project and contract at pleasure, which gives the creature a frightful and disagreeable countenance.

They bury themselves in the slushy bottoms of rivers and ponds, under the roots of flags and other aquatic herbage, leaving a hole or aperture just sufficient for their head to play through. To such places they withdraw themselves when hungry and there seize their prey by surprise, darting out their heads as quick as lightning upon the unwary animal that unfortunately strolls within their reach. They can extend their neck to a surprising length, which enables them to seize young fowl swimming on the surface of the water above them, which they instantly drag down. They are seen to raise their heads above the surface of the water, in the depths of the lakes and rivers, and blow, causing a faint puffing noise, somewhat like a porpoise; probably this is for pastime or to charge themselves with a proper supply of fresh air. They are carnivorous, feeding on any animal they can seize, particularly young ducks, frogs, and fish.

We had a large and fat one served up for our supper, which I at first apprehended we had made a very extravagant waste of, not being able to consume one half of its flesh, though excellently well cooked. My companions, however, seemed regardless, being in the midst of plenty and variety, at any time within our reach and to be obtained with little or no trouble or fatigue on our part; when herds of deer were feeding in the green meadows before us, flocks of turkeys walking in the groves around us, and myriads of fish, of the greatest variety and delicacy, sporting in the crystalline floods before our eyes.

The vultures and ravens were crouched on the crooked limbs of the lofty pines at a little distance from us, sharpening their beaks in low debate, waiting to regale themselves on the offals after our departure from camp.

Gopher Tortoise

[*In the sand hills west of Lake George, Florida. Ed.*]

We observed, as we passed over the same hills, the dens of the great land tortoise, called gopher. This strange creature remains yet undescribed by historians and travelers. The first signs of this animal's existence, as we travel southerly, are immediately after we cross the Savannah River. It is to be seen only on the high, dry sand hills. When arrived at its greatest magnitude, the upper shell is near eighteen inches in length and ten or twelve inches in breadth. The back is very high and the shell of a very hard, bony substance, consisting of many regular compartments united by sutures in the manner of the other species of tortoise, and covered with thin, horny plates. The nether or belly shell is large and regularly divided transversely into five parts: these compartments are not knit together like the sutures of the skull or the back shell of the tortoise, but adhere, or are connected together by a very ridgy horny cartilage, which serves as hinges for him to shut up his body within his shell at pleasure. The fore part of the belly shell towards its extremity is formed somewhat like a spade, extends forward near three inches, and is about an inch and a half in breadth; its extremity is a little bifid; the posterior division of the belly shell is likewise protended backwards considerably and is deeply bifurcated.

The legs and feet are covered with flat, horny squamæ; he seems to have no clefts in them or toes, but long flattish nails or talons, somewhat in resemblance to the nails of the human fingers, five on the fore feet; the hind legs or feet appear as if truncated, or as stumps of feet, armed all round with sharp, flattish, strong nails, the number undetermined or irregular; the head is of a moderate size; the upper mandible a little hooked, the edges hard and sharp; the eyes are large; the nose picked; the nostrils near together and very minute; the general color of the animal is a light ash or clay, and at a distance, unless it is in motion, anyone would disregard or overlook it as a stone or an old stump. It is astonishing what a weight one of these creatures will bear; it will easily carry any man standing on its back on level ground. They form great and deep dens in the sand hills, casting out incredible quantities of earth. They are esteemed excellent food. The eggs are larger than a musket ball, perfectly round, and the shell hard.

The Glass Snake

[*Really a legless lizard,* Ophisaurus ventralis. *Ed.*]

I observed near my feet the surprising glass snake (*Anguis fragilis*). It seems as innocent and harmless as a worm. It is, when full grown, two feet and a half in length, and three fourths of an inch in thickness. The abdomen or body part is remarkably short, and it seems to be all tail, which, though long, gradually attenuates to its extremity, yet not small and slender as in switch snakes. The color and texture of the whole animal is exactly like bluish-green glass, which, together with its fragility, almost persuades a stranger that it is in reality of that brittle substance: but it is only the tail part that breaks off, which it does like glass, by a very gentle stroke from a slender switch. Though it is quick and nimble in twisting about, yet it cannot run fast from one, but quickly secretes itself at the bottom of the grass or under leaves. It is a vulgar fable that it is able to repair itself after being broken into several pieces; which pieces, common report says, by a power or faculty in the animal, voluntarily approach each other, join, and heal again.[1]

14. Fish and Their Enemies

The Gold Fish (Bartram's Minnow) in a Creek Flowing into Broad River, Georgia

The waters at this place were still and shoal and flowed over a bed of gravel just beneath a rocky rapid. In this eddy shoal were a number of little gravelly pyramidal hills whose summits rose almost to the surface of the water, very artfully constructed by a species of small crayfish which inhabited them. Here seemed to be their citadel, or place of retreat for their young against the attacks and ravages of their enemy, the gold fish. These, in numerous bands, continually infested them, except at short intervals, when small detachments of veteran crayfish sallied out upon them from their cells within the gravelly pyramids, at which time a brilliant fight presented. The little gold fish instantly fled from every side, darting through the transparent waters like streams of lightning; some even sprang above the surface into the air, but all quickly returned to the charge, surrounding the pyramids as before, on the retreat of the crayfish; in this manner the war seemed to be continual.

The gold fish is about the size of the anchovy, nearly four inches long, of a neat slender form; the head is covered with a salade of an ultramarine blue, the back of a reddish brown,

the sides and belly of a flame or of the color of a fine red
lead; a narrow dusky line runs along each side, from the gills
to the tail; the eyes are large, with the iris like burnished
gold.

Trout Fishing in Lake George, Florida

[*Large-mouthed bass are generally called "trout" in the Southeast. Ed.*]

I found some of my companions fishing for trout, round
about the edges of the floating nymphæa, and not unsuccess-
fully, having then caught more than sufficient for us all. As
the method of taking these fish is curious and singular, I shall
just mention it.

They are taken with a hook and line, but without any
bait. Two people are in a little canoe, one sitting in the stern
to steer and the other near the bow, having a rod ten or
twelve feet in length, to one end of which is tied a strong
line about twenty inches in length, to which are fastened three
large hooks, back to back. These are fixed very securely and
covered with the white hair of a deer's tail, shreds of a red
garter, and some particolored feathers, all which form a tuft
or tassel, nearly as large as one's fist, and entirely cover and
conceal the hooks: this is called a bob. The steersman paddles
softly and proceeds slowly along shore, keeping the boat parallel to it, at a distance just sufficient to admit the fisherman
to reach the edge of the floating weeds along shore. He then
ingeniously swings the bob backwards and forwards, just
above the surface, and sometimes tips the water with it; when
the unfortunate cheated trout instantly springs from under the

weeds and seizes the supposed prey. Thus he is caught without a possibility of escape, unless he break the hooks, line, or rod, which he, however, sometimes does by dint of strength. To prevent this, the fisherman used to the sport is careful not to raise the reed suddenly up but jerks it instantly backwards, then steadily drags the sturdy, reluctant fish to the side of the canoe and with a sudden upright jerk brings him into it.

The head of this fish makes about one third of his length, and consequently the mouth is very large: birds, fish, frogs, and even serpents are frequently found in its stomach.

The trout is of a lead color, inclining to a deep blue, and marked with transverse waved lists of a deep slate color, and when fully grown, has a cast of red or brick color. The fins, with the tail, which is large and beautifully formed, are of a light reddish purple, or flesh color, the whole body is covered with large scales. But what is most singular, this fish is remarkably ravenous; nothing living that he can seize upon escapes his jaws; and the opening and extending of the branchiostega, at the moment he rises to the surface to seize his prey, discovering his bright red gills through the transparent waters, give him a very terrible appearance. Indeed it may be observed that all fish of prey have this opening and covering of the gills very large, in order to discharge the great quantity of water which they take in at their mouth, when they strike at their prey. This fish is nearly cuneiform, the body tapering gradually from the breast to the tail and lightly compressed on each side. They frequently weigh fifteen, twenty, and thirty pounds and are delicious food.

Fish in the Inland Lakes of Florida

The various kind of fish . . . that inhabit these inland lakes and waters may be mentioned here, as many of them here assembled pass and repass in the lucid grotto. First the great brown spotted gar, accoutered in an impenetrable coat of mail. This admirable animal may be termed a cannibal amongst fish, as fish are his prey. When fully grown he is from five to six feet in length and of proportionable thickness, of a dusky brown color, spotted with black. The Indians make use of their sharp teeth to scratch or bleed themselves with, and their pointed scales to arm their arrows. This fish is sometimes eaten, and to prepare them for food, they cover them whole in hot embers, where they bake them. The skin with the scales easily peels off, leaving the meat white and tender.

The mud fish is large, thick or round, and two feet in length. His meat is white and tender but soft and tastes of the mud, and is not much esteemed. The great devouring trout and catfish are in abundance, and the golden bream or sunfish, the red-bellied bream, the silver or white bream, the great yellow and great black or blue bream also abound here. The last of these mentioned is a large, beautiful, and delicious fish. When full grown they are nine inches in length and five to six inches in breadth; the whole body is of a dull blue or indigo color, marked with transverse lists or zones of a darker color, scatteringly powdered with sky blue, gold, and red specks; fins and tail of a dark purple or livid flesh color; the ultimate angle of the branchiostega forming a spatula, the extreme end of which is broad and circular, terminating like the feather of the peacock's train and having a brilliant spot or eye like it, being delicately painted with a fringed border of a fire color.

The great yellow particolored bream is in form and proportion much like the forementioned, but larger, from a foot to fifteen inches in length; his back from head to tail is of a dark clay and dusky color, with transverse dashes or blotches of reddish dull purple, or bluish, according to different exposures to light; the sides and belly of a bright pale yellow; the belly faintly stained with vermilion red, insensibly blended with the yellow on the sides, and all garnished with fiery, blue, green, gold, and silver specks on the scales; the branchiostega is of a yellowish clay or straw color; the lower edge or border next the opening of the gills is near a quarter of an inch in breadth, of a sea green or marine blue; the ulterior angle protends backwards to a considerable length, in the form of a spatula or feather, the extreme end dilated and circular, of a deep black or crow color, reflecting green and blue and bordered round with fiery red, somewhat like red sealing wax, representing a brilliant ruby on the side of the fish; the fins reddish, edged with a dove color: it is deservedly esteemed a most excellent fish.

The Yellow Bream or Warmouth

What a most beautiful creature is this fish before me! gliding to and fro and figuring in the still, clear waters, with his orient attendants and associates. It is the yellow bream or sun fish. It is about eight inches in length, nearly of the shape of the trout but rather larger in proportion over the shoulders and breast; the mouth large, and the branchiostega opens wide. The whole fish is of a pale gold (or burnished brass) color, darker on the back and upper sides; the scales are of a proportionable size, regularly placed, and everywhere variably powdered with red, russet, silver, blue, and green specks, so laid on the scales as to appear like real dust or opaque bodies, each apparent particle being so projected by light and shade and the various attitudes of the fish as to deceive the sight; for in reality nothing can be of a more plain and polished surface than the scales and whole body of the fish. The fins are of an orange color; and, like all the species of the bream, the ultimate angle of the branchiostega terminates by a little spatula, the extreme end of which represents a crescent of the finest ultramarine blue, encircled with silver and velvet black, like the eye in the feathers of a peacock's train. He is a fish of prodigious strength and activity in the water, a warrior in a gilded coat of mail, and gives no rest or quarter to small fish, which he preys upon. They are delicious food and in great abundance.

The Red-Belly

Towards the evening we made a little party at fishing. We chose a shaded retreat, in a beautiful grove of magnolias, myrtles, and sweet bay trees, which were left standing on the bank of a fine creek that, from this place, took a slow, serpentine course through the plantation. We presently took some fish, one kind of which is very beautiful; they call it the red-belly. It is as large as a man's hand, nearly oval, and thin, being compressed on each side. The tail is beautifully formed; the top of the head and back of an olive green, besprinkled with russet specks. The sides are of a sea green, inclining to azure, insensibly blended with the olive above, and beneath lightens to a silvery white, or pearl color, elegantly powdered with specks of the finest green, russet, and gold. The belly is of a bright scarlet red, or vermilion, darting up rays or fiery streaks into the pearl on each side. The ultimate angle of the branchiostega extends backwards with a long spatula, ending with a round or oval particolored spot, representing the eye in the long feathers of a peacock's train, verged round with a thin flame-colored membrane, and appears like a brilliant ruby fixed on the side of the fish; the eyes are large, encircled with a fiery iris; they are a voracious fish, and are easily caught with a suitable bait.

Multitudes of Fish in the Great Sink

[*On the Alachua Savannah, now Payne's Prairie, near Gainesville, Florida. Ed.*]

In and about the Great Sink are to be seen incredible numbers of crocodiles, some of which are of an enormous size and view the passenger with incredible impudence and avidity. At this time they are so abundant that, if permitted by them, I could walk over any part of the basin and the river upon their heads, which slowly float and turn about like knotty chunks or logs of wood, except when they plunge or shoot forward to beat off their associates, pressing too close to each other or taking up fish, which continually crowd in upon them from the river and creeks draining from the savannah, especially the great trout, mudfish, catfish, and the various species of bream. The gar are rather too hard for their jaws and rough for their throats, especially here, where they have a superfluous plenty and variety of those that are every way preferable: besides, the gar being, like themselves, a warlike, voracious creature, they seem to be in league or confederacy together, to enslave and devour the numerous defenseless tribes.

It is astonishing and incredible, perhaps, I may say, to relate what unspeakable numbers of fish repair to this fatal fountain or receptacle during the latter summer season and autumn, when the powerful sunbeams have evaporated the waters off the savannah. Those who are so fortunate as to effect a retreat into the conductor and escape the devouring jaws of the fearful alligator and armed gar descend into the earth through the wells and cavities or vast perforations of the rocks, and from thence are conducted and carried away by secret subterranean conduits and gloomy vaults to other distant lakes and rivers. And it does not appear improbable but that in some future day this vast savannah or lake of waters in the winter season will be discovered to be in a great measure filled with its finny inhabitants, who are strangers or adventurers from other lakes, ponds, and rivers, by subterraneous rivulets and communications to this rocky, dark door or outlet, whence they ascend to its surface, spread over and people the winter lake, where they breed, increase, and continue as long as it is under water, or during pleasure, for they are at all seasons to be seen ascending and descending through the rocks. Towards the autumn, when the waters have almost left the plains, they then crowd to the sink in such multitudes as at times to be seen pressing on in great banks into the basin, being urged by pursuing bands of alligators and gar, and when entering the great basin or sink are suddenly fallen upon by another army of the same devouring enemies, lying in wait for them. Thousands are driven on shore, where they perish and rot in banks, which was evident at the time I was there, the stench being intolerable, although then early in the summer. There are three great doors or vent holes through the rocks in the sink, two near the center and the other one near the rim, much higher up than the other two, which was conspicuous through the clear water. The beds of rocks lay in horizontal thick strata or laminæ, one over the other, where the sink holes or outlets are. These rocks are perforated by perpendicular wells or tubes four, five, and six feet in diameter, exactly circular as the tube of a cannon or a walled well. Many of these are broken into one another, forming a great ragged orifice, appearing fluted by alternate jambs and semicircular perpendicular niches or excavations.[1]

15. The Ways of Insects and Spiders

Locusts in Pennsylvania

[*By John Bartram. Ed.*]

O N THE 10th of May, 1749, in the morning, I observed (in the neighborhood of Philadelphia) abundance of Locusts, just escaped from their skins. Some had turned of a dark brown, others white, with their wings moist. Some were creeping out; some were on the grass, on the bushes, rails, and bodies of trees.

11th and 12th. Abundance came out. *13th.* They begin to make noise. *14th.* Many still come out. *15th.* They still come out, in great numbers and there is a continual noise all over our woods and orchards from morning to evening. They fly about and copulate. *16th.* They begin to dart the twigs and lay their eggs, and continued until June, when they came no more out of the ground. By the 8th of this month they were all gone.

In the latter end of April, this year, the locusts came so near the surface of the ground that the hogs rooted up the ground for a foot deep all about the hedges and fences, under trees, in search of them. They were then full of a thick white matter, like cream. Yet, in a few hours, the air changed them into a dark brown.

It is only the males that make a noise. This they do by a tremendous motion of two air bladders under their wings. The male, in the act of copulation, enters the body of the female, just between the rings of her belly and the root of her dart, by two crooked bodies at the extremity of his tail. As these bodies spread within the female, the sexes are held together for a long time; for there are a great many eggs to impregnate. I think each individual copulates but once. I killed two of them in the beginning of the act and was surprised that the agonies of death did not part them, though they had been a quarter of an hour together.

Soon after copulation, they begin to dart the twigs and lay their eggs, to a great number. It is surprising how soon they will work into the solid wood and crowd it full of eggs, arranged close together, with one end close to the solid wood. How they directed the eggs in such order, I was puzzled to know; for they seemed so shy that when I came near enough to observe, they would fly away. One day, however, my son caught one of them in the beginning of the operation and, taking a strong stalk of a weed, presented it to her. She directly fell to work while he held the stalk in his hand. He carefully observed how she worked her dart into the stalk and found that she did not touch it, all the time, with her belly. He permitted her to dart two or three places and then searched and found that she had laid eight or nine eggs. He therefore concluded that she must convey the eggs into the stalk through her dart, which we have always found to be hollow.

All kinds of wood, as well forest as orchard, were darted by them. I think they began with sassafras (Laurus sassafras), this being a soft wood. Generally they made choice of the second or third year's shoot.[1]

The Mosquitoes in Charleston

[By John Bartram. Ed.]

Where we found them the most intolerable of any place hitherto in all our travels; for here [Charleston] they torment us all night. In most other places they are not very troublesome after bedtime. At the Savannah town they bite sharp and sting like nettles in the beginning of the night, but after bedtime they were not very troublesome. But, for 100 miles up the Savannah River, the great gray sort were very troublesome in their swamps and low lands — especially in the morning — but their bite was not so stinging as the little brown sorts. At Augustine they now pester us both night and day: a very small, brown sort and so shy that it's very hard to kill one, but they are now tolerable enough to be endured. Their bite does not itch very much after they withdraw. I suppose they have been worse in hot weather, but I have suffered more by them in Jersey and our lower counties than in all this journey. . . . As for the spotted-winged and green flies so troublesome to horses in Jersey, we saw very few of them. As for the indigo flies which people make such a spunk about, they were no disturbance to us. I believe they are bad enough in or near the indigo fields, but many people love to tell wonders.[2]

Ephemera (May Flies) Emerge from St. John's River

[*William Bartram's narrative is resumed. Ed.*]

I observed this day, during my progress up the river, incredible numbers of small flying insects, of the genus termed by naturalists Ephemera. They continually emerged from the shallow water near shore, some of them immediately taking their flight to the land, whilst myriads crept up the grass and herbage, where remaining for a short time as they acquired sufficient strength, they took their flight also, following their kindred to the mainland. This resurrection from the deep, if I may so express it, commences early in the morning and ceases after the sun is up. At evening they are seen in clouds of innumerable millions, swarming and wantoning in the still air, gradually drawing near the river. They descend upon its surface, and there quickly end their day, after committing their eggs to the deep; which, being for a little while tossed about, enveloped in a viscid scum, are hatched, and the little larvæ descend into their secure and dark habitation in the oozy bed beneath, where they remain gradually increasing in size until the returning spring. They then change to a nymph, when the genial heat brings them, as it were, into existence, and they again arise into the world. This fly seems to be delicious food for birds, frogs, and fish. In the morning, when they arise, and in the evening, when they return, the tumult is great indeed, and the surface of the water along shore broken into bubbles or spirited into the air by the contending aquatic tribes; and such is the avidity of the fish and frogs that they spring into the air after this delicious prey.

Early in the evening, after a pleasant day's voyage, I made a convenient and safe harbor in a little lagoon, under an elevated bank, on the west shore of the river; where I shall entreat the reader's patience whilst we behold the closing scene of the short-lived Ephemera and communicate to each other the reflections which so singular an exhibition might rationally suggest to an inquisitive mind. Our place of observation is happily situated under the protecting shade of majestic live oaks, glorious magnolias, and the fragrant orange, open to the view of the great river and still waters of the lagoon just before us.

At the cool eve's approach, the sweet, enchanting melody of the feathered songsters gradually ceases, and they betake themselves to their leafy coverts for security and repose.

Solemnly and slowly move onward, to the river's shore, the rustling clouds of the Ephemera. How awful the procession! Innumerable millions of winged beings voluntarily verge on to destruction, to the brink of the grave, where they behold bands of their enemies with wide-open jaws ready to receive them. But as if insensible of their danger, gay and tranquil, each meets his beloved mate in the still air, inimitably bedecked in their new nuptial robes. What eye can trace them, in their varied, wanton, amorous chases, bounding and fluttering on the odoriferous air! With what peace, love, and joy do they end the last moments of their existence!

I think we may assert, without any fear of exaggeration, that there are annually, of these beautiful winged beings which rise into existence and for a few moments take a transient view of the glory of the Creator's works, a number greater than the whole race of mankind that have ever existed since the creation; and that, only from the shores of this river. How many then must have been produced since the creation, when we consider the number of large rivers in America, in comparison with which this river is but a brook or rivulet.

The importance of the existence of these beautiful and delicately formed little creatures, whose frame and organization are equally wonderful, more delicate, and perhaps as complicated as those of the most perfect human being, is well worth a few moments' contemplation; I mean particularly when they appear in the fly state. And if we consider the very short period of that stage of existence, which we may reasonably suppose to be the only space of their life that admits of pleasure and enjoyment, what a lesson doth it not afford us of the vanity of our own pursuits!

Their whole existence in this world is but one complete year. At least three hundred and sixty days of that time, they are in the form of an ugly grub, buried in mud, eighteen inches under water, and in this condition scarcely locomotive, as each larva or grub has but its own narrow, solitary cell, from which it never travels or moves but in a perpendicular progression of a few inches, up and down, from the bottom to the surface of the mud, in order to intercept the passing atoms for its food and get a momentary respiration of fresh air. Even here it must be perpetually on its guard in order to escape the troops of fish and shrimps watching to catch it, and from whom it has no escape but by instantly retreating back into its cell. One would be apt almost to imagine them created merely for the food of fish and other animals.

Flies, Heat, and Storm

[This uncomfortable experience took place while traveling across Georgia on the trade route from Augusta to Mobile. Ed.]

Next day we traveled but a few miles; the heat and the burning flies tormenting our horses to such a degree as to excite compassion even in the hearts of pack-horse men. These biting flies are of several species, and their numbers incredible. We traveled almost from sunrise to his setting amidst a flying host of these persecuting spirits, who formed a vast cloud around our caravan so thick as to obscure every distant object. Our van always bore the brunt of the conflict, and the heads, necks, and shoulders of the leading horses were continually in a gore of blood. Some of these flies were near as large as bumblebees; this is the Hippobosca. They are armed with a strong, sharp beak, or proboscis, shaped like a lancet and sheathed in flexible thin valves. With this beak they instantly pierce the veins of the creatures, making a large orifice from whence the blood springs in large drops, rolling down as tears, causing a fierce pain or aching for a considerable time after the wound is made. There are three or four species of this genus of less size but equally vexatious, as they are vastly more numerous, active, and sanguinous — particularly, one about half the size of the first mentioned, the next less, of a dusky color with a green head. Another is yet somewhat less, of a splendid green and the head of a gold color. The sting of this is intolerable — no less acute than a prick from a red-hot needle or a spark of fire on the skin. These are called the burning flies. Besides the preceding tormentors, there are three or four species of smaller biting flies; one of grayish dusky color; another much of the same color, having spotted wings and a green head; and another very small and perfectly black. This last species lies in ambush in shrubby thickets and cane brakes near water. Whenever we approach the cool shades near creeks, impatient for repose and relief, almost sinking under the persecutions from the evil spirits who continually surround and follow us over the burning desert ridges and plains, and here are in some hopes of momentary peace and quietness under cover of the cool, humid groves, we are surprised and quickly invested with dark clouds of these persecuting demons, besides mosquitoes and gnats.

The next day, being in like manner oppressed and harassed by the stinging flies and heats, we halted at noon, being unable longer to support ourselves under such grievances, even in our present situation, charming to the senses, on the acclivity of a high, swelling ridge planted with open, airy groves of the superb terebinthine pines, glittering rills playing beneath, and pellucid brooks meandering through an expansive green savannah, their banks ornamented with coppices of blooming aromatic shrubs and plants perfuming the air. The meridian heats just allayed, the sun is veiled in a dark cloud, rising northwestward; the air still, gloomy, and sultry; the animal spirits sink under the conflict, and we fall into a kind of mortal torpor rather than refreshing repose; and startled or terrified at each other's plaintive murmurs and groans.

Now the earth trembles under the peals of incessant distant thunder, the hurricane comes on roaring, and I am shocked again to life. I raise my head and rub open my eyes, pained with gleams and flashes of lightning; when, just attempting to wake my afflicted brethren and companions, almost overwhelmed with floods of rain, the dark cloud opens over my head, developing a vast river of the ethereal fire. I am instantly struck dumb, inactive, and benumbed. At length the pulse of life begins to vibrate, the animal spirits begin to exert their powers, and I am by degrees revived.[3]

Silk Spiders in Florida

There are several species of spiders but [I] never heard of any hurt from them. The most remarkable are the great yellow-and-black-streaked spiders. They spin or weave a vast web or net between the tops of very high trees in the low lands and shady groves, even when the trees are fifteen or twenty feet, one limb from another. The web is very strong and knitted or woven in a very beautiful and ingenious manner. They place themselves in the center. They catch large insects such as the cicada, Cervus volans, small birds, etc.

When they have sucked all the substance out of these creatures, they are careful to bite off the web or thread that entangled them and let the dry skeleton drop to the ground and afterwards repair their net for fresh service.

Their body is about the size of a pigeon egg, something longer, their legs very long and armed with prickles of stiff black hair. The two forelegs are the longest, flared and broad at the middle joint. When the unhappy insect or bird is entangled in the net and the spider finds by his struggles that he can't disengage himself, he runs speedily up and spurts out a thick white web near as thick as a goose quill upon his prey, which spreads like a cloud or white mist over him. This soon puts an end to the struggle.[4]

A Spider in East Florida

As I was gathering specimens of flowers from the shrubs, I was greatly surprised at the sudden appearance of a remarkably large spider on a leaf. At sight of me he boldly faced about and raised himself up, as if ready to spring upon me. His body was about the size of a pigeon's egg, of a buff color, and, with his legs, was covered with short silky hair; on the top of the abdomen was a round red spot or ocelle, encircled with black. After I had recovered from the surprise, observing that the wary hunter had retired under cover, I drew near again and presently discovered that I had surprised him on predatory attempts against the insect tribes. I was therefore determined to watch his proceedings. I soon noticed that the object of his wishes was a large fat bumblebee that was visiting the flowers and piercing their nectariferous tubes. This cunning, intrepid hunter conducted his subtle approaches with the circumspection and perseverance of a Seminole when hunting a deer, advancing with slow steps obliquely, or under cover of dense foliage, and behind the limbs, and when the bee was engaged in probing a flower, he would leap nearer and then instantly retire out of sight, under a leaf or behind a branch, at the same time keeping a sharp eye upon me. When he had now gotten within two feet of his prey, and the bee was intent on sipping the delicious nectar from a flower, with his back next the spider, he instantly sprang upon him and grasped him over the back and shoulder, when for some moments they both disappeared. I expected the bee had carried off his enemy, but to my surprise they both together rebounded back again, suspended at the extremity of a strong, elastic thread or web which the spider had artfully let fall or fixed on the twig the instant he leaped from it. The rapidity of the bee's wings, endeavoring to extricate himself, made them both together appear as a moving vapor, until the bee became fatigued by whirling round, first one way and then back again. At length, in about a quarter of an hour, the bee, quite exhausted by his struggles and the repeated wounds of the butcher, became motionless and quickly expired in the arms of the devouring spider who, ascending the rope with his game, retired to feast on it under cover of the leaves; and perhaps before night became himself the delicious evening repast of a bird or lizard.[5]

16. William Bartram as an Ornithologist

Birds of the Alachua Savannah

[*The "sonorous stork" was the whooping crane. Fewer than thirty individuals remain alive in the world today. Here the sandhill crane is called a whooping crane. Ed.*]

BEHOLD a vast plain of water in the middle of a pine forest, fifteen miles in extent and near fifty miles in circumference, verged with green, level meadows in the summer season, beautifully adorned with jetting points and promontories of high land. The prospect is greatly beautified by the prodigious numbers of wild fowl of various kinds, such as cranes, herons, bitterns, plovers, coots. There are also vast herds of cattle, horses, and deer which we see far distant in detachments over the vast plain. The upper regions of the air contribute to this joyful scene. The silver-plumed heron, early in the morning hastening to their fisheries, crowd to the watery plain. The sonorous stork and whooping cranes proclaim the near approach of the summer heat [and] descend from the skies in musical squadrons . . . spreading themselves over the wide green. All these gay inhabitants at eventide retire to the surrounding groves.

This vast plain in the winter season is a beautiful lake of

Heron Rookery

water, visited by incredible numbers of wild fowl: the great Canada goose, brant, and gray goose, with an endless variety of ducks.

In the month of November, when cold north and northeast winds reach this country, the winged inhabitants of North America begin to assemble here, especially water fowl, who make this country of East Florida their winter retreat and this vast savannah, on account of its great extent affording proper food: grass, snails, periwinkles, water insects, fish, and reptiles. It may be termed the Elysium of Birds, and happy was he that reached it, as the Indians never molest them. But lately the white people, traders, take incredible numbers of them.

Here they assemble in such prodigious numbers, approaching like clouds in the air, and spread themselves over the waters. A gun being fired amongst them in the evening or morning, the effect is altogether astonishing. They rise in that quarter like a vast dark thunderstorm and shake the air as a rushing tempest. But on being disturbed in the night, the multitudes rise from all quarters; the thunder of their wings, with their united squalling tongues, exhibit a scene of confusion and a babbling as if the dissolution of nature was at hand.[1]

The Sandhill Crane

[*The ranks of the sandhill crane in Florida have thinned greatly since Bartram's day. Seldom indeed does one see such squadrons of them as he here describes. Ed.*]

The wary, sharp-sighted crane circumspectly observed our progress. We saw a female of them sitting on her nest, and

Sandhill Cranes

the male, her mate, watchfully traversing backwards and forwards at a small distance. They suffered us to approach near them before they arose, when they spread their wings, running and tipping the ground with their feet sometime; and then mounted aloft, soaring round and round over the nest. They sit upon only two eggs at a time, which are very large, long, and pointed at one end, of a pale ash color powdered or speckled with brown. The manner of forming their nests and sitting is very singular. They chose a tussock and there form a rude heap of dry grass or such like materials near as high as their body is from the ground, when standing upon their feet; on the summit of this they form their nest of fine, soft, dry grass.

After some refreshment, our hunters went out into the forest and returned towards evening. Amongst other game, they brought with them a savannah crane which they shot in the adjoining meadows. This stately bird is about six feet in length from the toes to the extremity of the beak when extended, and the wings expand eight or nine feet; it is about five feet high when standing erect. The tail is remarkably short, but the flag or pendant feathers which fall down off the rump on each side are very long and sharp-pointed, of a delicate texture and silky softness. The beak is very long, straight, and sharp-pointed. The crown of the head, bare of feathers, is of a reddish rose color, thinly barbed with short, stiff black hair. The legs and thighs are very long and bare of feathers a great space above the knees. The plumage of this bird is generally of a pale ash color, with shades or clouds of pale brown and sky blue; the brown prevails on the shoulders and back; the barrels of the prime quill feathers are long and of a large diameter, leaving a large cavity when extracted from the wing. All the bones of this bird have a thin shell and consequently a large cavity or medullary receptacle. When these birds move their wings in flight, their strokes are slow, moderate, and regular; and even when at a considerable distance or high above us, we plainly hear the quill feathers; their shafts and webs upon one another creak as the joints or working of a vessel in a tempestuous sea.

We had this fowl dressed for supper, and it made excellent soup. Nevertheless, as long as I can get any other necessary food, I shall prefer their seraphic music in the ethereal skies, and my eyes and understanding gratified in observing their economy and social communities in the expansive green savannahs of Florida. . . .

Behold how gracious and beneficent shines the roseate morn! Now the sun arises and fills the plains with light; his glories appear on the forests, encompassing the meadows, and gild the top of the terebinthine pine and exalted palms, now gently rustling by the pressure of the waking breezes. The music of the seraphic cranes resounds in the skies; in separate squadrons they sail, encircling their precincts, slowly descend beating the dense air, and alight on the green, dewy verge of the expansive lake; its surface yet smoking with the gray ascending mists which, condensed aloft in clouds of vapor, are borne away by the morning breezes and at last gradually vanish on the distant horizon. All nature awakes to life and activity. . . .

Induced by the beautiful appearance of the green meadows, which open to the eastward, I determined not to pass this Elysium without a visit. Behold the loud, sonorous, watchful savannah cranes, with musical clangor, in detached squadrons. They spread their light, elastic sail. At first they move from the earth heavy and slow; they labor and beat the dense air; they form the line with wide-extended wings, tip to tip; they all rise and fall together as one bird; now they mount aloft, gradually wheeling about; each squadron performs its evolution, encircling the expansive plains, observing each one its own orbit. Then, lowering sail, they descend on the verge of some glittering lake; whilst other squadrons, ascending aloft in spiral circles, bound on interesting discoveries, wheel round and double the promontory, in the silver regions of the clouded skies where, far from the scope of eye, they carefully observe the verdant meadows on the borders of the East Lake; then contract their plumes and descend to the earth, where, after resting a while on some verdant eminence near the flowery border of the lake, they, with dignified, yet slow, respectful steps, approach the kindred band, confer, and treat for habitation; the bounds and precincts being settled, they confederate and take possession.

Passenger Pigeons

[*At the Bryan villa by the Savannah River. The passenger pigeon, once unbelievably abundant, became extinct when the last individual died in the Cincinnati Zoological Park in 1914. Ed.*]

At night, soon after our arrival, several of his [Mr. Bryan's] servants came home with horse loads of wild pigeons, which it seems they had collected in a short space of time at a neighboring bay swamp. They take them by torchlight; the birds have particular roosting places, where they associate in incredible multitudes at evening, on low trees and bushes, in hummocks or higher knolls in the interior parts of vast swamps. Many people go out together on this kind of sport, when dark. Some take with them little fascines of fat-pine splinters for torches; others, sacks or bags; and

others furnish themselves with poles or staves. Thus accoutered and prepared, they approach the roosts. The sudden
blaze of light confounds, blinds, and affrights the birds,
whereby multitudes drop off the limbs to the ground and
others are beaten off with the staves, being by the sudden
consternation entirely helpless and easily taken and put into
the sacks. It is chiefly the sweet, small acorns of the Quercus
phillos, Quercus aquatica, Quercus sempervirens, Quercus
flammula, and others which induce these birds to migrate in
the autumn to those Southern regions, where they spend
their days agreeably and feast luxuriously during the rigor
of the colds in the North, whither they return at the approach
of summer to breed.

The Carolina Paroquet

[*Killed by farmers because it took fruit, bagged in great numbers
by bird catchers, killed for its plumage, and wantonly slaughtered
by so-called sportsmen were the reasons given by the late Dr. Frank
M. Chapman for its extinction. Ed.*]

The parakeets (Psittacus caroliniensis) never reach so far
north as Pennsylvania, which to me is unaccountable, considering they are a bird of such singularly rapid flight that
they could easily perform the journey in ten or twelve hours
from North Carolina, where they are very numerous, and we
abound with all the fruits which they delight in.

I was assured in Carolina that these birds, for a month or
two in the coldest winter weather, house themselves in
hollow cypress trees, clinging fast to each other like bees in a
hive, where they continue in a torpid state until the warmth
of the returning spring reanimates them, when they issue

forth from their late, dark, cold winter cloisters. But I lived several years in North Carolina and never was witness to an instance of it; yet I do not at all doubt but there have been instances of belated flocks thus surprised by sudden severe cold and forced into such shelter, and the extraordinary severity and perseverance of the season might have benumbed them into a torpid sleepy state; but that they all willingly should yield to so disagreeable and hazardous a situation does not seem reasonable or natural, when we consider that they are a bird of the swiftest flight and impatient of severe cold. They are easily tamed, when they become docile and familiar, but never learn to imitate the human language.[2]

The Gray Eagle, the Bald Eagle, and the Fishing Eagle

[Bartram's gray eagle was the immature southern bald eagle and at that age is not likely to nest at all. After the nesting season (in the winter months in Florida) both the immature and the adult bald eagles wander far north of their breeding range. His fishing eagle or fishing hawk is now called osprey. Ed.]

The greatest gray eagle. These are large strong birds. They prey upon all animals they can conquer, resort to the seacoast and the banks of great waters. Sitting on some eminence, they watch the flux and reflux of the sea, observing the success of other birds of prey, which they pursue and cause them to drop the produce of their labors, which they commonly catch ere it touches the earth.

The fishing eagle [the osprey], however, often eludes his utmost vigilance and power for, being much lighter and active on the wing, he mounts aloft with greater ease. But if the eagle gets above him, the struggle is quickly over. High up in the airy regions, the contest is quickly decided. The hawk is forced to quit his prey when the eagle closes the points of his wings towards his body and, with collected power, cleaves the elastic air and seems to rend the skies, which indeed can only be equaled by the terror of sudden and unexpected thunder.

Early in the spring they arrive from the south and build their nests on lofty pine trees. In the autumn they return south, but others arrive from the north and stay with us all winter, so they are to be seen all the year in this Province.

The great bald eagles are strong birds. They, like the gray eagle, prey upon all animals they can take but receive large contribution from the fishing eagle and other smaller birds of prey. This likewise is a bird of passage, but breeds and sometimes continues here during the winter, coming here from the north.

The fishing eagle [is] commonly called the fishing hawk, though in the make and structure of his body he is perfectly aquiline yet more slender and delicately formed than any of the eagles, his wings very long and sharp pointed. They keep continually about rivers and waters and feed only on fish.

They build large nests on the highest summits of dead trees by the water, are extremely fierce and watchful about the time of incubation. They are birds of passage, retiring south at the approach of winter, but in the spring appear in great numbers and soon after pair together and begin to erect their nests.

This bird is the eagle's purveyor and it is said, as soon as he takes a fish, he hallos out to give notice to the eagle but this is certainly a mistaken notion, but squeals out for fear of the eagle, which he continues to do during the contest as they mount up, even to such a height in the air as to be nearly out of sight or hearing.[3]

Two Vultures

[*For years scientists discounted William Bartram's description of what must have been the king vulture in Florida. Studies by Dr. Alexander Wetmore of material excavated from the Pleistocene deposits in Florida have revealed the presence then of such unlikely species as the California condor, jabiru stork, and trumpeter swan, as well as of other remarkable birds. Knowing how quickly a species can disappear from an area, few now doubt that king vultures were observed by Bartram. His coped vulture is now called black vulture. Ed.*]

There are two species of vultures in these regions, I think not mentioned in history. The first we shall describe is a beautiful bird, near the size of a turkey buzzard, but his wings are much shorter, and consequently he falls greatly below that admirable bird in sail. I shall call this bird the painted vulture. The bill is long and straight almost to the point, when it is hooked or bent suddenly down and sharp. The head and neck are bare of feathers nearly down to the stomach, when the feathers begin to cover the skin and soon become long and of a soft texture, forming a ruff or tippet in which the bird, by contracting his neck, can hide that as well as his head. The bare skin on the neck appears loose and wrinkled and is of a deep bright-yellow color, intermixed with coral red. The hinder part of the neck is nearly covered with short, stiff hair; and the skin of this part of the neck is of a dun-purple color, gradually becoming red as it approaches the yellow of the sides and fore part. The crown of the head is red; there are lobed lappets of a reddish-orange color, which lie on the base of the upper mandible. But, what is singular, a large portion of the stomach* hangs down on the breast of the bird, in the likeness of a sack or half wallet, and seems to be a duplicature of the craw, which is naked and of a reddish flesh color. This is partly concealed by the feathers of the breast, unless when it is loaded with food (which is commonly, I believe, roasted reptiles), and then it appears prominent. The plumage of the bird is generally white or cream color, except the quill feathers of the wings and two or three rows of the coverts, which are of a beautiful dark brown. The tail, which is large and white, is tipped with this dark brown or black; the legs and feet of a clear white; the eye is encircled with a gold-colored iris; the pupil black.

The Creeks or Muscogulges construct their royal standard of the tail feather of this bird, which is called by a name signifying the eagle's tail. This they carry with them when they go to battle, but then it is painted with a zone of red within the brown tips; and in peaceable negotiations it is displayed new, clean, and white. This standard is held most sacred by them on all occasions and is constructed and ornamented with great ingenuity. These birds seldom appear but when the deserts are set on fire (which happens almost every day throughout the year, in some part or other, by the Indians, for the purpose of rousing the game, as also by the lightning). They are seen at a distance soaring on the wing, gathering from every quarter, and gradually approaching the burnt plains, where they alight upon the ground yet smok-

---

* An error; it is not connected to the stomach. [Ed.]

ing with hot embers. They gather up the roasted serpents, frogs, and lizards, filling their sacks with them. At this time a person may shoot them at pleasure; they not being willing to quit the feast and indeed seeming to brave all danger.

The other species may very properly be called the coped vulture and is by the inhabitants called the carrion crow. As to bulk or weight, he is nearly equal to either of the others beforementioned. His wings are not long and sharp-pointed but broad and round at their extremities, having a clumsy appearance; the tail is remarkably short, which he spreads like a little fan when on the wing. They have a heavy, laborious flight, flapping their wings, then sail a little and then flap their wings again, and so on as if recovering themselves when falling. The beak is very long and straight, until it makes a sudden hook at the point, in the manner of the other vultures. The whole bird is of a sable or mourning color; the head and neck down to the breast is bare of feathers, and the skin wrinkled; this unfeathered skin is of a deep, livid purple, appearing black and thinly set with short black hair. He has a ruff or tippet of long, soft feathers, like a collar, bearing on his breast.

Limpkins, White Ibis, and Wood Ibis

[*William Bartram was correct in not placing the limpkin in a European family. Closely allied to the rails, it belongs to a strictly American family of which two species are known; one in South America, the other found in Central America, Mexico, Cuba, Florida, and occasionally in southern Georgia.*

[*The dark, immature white ibis (here called Spanish curlew) was believed to be a distinct species until Audubon's time and even later.*

[*The wood ibis (wood pelican) is our only stork. It is often solitary after breeding, but during the nesting season it gathers in enormous colonies, especially in the Everglades. Ed.*]

There is inhabiting the low shores and swamps of this river and the lakes of Florida, as well as Georgia, a very curious bird, called by an Indian name which signifies in our language the crying bird. I cannot determine what genus of European birds to join it with. It is about the size of a large domestic hen. All the body, above and beneath, is of a dark lead color, every feather edged or tipped with white, which makes the bird appear speckled on a near view. The eye is large and placed high on the head, which is very prominent; the bill or beak is five or six inches in length, arched or bent gradually downwards, in that respect to be compared to one half of a bent bow. It is large or thick near the base, compressed on each side, and flatted at top and beneath, which makes it appear foursquare for more than an inch where the nostrils are placed, from whence, to their tips, both mandibles are round, gradually lessening or tapering to their extremities, which are thicker for about half an inch than immediately above, by which the mandibles never fit

Limpkin, Bartram's "Crying Bird"

quite close their whole length. The upper mandible is a small matter longer than the under; the bill is of a dusky-green color, more bright and yellowish about the base and angles of the mouth. The tail is very short and the middle feather the longest; the others on each side shorten gradually and are of the color of the rest of the bird, only somewhat darker. The two shortest or outermost feathers are perfectly white, which the bird has a faculty of flirting out on either side as quick as a flash of lightning, especially when he hears or sees anything that disturbs him, uttering at the same instant an extreme harsh and loud shriek. His neck is long and slender; and his legs are also long and bare of feathers above the knee, like those of the bittern, and are black or of a dark-lead color.

There are two other species of this genus, which agree in almost every particular with the above description, except in size and color. The first of these I shall mention is a perfect white, except the prime quill feathers, which are as black as those of a crow; the bill and legs of a beautiful clear red, as also a space clear of feathers about the eyes. The other species is black on the upper side, the breast and belly white, and the legs and beak as white as snow. Both these species are about half the size of the crying bird. They fly in large flocks or squadrons, evening and morning, to and from their feeding place or roosts; both species are called Spanish curlews; these and the crying bird feed chiefly on crayfish; whose cells they probe, and with their strong pinching bills drag them out. All the three species are esteemed excellent food.

It is a pleasing sight at times of high winds and heavy thunderstorms to observe the numerous squadrons of these Spanish curlews driving to and fro, turning and tacking about, high up in the air, when by their various evolutions in the different and opposite currents of the wind high in the clouds their silvery-white plumage gleams and sparkles like the brightest crystal, reflecting the sunbeams that dart upon them between the dark clouds.

Since I have turned my observations upon the birds of this country, I shall notice another very singular one, though already most curiously and exactly figured by Catesby, which seems to be nearly allied to those before mentioned. I mean the bird which he calls the wood pelican. This is a large bird, perhaps near three feet high when standing erect. The bill is very long and strong, bending with a moderate curve from the base to the tip; the upper mandible is the largest, and receives the edges of the nether one into its whole length; the edges are very sharp and firm, the whole of a dark ash or horn color; the forehead round the base of the beak and sides of the head is bare of feathers and of a dark-greenish color, in which space is placed the eyes, which are very large. The remainder of the head and neck is of a nut-brown color; the back of a light-bluish gray; upper part of the wings, breast, and belly, almost white, with some slight dashes of gray. The quill feathers and tail, which are very short, are of a dark slate color, almost black; the legs, which are very long and bare of feathers a great length above the knees, are of a dark, dull-greenish color. It has a small bag or pouch under its throat and it feeds on serpents, young alligators, frogs, and other reptiles.

This solitary bird does not associate in flocks but is generally seen alone; commonly near the banks of great rivers, in vast marshes or meadows, especially such as are caused by inundations; and also in the vast, deserted rice plantations.

He stands alone on the topmost limb of tall, dead cypress trees, his neck contracted or drawn in upon his shoulders, and beak resting like a long scythe upon his breast: in this pensive posture and solitary situation, he looks extremely grave, sorrowful, and melancholy, as if in the deepest thought. They are never seen on the salt-sea coast and yet are never found at a great distance from it. I take this bird to be of a different genus from the tantalus, and perhaps it approaches the nearest to the Egyptian ibis of any other bird yet known.[4]

Snail Eggs

[*These were the eggs of* Pomacea paludosa. *Both the limpkins and the extremely rare everglade kite feed almost exclusively on the snails that lay these large, pearl-like eggs. Ed.*]

Drove through a large savannah and pond (the water shallow). Took notice of abundance [of] large snail shells round about the shore, some half as big as my fist, and on examination found multitudes of them in the mud and slush at the bottom of the pond in the savannah. They breed here in prodigious numbers, fixing their spawn or ovule in clusters round about bulrushes, reeds, and sticks in the water, two or three hundred in a cluster. They are perfectly round, of the size of peas, the shell thin, hard, and brittle. They look clear, like pearls.

These vast periwinkles or snails are bred in vast numbers in the muddy shores of this river* and great St. Juan, insomuch that the rushes, reeds, sticks, and trees near the waters

* Suwannee River. [Ed.]

Wood Ibis, Bartram's "Wood Pelican"

are white, being almost covered with their eggs a foot or eighteen inches above the water, and afford food for fish and young alligators.[5]

The Anhinga

[*There are four species of anhinga (also called snake bird and water turkey) in the whole world; one each in Africa, Asia, Australia, and tropical and semitropical America. The fact that William Bartram recognized them as like birds he had seen in Oriental paintings gives us a clue to his artistic education. Ed.*]

Here is in this river and in the waters all over Florida a very curious and handsome species of birds; the people call them snake birds. I think I have seen paintings of them on the Chinese screens and other India pictures. They seem to be a species of cormorant or loon, but far more beautiful and delicately formed than any other species that I have ever seen. The head and neck of this bird are extremely small and slender, the latter very long indeed, almost out of all proportion. The bill long, straight, and slender, tapering from its ball to a sharp point. All the upper side, the abdomen and thighs, are as black and glossy as a raven's, covered with feathers so firm and elastic that they in some degree resemble fish scales. The breast and upper part of the belly are covered with feathers of a cream color. The tail is very long, of a deep black, and tipped with a silvery white, and when spread represents an unfurled fan. They delight to sit in little peaceable communities, on the dry limbs of trees, hanging over the still waters, with their wings and tails expanded, I suppose to cool and air themselves, when at the same time they behold their images in the watery mirror. At such times, when we approach them, they drop off the limbs into the water as if dead, and for a minute or two are not to be seen; when on a sudden, at a vast distance, their long slender head and neck only appear and have very much the appearance of a snake, and no other part of them is to be seen when swimming in the water, except sometimes the tip end of the tail. In the heat of the day they are seen in great numbers, sailing very high in the air, over lakes and rivers.

I doubt not but if this bird had been an inhabitant of the Tiber in Ovid's days, it would have furnished him with a subject for some beautiful and entertaining metamorphoses. I believe it feeds entirely on fish, for its flesh smells and tastes intolerably strong of it; it is scarcely to be eaten, unless [one is] constrained by insufferable hunger.

Dawn Chorus of Turkey Cocks

Having rested very well during the night, I was awakened in the morning early by the cheering converse of the wild turkey cocks saluting each other from the sun-brightened tops of the lofty cypresses and magnolias. They begin at early dawn and continue till sunrise, from March to the last of April. The high forests ring with the noise, like the crowing of the domestic cock, of these social sentinels; the watchword being caught and repeated from one to another for hundreds of miles around; insomuch that the whole country is for an hour or more in a universal shout. A little after sunrise their crowing gradually ceases, they quit their high lodging places and alight on the earth where, expanding their silver-bordered train, they strut and dance round about the coy female, while the deep forests seem to tremble with their shrill noise.

A Bird Roost at the Mouth of St. John's River, Florida

Being now in readiness to prosecute our voyage to St. John's, we set sail in a handsome pleasure boat manned with four stout Negro slaves, to row in case of necessity. After passing Amelia Narrows, we had a pleasant run across Fort George's Sound where, observing the pelicans fishing, Mr. Egan shot one of them, which he took into the boat. I was greatly surprised on observing the pouch, or sack, which hangs under the bill. It is capable of being expanded to a prodigious size. One of the people on board said that he had seen more than half a bushel of bran crammed into one of their pouches. The body is larger than that of a tame goose, the legs extremely short, the feet webbed, the bill of a great length, bent inwards like a scythe, the wings extend near seven feet from tip to tip; the tail is very short, the head, neck, and breast nearly white, the body of a light-bluish gray, except the quill feathers of the wings, which are black. They seem to be of the gull kind, both in form and structure, as well as manner of fishing. The evening following, we landed on the main. It was a promontory of high land, covered with orange trees and projecting into the sound, forming a convenient port. We pitched our tent under the shelter of a forest of live oaks, palms, and sweet bays; and having, in the course of the day, procured plenty of sea fowl, such as curlews, willets, snipes, sand birds, and others, we had them

Anhinga, or Snake Bird

dressed for supper and seasoned with excellent oysters, which lay in heaps in the water, close to our landing place. The shrub Capsicum, growing here in abundance, afforded us a very good pepper. We drank of a well of fresh water just at hand, amidst a grove of myrtles (Myrica cerifera). Our repose, however, was incomplete, from the stings of mosquitoes, the roaring of crocodiles, and the continual noise and restlessness of the sea fowl, thousands of them having their roosting places very near us, particularly loons of various species, herons, pelicans, Spanish curlews, etc., all promiscuously lodging together, and in such incredible numbers that the trees were entirely covered. They roost in inaccessible islets in the salt marshes, surrounded by lagoons and shallow water.

The Migration of Birds

[*Some of the illustrations in Edwards's works on American birds (and used by Linnæus in giving them names) were from drawings made by William Bartram when very young or from dried skins of "birds of quick passage" that he collected for Edwards. Ed.*]

There are but few [birds] that have fallen under my observation but have been mentioned by the zoologists, and most of them very well figured in Catesby's or Edwards's works.

But these authors have done very little towards elucidating the subject of the migration of birds or accounting for the annual appearance and disappearance and vanishing of these beautiful and entertaining beings who visit us at certain stated seasons. Catesby has said very little on this curious subject; but Edwards more, and perhaps all, or as much as could be said in truth, by the most able and ingenious, who had not the advantage and opportunity of ocular observation; which can only be acquired by traveling, and residing a whole year at least in the various climates from north to south, to the full extent of their peregrinations; or minutely examining the tracts and observations of curious and industrious travelers who have published their memoirs on this subject. There may perhaps be some persons who consider this inquiry not to be productive of any real benefit to mankind, and pronounce such attention to natural history merely speculative and only fit to amuse and entertain the idle virtuoso. However, the ancients thought otherwise: for, with them, the knowledge of the passage of birds was the study of their priests and philosophers and was considered a matter of real and indispensable use to the state, next to astronomy; as we find their system and practice of agriculture was in a great degree regulated by the arrival and disappearance of birds of passage; and perhaps a calendar under such a regulation at this time might be useful to the husbandman and gardener.

But, however attentive and observant the ancients were on this branch of science, they seem to have been very ignorant or erroneous in their conjectures concerning what became of birds after their disappearance until their return again. In the southern and temperate climates some imagined they went to the moon; in the northern regions they supposed that they retired to caves and hollow trees for shelter and security, where they remained in a dormant state during the cold seasons; and even at this day very celebrated men have asserted that swallows, at the approach of winter, voluntarily plunge into lakes and rivers, descend to the bottom, and there creep into the mud and slime, where they continue overwhelmed by ice in a torpid state until the returning summer warms them again into life; when they rise, return to the surface of the water, immediately take wing, and again people the air. This notion, though the latest, seems the most difficult to reconcile to reason and common sense, respecting a bird so swift of flight that it can with ease and pleasure move through the air even swifter than the winds and in a few hours' time shift twenty degrees from north to south, even from frozen regions to climes where frost is never seen and where the air and plains are replenished with flying insects of infinite variety, its favorite only food.

Pennsylvania and Virginia appear to me to be the climates in North America where the greatest variety and abundance of these winged emigrants choose to celebrate their nuptials and rear their offspring, which they annually return with to their winter habitations in the southern regions of North America; and most of those beautiful creatures which annually people and harmonize our forests and groves in the spring and summer seasons are birds of passage from the southward. . . .

Very few tribes of birds build, or rear their young, in the south or maritime parts of Virginia and Carolina, Georgia and Florida; yet all these numerous tribes, particularly of the soft-billed kinds, which breed in Pennsylvania, pass in the spring season through these regions in a few weeks' time, making but very short stages by the way; and again, but few of them winter there, on their return southerly; and as I have never traveled the continent south of New Orleans or the point of Florida, where few or none of them are to be seen in the winter, I am entirely ignorant how far southward they continue their route, during their absence from Pennsylvania; but perhaps none of them pass the tropic.

When in my residence in Carolina and Florida, I have seen vast flights of the house swallow and bank martin passing onward north toward Pennsylvania, where they breed in the spring, about the middle of March, and likewise in the autumn in September or October, and large flights on their return southward. And it is observable that they always avail themselves of the advantage of high and favorable winds, which likewise do all birds of passage. The pewit, or blackcap flycatcher of Catesby, is the first bird of passage which appears in the spring in Pennsylvania, which is generally about the first or middle of March; and then, wherever they appear, we may plant peas and beans in the open grounds, French beans, sow radishes, lettuce, onions, and almost every kind of esculent garden seeds without fear or danger from frosts; for, although we have sometimes frosts after their first appearance for a night or two, yet not so severe as to injure the young plants.

In the spring of the year the small birds of passage appear very suddenly in Pennsylvania, which is not a little surprising, and no less pleasing. At once the woods, the groves, and meads are filled with their melody, as if they dropped down from the skies. The reason or probable cause is their setting off with high and fair winds from the southward; for a strong south and southwest wind about the beginning of April never fails bringing millions of these welcome visitors.

Bobolinks

[*In autumn, male bobolinks, that in spring are so colorful in their black, white, and yellow plumage, and the immature birds as well, resemble the drab brown-and-clay-colored females. The*

*males move northward in spring in conspicuous flocks well ahead
of the dull females. Ed.*]

I shall first mention the rice bird. It is the commonly received opinion that they are male and female of the same
species, i.e., the black pied rice bird the male, and a yellowish clay-colored one the female. The last mentioned appears
only in the autumn, when the oryza zizania are about ripening; yet, in my opinion there are some strong circumstances
which seem to operate against such a conjecture, though
generally believed.

In the spring, about the middle of May, the black pied
rice bird (which is called the male) appears in Pennsylvania. At that time the great yellow ephemera, called May fly,
and a species of locust appear in incredible multitudes, the
favorite delicious food of these birds, when they are sprightly,
vociferous, and pleasingly tuneful.

When I was at St. Augustine, in East Florida, in the
beginning of April, the same species of grasshoppers were
in multitudes on the fields and commons about the town.
When great flights of these male rice birds suddenly arrived
from the South and by feeding on these insects became
extremely fat and delicious. They continued here two or
three weeks, until their food became scarce, when they disappeared, I suppose pursuing their journey north after the
locust and ephemera. There were a few of the yellow kind, or
true rice bird, to be seen amongst them. Now these pied rice
birds seem to observe the same order and time in their
migrations northerly with the other spring birds of passage, and are undoubtedly on their way to their breeding
place; but then there are no females with them, at least not
one to ten thousand of the male color, which cannot be sup-

posed to be a sufficient number to pair and breed by. Being in Charleston in the month of June, I observed at a gentleman's door a cage full of rice birds, that is, of the yellow or female color, who were very merry and vociferous, having the same variable music with the pied or male kind, which I thought extraordinary; and observing it to the gentleman, he assured me that they were all of the male kind, taken the preceding spring, but had changed their color and would be next spring of the color of the pied, thus changing color with the seasons of the year. If this is really the case, it appears they are both of the same species intermixed, spring and fall. In the spring they are gay, vociferous, and tuneful birds.[6]

An American Species of Certhia

[*Though Bonaparte's (1803-1857) description of the brown creeper is recognized by ornithologists, William Bartram's description and name antedate it by many years. These notes on the habits of the American creeper are included with the scientific description. Ed.*]

This species of Certhia is an autumnal bird of passage from the North. They arrive and appear in the environs of Philadelphia about the first of October (sooner or later, according to the severity of the season) and continue with us during the winter, if it be temperate. Or they pass on southerly as far as Carolina and Florida, where they winter, but return northerly in the spring to breed and rear their young. I have not heard of their breeding in Pennsylvania, yet they may breed in the most northern district of the state.

Their place of residence is in the woods or high forests,

where we see them climbing up and running about the trunks of large trees, searching the crevices of the bark for spiders and other insects, which constitute their food. And for this purpose, their slender, curved beak is well adapted. They utter a feeble, chirping note.

This species of Certhia has the form and habits of the woodpecker, except in the position of its toes. Neither is its bill like that of the woodpecker, strong and shaped for the purpose of perforating wood.[7]

Bird-Migration Records of William Bartram*

There is preserved in the library of the Academy of Natural Sciences of Philadelphia a well-worn manuscript volume with pages about four by six inches and a pasteboard cover upon which is inscribed in almost illegible characters "Calendar of Natural History, Memorable Events &," while page 1 bears the heading "Calendar of the Year of Our Lord 1802."

There follows a daily record of the state of the weather, the blooming of plants and trees, and the appearance of birds, insects, and other forms of animal life, after the manner of Gilbert White's Calendar in his *Natural History of Selbourne*.

An insert informs us that this is the manuscript of William Bartram during the years of 1802 to 1822, kept at the old Bartram homestead on the Schuylkill in Kingsessing, now a part of the city of Philadelphia, though at that time several miles out in the country.

The Bartram place, established by John Bartram, father of

* By Witmer Stone, from *The Auk,* Vol. XXX, No. 3, 1913.

William and, like him, a famous botanist, is now preserved as a city park under the name of Bartram's Garden. Here one can still see the old house built by the elder Bartram with his own hands and can walk along the box-bordered paths and admire the various trees, shrubs, and herbs brought by the Bartrams from various parts of the Middle and Southern states, or raised from seed obtained in exchange from more remote countries.

What is more interesting to the ornithologist is the fact that to this same garden came Alexander Wilson, the Scottish schoolmaster, from his little country schoolhouse which stood nearby. Largely under the influence of William Bartram and the famous garden, he became the noted American ornithologist.

The diary begins with the very year that Wilson came to Kingsessing. Had Bartram only seen fit to record his impressions of the young schoolmaster and his subsequent activities, what a historical storehouse this little volume would be! He kept it strictly a "Calendar of Nature," however, and so far as we can gather from its pages, such a man as Alexander Wilson never even lived.

But there is a mine of information in these closely written pages, and the data on bird migration constitute, we believe, the oldest record, covering a series of years, that we have for any part of North America. The record is by no means complete, and every year one or more common birds are omitted. We must remember, of course, that Bartram was familiar with only a portion of our native birds and made no pretense of being an ornithologist.

The diary is not continuous, and the writer, like many another keeper of journals, found that it was easy to start faithfully on New Year's but not so easy to continue the record day after day. It runs from January 1, 1802, to September 20, 1808, missing here and there a few days or, in one case, an entire month. It is always more detailed in winter and spring than later in the year. There is a gap from September 20, 1808, to January 1, 1814, and another from February 13, 1814, to January 1, 1818, from which point it continues until December 31, 1822, about seven months before the death of the writer. His increasing feebleness is reflected in the wavering lines of the handwriting. Eleven spring seasons are thus included, but only the most familiar birds are noted each year. Bartram was sixty-three at the opening of the calendar and eighty-four at the close, but his constant outdoor life and the favorable situation of the garden offset any lack of ability due to age and make it probable that he recorded the common species as soon as they came about the house. These I have arranged systematically, and now, through the courtesy of Dr. Edward J. Nolan, librarian of the Academy of Natural Sciences of Philadelphia, I am able to present them to the readers of *The Auk* with such comments as seem pertinent.

As these data, separated from the botanical and meteorological information with which they were originally associated, give one no idea of the character of the daily entries, I have reproduced verbatim the greater part of the record for January 1802 and the more important zoological data for the remainder of that year.

From these the reader will be brought into sympathy with the writer and will be enabled to picture the gentle old man, looking after his farm and pottering about his beautiful garden on the river shore, and each evening by candle light jotting down in his little book the events of the day that stood out most prominently in his simple life.

[*The following are a few samples of Bartram's manner of entering data in his diary. Ed.*]

Calendar for the Year of Our Lord 1802

Jany. 1. The weather is serene and as warm as in the month of May after a white frost in the morning. The fields and gardens green with growing vegetables, several species in flower, and abundance of insects darting in the air and birds singing as in spring of the year, frogs lively in the springs. Wind S.E.

2. Slight white frost, the day exceedingly warm and pleasant as yesterday. Wind S.W. Spiders darting their webs, wasps flying about (Vespa anularis), the blue bird sings (Motacilla sialis). Evening calm and warm.

6. White frost this morning and some ice but midday very warm and pleasant. Afternoon cloudy, evening hazy, warm and thawy, wind E. Birds numerous, snow birds, sparrows, woodpeckers, golden crowned wren, titmice (Parus atricapillus, P. cristatus), Nut hatch (Sitta canadensis). Crows numerous. Hawks of various species. Blue bird, robins (Turdus migratorius), and an endless variety of insects.

15. Clear and warm as a May day, no ice to be seen in the river, the bees out till evening flying about. Sparrow hawk & blue bird. Crocus verna, narcissus, snow-drop, tulip above ground. Hamamelis in full bloom. Wind S.W.

27. Large flight of crows to the southward (Corvus frugivorus).

31. Clear, pleasant, and moderate weather, no frost, the field and pasture green as in spring. Grass and grain growing as in the spring. Spring aconite (heleborus) in flower in the garden. Large flocks of ducks in the river Schuylkill. The face of the earth exhibits more the appearance of spring than winter.

February 1. A large flock of blue birds passed by from the southward.

14. A small flock of red-wings (Oriolus phoenicis). The blue birds begin to pair.

17. The ground squirrel came out of his winter quarters frisking about in the warm sun. The crow blackbird (Gracula barita) arrived from the southward. The alder in blossom.

March 2. Flights of red-wing passing from the southward and flocks of cedarbirds.

5. Wild geese passing northerly.

11. Spring frogs whistle, flocks of various kinds of ducks in Schuylkill from the southward.

26. Snow lies three inches deep and trees loaded with it.

May 5. A bull frog swallowed a large mole instantly.

21. The lightning fly sparkles in the night.

August 7. Malignous fever rages in Philadelphia and Baltimore. The inhabitants on recommendation of the Board of Health are moving out into the country.

Sept. 9. Whip-poor-will crys this evening. They are now on their passage to the South.

December 13. Schuylkill scaled over with ice. Yet Picus auratus (*Flicker*), yellow rump (*Myrtle warbler*), blue bird, butcher bird, and mock-bird are with us.

24. Evening serene and calm. A very small owl was caught having no horns, not much exceeding the size of a sparrow, much like one figured by Edwards a native of Hudson's Bay.

31. Cleared last night. Morning cool. Blue bird, butcher bird, Fringilla tristis (*goldfinch*), Regulus cristatus (*golden-*

crowned kinglet). No ice in Schuylkill. Wasps flying. Moles throw up the earth. Frogs in springy places. Dracontium foetidum above ground.[8]

Anecdotes of an American Crow

It is a difficult task to give a history of our crow. And I hesitate not to aver that it would require the pen of a very able biographer to do justice to his talents.

Before I enter on this subject minutely, it may be necessary to remark that we do not here speak of the crow collectively, as giving an account of the whole race (since I am convinced that these birds differ as widely as men do from each other in point of talents and acquirements), but of a particular bird of that species which I reared from the nest.

He was for a long time comparatively a helpless, dependent creature, having a very small degree of activity or vivacity, every sense seeming to be asleep, or in embryo, until he had nearly attained his finished dimensions and figure and the use of all his members. Then we were surprised and daily amused with the progressive development of his senses, expanding and maturating as the wings of the youthful phalaena when disengaged from its nympha shell.

These senses, however, seemed, as in man, to be only the organs or instruments of his intellectual powers and of their effects, as directed towards the accomplishment of various designs and the gratification of the passions.

This was a bird of a happy temper and good disposition. He was tractable and benevolent, docile and humble, whilst his genius demonstrated extraordinary acuteness and lively sensations. All these good qualities were greatly in his favor, for they procured him friends and patrons, even among *men,* whose society and regard contributed to illustrate the powers of his understanding. But, what appeared most extraordinary, he seemed to have the wit to select and treasure up in his mind, and the sagacity to practice, that kind of knowledge which procured him the most advantage and profit.

He had great talents and a strong propensity to imitation. When I was engaged in weeding in the garden, he would often fly to me, and after very attentively observing me in pulling up the small weeds and grass, he would fall to work and with his strong beak pluck up the grass; and the more so when I complimented him with encouraging expressions. He enjoyed great pleasure and amusement in seeing me write, and would attempt to take the pen out of my hand and my spectacles from my nose. The latter article he was so pleased with that I found it necessary to put them out of his reach, when I had done using them. But, one time in particular, having left them a moment, the crow being then out of my sight, recollecting the bird's mischievous tricks, I returned quickly and found him upon the table, rifling my inkstand, books, and paper. When he saw me coming, he took up my spectacles, and flew off with them. I found it vain to pretend to overtake him; but, standing to observe his operations with my spectacles, I saw him settle down at the root of an apple tree where, after amusing himself for a while, I observed that he was hiding them in the grass and covering them with chips and sticks, often looking round about to see whether I was watching him. When he thought he had sufficiently secreted them, he turned about, advancing towards me at my call. When he had come near me, I ran towards the tree to regain my property. But he, judging of my intentions by my actions, flew, and arriving there before me, picked them up again and flew off with them into another apple tree. I now almost despaired of ever getting them again. However, I returned back to the house, a little distance off, and there secreting myself, I had a full view of him and waited to see the event. After some time had elapsed, during which I heard a great noise and talk from him, of which I understood not a word, he left the tree with my spectacles dangling in his mouth and alighted with them on the ground. After some time and a great deal of caution and contrivance in choosing and rejecting different places, he hid them again, as he thought very effectually, in the grass, carrying and placing over them chips, dry leaves, etc., and often pushing them down with his bill. After he had finished his work, he flew up into a tree, hard by, and there continued for a long time talking to himself and making much noise; bragging, as I supposed, of his achievements. At last, he returned to the house where, not finding me, he betook himself to other amusements. Having noted the place where he had hid my spectacles, I hastened thither and after some time recovered them.

This bird had an excellent memory. He soon learned the name which we had given him, which was Tom, and would commonly come when he was called, unless engaged in some favorite amusement, or soon after correction; for when he had run to great lengths in mischief, I was under the necessity of whipping him; which I did with a little switch. He would, in general, bear correction with wonderful patience and humility, supplicating with piteous and penitent cries and actions. But sometimes, when chastisement became intolerable, he would suddenly start off and take refuge in the next tree. Here he would console himself with chattering and adjusting his feathers, if he was not lucky enough to carry off with him some of my property, such as a penknife or a piece of paper; in this case, he would boast and brag very loudly. At other times, he would soon return and with every token of penitence and submission approach me for forgiveness and reconciliation. On these occasions, he would sometimes return and settle on the ground near my feet and diffidently advance, with soft, soothing expressions and a sort of circumlocution; and sit silently by me for a considerable time. At other times, he would confidently come and settle upon my shoulder and there solicit my favor and pardon, with soothing expressions and caressing gesticulations; not omitting to tickle me about the neck, ears, etc.

Tom appeared to be influenced by a lively sense of domination (an attribute prevalent in the animal creation); but, nevertheless, his ambition in this respect seemed to be moderated by a degree of reason, or reflection. He was certainly by no means tyrannical or cruel. It must be confessed, however, that he aimed to be master of every animal around him in order to secure his independence and his self-preservation, and for the acquisition and defense of his natural rights. Yet, in general, he was peaceable and social with all the animals about him.

He was the most troublesome and teasing to a large dog, whom he could never conquer. This old dog, from natural fidelity and a particular attachment, commonly lay down near me when I was at rest, reading, or writing under the shade of a pear tree in the garden near the house. Tom (I believe from a passion of jealousy) would approach me with his usual caresses and flattery, and after securing my notice and regard, he would address the dog in some degree of complaisance and by words and actions; and if he could obtain access to him, would tickle him with his bill, jump upon him, and compose himself for a little while. It was evident, however, that this seeming sociability was mere artifice to gain an opportunity to practice some mischievous trick; for no sooner did he observe the old dog dozing than he would be sure to pinch his lips and pluck his beard. At length, however, these bold and hazardous achievements had nearly cost him his life; for, one time, the dog being highly provoked, he made so sudden and fierce a snap that the crow narrowly escaped with his head. After this, Tom was wary and used every caution and deliberation in his approaches, examining the dog's eyes and movements, to be sure that he was really asleep, and at last would not venture nearer than his tail, and then by slow, silent, and wary steps, in a sideways or oblique manner, spreading his legs and reaching forward. In this position he would pluck the long hairs of the dog's tail. But he would always take care to place his feet in such a manner as to be ready to start off when the dog was aroused and snapped at him.

It would be endless . . . to recount instances of this bird's understanding, cunning, and operations, which certainly exhibited incontestible demonstrations of a regular combination of ideas, premeditation, reflection, and contrivance, which influenced his operations.[9]

17. Indian Ruins and Indians of William Bartram's Day

A Remarkable Indian Dog

WE PASSED along the verge of an extensive savannah and meadows many miles in circumference, edged on one border with detached groves and pompous palms and embellished with a beautiful sparkling lake. Its verges were decorated with tall, waving grass and floriferous plants; the pellucid waters gently rolling on to a dark, shaded grotto, just under a semicircular, swelling, turfy ascent or bank skirted by groves of magnolias, oaks, laurels, and palms. In these expansive and delightful meadows were feeding and roving troops of the fleet Seminole horse. We halted a while at this grotto; and, after refreshing ourselves, we mounted horse and proceeded across a charming lawn, part of the savannah, entering on it through a dark grove. In this extensive lawn were several troops of horse, and our company had the satisfaction of observing several belonging to themselves. One occurrence remarkable here was a troop of horse under the control and care of a single black dog, which seemed to differ in no respect from the wolf of Florida except his being able to bark as the common dog. He was very careful and industrious in keeping them together; and if any one strolled from the rest at too great a distance, the dog would spring up, head the horse, and bring him back to the company. The proprietor of these horses is an Indian in Talahasochte, about ten miles' distance from this place, who, out of humor and experiment, trained his dog up from a puppy to this business. He follows his master's horses only, keeping them in a separate company where they range; and when he is hungry or wants to see his master, in the evening he returns to town, but never stays at home a night.

The Beautiful Women of the Okefenokee Swamp

The river St. Mary has its source from a vast lake, or marsh, called Ouaquaphenogaw, which lies between Flint and Ocmulgee Rivers and occupies a space of near three hundred miles in circuit. This vast accumulation of waters, in the wet season, appears as a lake and contains some large islands or knolls of rich high land; one of which the present generation of the Creeks represent to be a most blissful spot of the earth. They say it is inhabited by a peculiar race of Indians whose women are incomparably beautiful. They also tell you that this terrestrial paradise has been seen by some of their enterprising hunters when in pursuit of game, who, being lost in inextricable swamps and bogs and on the point of perishing, were unexpectedly relieved by a company of beautiful women, whom they call daughters of the sun, who kindly gave them such provisions as they had with them, which were chiefly fruit, oranges, dates, etc. and some corn cakes, and then enjoined them to fly for safety to their own country, for their husbands were fierce men, and cruel to strangers. They further say that these hunters had a view of

their settlements, situated on the elevated banks of an island, or promontory, in a beautiful lake; but that in their
endeavors to approach it they were involved in perpetual
labyrinths and, like enchanted land, still as they imagined
they had just gained it, it seemed to fly before them, alternately appearing and disappearing. They resolved at length
to leave the delusive pursuit and to return; which, after a
number of inexpressible difficulties, they effected. When
they reported their adventures to their countrymen, their
young warriors were inflamed with an irresistible desire to
invade and make a conquest of so charming a country; but all
their attempts hitherto have proved abortive, never having
been able again to find that enchanting spot nor even any
road or pathway to it. Yet, they say that they frequently meet
with certain signs of its being inhabited, as the building of
canoes, footsteps of men, etc. They tell another story concerning the inhabitants of this sequestered country, which
seems probable enough, which is that they are the posterity
of a fugitive remnant of the ancient Yamasees, who escaped
massacre after a bloody and decisive conflict between them
and the Creek nation (who, it is certain, conquered and
nearly exterminated that once powerful people) and here
found an asylum, remote and secure from the fury of their
proud conquerors. It is, however, certain that there is a vast
lake, or drowned swamp, well known and often visited both
by white and Indian hunters, and on its environs the most
valuable hunting grounds in Florida, well worth contending
for, by those powers whose territories border upon it. From
this great source of rivers, St. Mary arises and meanders
through a vast plain and pine forest near a hundred and fifty
miles to the ocean, with which it communicates, between

the points of Amelia and Talbert islands; the waters flow deep and gently down from its source to the sea.

Indians and Englishmen Join in a Bacchanalian Revel

[*At Spalding's Upper Store on St. John's River. Near present site of Astor. Ed.*]

At the trading house I found a very large part of the Lower Creeks encamped in a grove, just without the palisados. This was a predatory band of the Seminoles, consisting of about forty warriors destined against the Choctaws of West Florida. They had just arrived here from St. Augustine, where they had been with a large troop of horses for sale, and furnished themselves with a very liberal supply of spirituous liquors, about twenty kegs, each containing five gallons.

These sons of Mars had the continence and fortitude to withstand the temptation of even tasting a drop of it until their arrival here, where they purposed to supply themselves with necessary articles to equip them for the expedition and proceed on directly; but here meeting with our young traders and pack-horse men, they were soon prevailed on to broach their beloved nectar; which in the end caused some disturbance and the consumption of most of their liquor; for after they had once got a smack of it, they never were sober for ten days, and by that time there was but little left.

In a few days this festival exhibited one of the most ludicrous bacchanalian scenes that is possible to be conceived. White and red men and women without distinction passed the day merrily with these jovial, amorous topers, and the nights in convivial songs, dances, and sacrifices to Venus, as long as they could stand or move. In these frolics both sexes take such liberties with each other and act without constraint or shame such scenes as they would abhor when sober or in their senses; and would endanger their ears and even their lives: but at last their liquor running low, and being most of them sick through intoxication, they became more sober; and now the dejected, lifeless sots would pawn everything they were in possession of for a mouthful of spirits to settle their stomachs, as they termed it. This was the time for the wenches to make their market, as they had the fortitude and subtilty by dissimulation and artifice to save their share of the liquor during the frolic, and that by a very singular stratagem; for, at these riots, every fellow who joins in the club has his own quart bottle of rum in his hand, holding it by the neck so sure that he never looses hold of it day or night, drunk or sober, as long as the frolic continues; and with this, his beloved friend, he roves about continually, singing, roaring, and reeling to and fro, either alone or arm in arm with a brother toper, presenting his bottle to every-one, offering a drink; and is sure to meet his beloved female if he can, whom he complaisantly begs to drink with him. But the modest fair, veiling her face in a mantle, refuses at the beginning of the frolic; but he presses and at last insists. She, being furnished with an empty bottle concealed in her mantle, at last consents and, taking a good long draught, blushes, drops her pretty face on her bosom, and artfully discharges the rum into her bottle, and by repeating this artifice soon fills it. This she privately conveys to her secret store, and then returns to the jovial game, and so on during the festival; and when the comic farce is over, the wench retails this precious cordial to them at her own price.

There were a few of the chiefs, particularly the Long Warrior, their leader, who had the prudence and fortitude to resist the alluring temptation during the whole farce; but though he was a powerful chief, a king, and a very cunning man, he was not able to control these madmen, although he was acknowledged by the Indians to have communion with powerful invisible beings or spirits, and on that account esteemed worthy of homage and great respect.

An Indian Banquet at Cuscowilla

[*This large Indian town was located on the Alachua Savannah (Payne's Prairie) just east of Micanopy, close to the northwest corner of Lake Tuscowilla, Florida. Ed.*]

Upon our arrival we repaired to the public square or council house, where the chiefs and senators were already convened. The warriors and young men assembled soon after, the business being transacted in public. As it was no more than a ratification of the late treaty of St. Augustine, with some particular commercial stipulations with respect to the citizens of Alachua, the negotiations soon terminated to the satisfaction of both parties.

The banquet succeeded; the ribs and choicest fat pieces of the bullocks, excellently well barbecued, were brought into the apartment of the public square, constructed and appointed for feasting. Bowls and kettles of stewed flesh and broth were brought in for the next course, and with it a very singular dish the traders call tripe soup; it is made of the belly or paunch of the beef, not overcleansed of its contents, cut and minced pretty fine, and then made into a thin soup, seasoned well with salt and aromatic herbs; but the seasoning not quite strong enough to extinguish its original flavor and scent. This dish is greatly esteemed by the Indians but is, in my judgment, the least agreeable they have amongst them.

The town of Cuscowilla, which is the capital of the Alachua tribe, contains about thirty habitations, each of which consists of two houses nearly the same size, about thirty feet in length, twelve feet wide, and about the same in height. The door is placed midway on one side or in the front. This house is divided equally across into two apartments, one of which is the cook room and common hall, and the other the lodging room. The other house is nearly of the same dimensions, standing about twenty yards from the dwelling house, its end fronting the door. The building is two stories high and constructed in a different manner. It is divided transversely, as the other, but the end next the dwelling house is open on three sides, supported by posts or pillars. It has an open loft or platform, the ascent to which is by a portable stair or ladder: this is a pleasant, cool, airy situation, and here the master or chief of the family retires to repose in the hot seasons and receives his guests or visitors. The other half of this building is closed on all sides by notched logs; the lowest or ground part is a potato house and the upper story over it a granary for corn and other provisions. Their houses are constructed of a kind of frame. In the first place, strong corner pillars are fixed in the ground, with others somewhat less, ranging on a line between; these are strengthened by cross pieces of timber, and the whole with the roof is covered close with the bark of the cypress tree. The dwelling stands near the middle of a square yard, encompassed by a low bank, formed with the earth taken out of the yard, which is always carefully swept. Their towns are clean, the inhabitants being particular in laying their filth at a proper distance from their dwellings, which undoubtedly contributes to the healthiness of their habitations.

The town stands on the most pleasant situation that could be well imagined or desired, in an inland country; upon a high swelling ridge of sand hills, within three or four hundred yards of a large and beautiful lake, the circular shore of which continually washes a sandy beach, under a moderately high sloping bank, terminated on one side by extensive forests consisting of orange groves, overtopped with grand magnolias, palms, poplar, tilia, live oaks, and others already noticed; and the opposite point of the crescent gradually retires with hummocky projecting points, indenting the grassy marshes, and lastly terminates in infinite green plains and meadows, united with the skies and waters of the lake. Such a natural landscape, such a rural scene, is not to be imitated by the united ingenuity and labor of man. At present the ground betwixt the town and the lake is adorned by an open grove of very tall pine trees which, standing at a considerable distance from each other, admit a delightful prospect of the sparkling waters. The lake abounds with various excellent fish and wild fowl; there are incredible numbers of the latter, especially in the winter season, when they arrive here from the north to winter.

The Indians abdicated the ancient Alachua town on the borders of the savannah and built here, calling the new town Cuscowilla: their reasons for removing their habitation were on account of its unhealthiness, occasioned, as they say, by the stench of the putrid fish and reptiles in the summer and autumn, driven on shore by the alligators, and the exhalations from marshes of the savannah, together with the persecutions of the mosquitoes.

They plant but little here about the town; only a small garden plot at each habitation, consisting of a little corn, beans, tobacco, citruls, etc. Their plantation, which supplies them with the chief of their vegetable provisions . . . lies on the rich, prolific lands bordering on the great Alachua savannah, about two miles' distance. This plantation is one common enclosure and is worked and tended by the whole community; yet every family has its particular part, according to its own appointment, marked off when planted. This portion receives the common labor and assistance until ripe, when each family gathers and deposits in its granary its own proper share, setting apart a small gift or contribution for the public granary, which stands in the center of the plantation.

The youth, under the supervisal of some of their ancient people, are daily stationed in the fields and are continually whooping and hallooing, to chase away crows, jackdaws, blackbirds, and such predatory animals. The lads are armed with bows and arrows and, being trained up to it from their early youth, are sure at a mark, and in the course of the day load themselves with squirrels, birds, etc. The men in turn patrol the cornfields at night, to protect their provisions from the depredations of night rovers, as bears, raccoons, and deer; the two former being immoderately fond of young corn, when the grain is filled with a rich milk, as sweet and nourishing as cream; and the deer are as fond of the potato vines.

After the feast was over, we returned to our encampment on the great savannah towards the evening. Our companions, whom we left at the camp, were impatient for our return, having been out horse hunting in the plains and groves during our absence. They soon left us, on a visit to the town, having there some female friends with whom they were anxious to renew their acquaintance. The Seminole girls are by no means destitute of charms to please the rougher sex. The white traders are fully sensible how greatly it is to their advantage to gain their affections and friendship in matters of trade and commerce; and if their love and esteem for each other is sincere and upon principles of reciprocity, there are but few instances of their neglecting or betraying the interests and views of their temporary husbands; they labor and watch constantly to promote their private interests and detect and prevent any plots or evil designs which may threaten their persons or operate against their trade or business.

Bartram Meets an Indian Prince

[*The town of Talahasochte was on the Suwannee River, probably where New Clay Landing is located, a few miles from Chiefland, Florida. Ed.*]

On our return to camp in the evening, we were saluted by a party of young Indian warriors, who had pitched their camp on a green eminence near the lake and at a small distance from our camp, under a little grove of oaks and palms. This company consisted of seven young Seminoles under the conduct of a young prince or chief of Talahasochte, a town southward on the isthmus. They were all dressed and painted with singular elegance and richly ornamented with silver plates, chains, etc., after the Seminole mode, with waving plumes of feathers on their crests. On our coming up to them, they arose and shook hands; we alighted and sat a while with them by their cheerful fire.

The young prince informed our chief that he was in pursuit of a young fellow who had fled from the town, carrying off with him one of his favorite young wives or concubines. He said merrily he would have the ears of both of them before he returned. He was rather above the middle stature and the most perfect human figure I ever saw; of an amiable, engaging countenance, air, and deportment; free and familiar in conversation, yet retaining a becoming gracefulness and dignity. We arose, took leave of them, and crossed a little vale covered with a charming green turf, already illuminated by the soft light of the full moon.

Soon after joining our companions at camp, our neighbors, the prince and his associates, paid us a visit. We treated them with the best fare we had, having till this time preserved some of our spirituous liquors. They left us with perfect cordiality and cheerfulness, wishing us a good repose, and retired to their own camp. Having a band of music with them, consisting of a drum, flutes, and a rattle gourd, they entertained us during the night with their music, vocal and instrumental.

There is a languishing softness and melancholy air in the Indian convivial songs, especially of the amorous class, irresistibly moving, attractive, and exquisitely pleasing, especially in these solitary recesses, when all nature is silent.[1]

The White King's Feast

[*The closest approach by a main highway to the site of the ancient Indian town of Talahasochte is on Route 19, where the bridge spans the Suwannee. Ed.*]

Parties of Indians came in loaded with venison, bear meat, and honey. We were informed the White King, chief of this settlement, was coming in. At night a large fire was kindled in the middle of the square, which was soon surrounded by Indians dancing and singing. We soon heard the drum beat in the square, and a messenger came to invite us to eat bear ribs and honey, it being the king's treat, having killed some bear. They never eat the ribs when out, but bring them to the town, where they make a feast in the square for the warriors and hunters.

We accordingly repaired to the square where the men were assembling. They made way for us and placed us near where the barbecued ribs were served up in large platters or wooden bowls in one of the chief houses of the square. We had kettles of honey and water, with a great wooden family spoon in each kettle. Everyone in turn took a sup or quaff, discoursing of cheerful subjects as he liked, as hunting, adventure, joking, news of love, intrigues, and so on. The youth and young fellows dancing, singing, and wrestling about the fire.

When everyone seemed satisfied with eating and drinking, we repaired to the fire, where the king appeared and joined us in a circle seated about the fire. The youths ceased their jollity and withdrew at some distance. The men passed the pipe about the ring and discoursed of more serious affairs with the greatest gravity and decorum. The king received us with great seeming satisfaction and joy and, being informed of our business by our trader, he expressed the warmest wishes and hopes for the store being settled again in his town, declaring how wretched they would be if the white people withdrew their friendship and protection from their town.

The king went home. We returned to the feast and, after taking another whet at the bear ribs and talking over the news of the times, broke up in peace and mirth, everyone taking his steps as his inclination led him. The Old Chief, who was their priest, or conjurer, carried off the remains of the victuals and retired. I continued for some time in the square, till the youth broke up their dancing and mirth. . . . These people spend a great part of their time in feasting and dancing. A Seminole comes in from the chase, he lays his game down before his hywah and throws himself on his bearskin spread for him under the shade. In the evening, his friends repair to his repast, sing and dance over his war and hunting exploits till tired, fall asleep. In the night he awakes, stretches himself along his back, sings himself to sleep again; thus they divide their time. . . .[2]

The Indian and the Compass at Buffalo Lick

[*William Bartram attended the Cherokee-Creek Congress of 1773 to determine new boundaries between the whites and Indians. From Augusta, he visited Wrightsborough, near the Little River in northwestern McDuffie County. The survey party went on to Great Buffalo Lick, which is about half a mile east of Philomath in the southern part of Oglethorpe County, then went northwest, passing west of Lexington to just southeast of Athens at Cherokee*

Corner on the Clarke-Oglethorpe line, then almost straight north, passing west of Danielsville to the Madison-Franklin line on the Broad River, then northeast across Hart County to the mouth of the Keowe River. Ed.]

After four days' moderate and pleasant traveling, we arrived in the evening at the Buffalo Lick. This extraordinary place occupies several acres of ground at the foot of the southeast promontory of the Great Ridge, which divides the rivers Savannah and Altamaha. A large cane swamp and meadows, forming an immense plain, lie southeast from it. In this swamp I believe the head branches of the great Ogeechee River take their rise. The place called the Lick contains three or four acres, is nearly level, and lies between the head of the cane swamp and the ascent of the Ridge. The earth, from the superficies to an unknown depth, is an almost white or cinereous-colored, tenacious, fattish clay, which all kinds of cattle lick into great caves, pursuing the delicious vein. It is the common opinion of the inhabitants that this clay is impregnated with saline vapors arising from fossil salts deep in the earth. I could discover nothing saline in its taste, but I imagined an insipid sweetness. Horned cattle, horses, and deer are immoderately fond of it, insomuch that their excrement, which almost totally covers the earth to some distance round this place, appears to be perfect clay; which, when dried by the sun and air, is almost as hard as brick.

We were detained at this place one day in adjusting and planning the several branches of the survey. A circumstance occurred during this time which was a remarkable instance of Indian sagacity and had nearly disconcerted all our plans and put an end to the business. The surveyor fixed his compass on the staff . . . to ascertain the course from our place of departure, which was to strike the Savannah River at the confluence of a certain river about seventy miles' distance from us. Just as he had determined upon the point, the Indian chief came up and, observing the course he had fixed upon, spoke and said it was not right; but that the course to the place was so and so, holding up his hand and pointing. The surveyor replied that he himself was certainly right, adding that that little instrument (pointing to the compass) told him so, which, he said, could not err. The Indian answered he knew better and that the little wicked instrument was a liar; and he would not acquiesce in its decisions, since it would wrong the Indians out of their land. This mistake (the surveyor proving to be in the wrong) displeased the Indians. The dispute arose to that height that the chief and his party had determined to break up the business and return the shortest way home, and forbade the surveyors to proceed any farther. However, after some delay, the complaisance and prudent conduct of the colonel made them change their resolution. The chief became reconciled upon condition that the compass should be discarded and rendered incapable of serving on this business; that the chief himself should lead the survey and, moreover, receive an order for a very considerable quantity of goods.

An Angry Seminole

[*Somewhere between the Satilla and the St. Mary's. Ed.*]

I had now passed the utmost frontier of the white settlements on that border. It was drawing on towards the close of day, the skies serene and calm, the air temperately cool, and gentle zephyrs breathing through the fragrant pines; the prospect around enchantingly varied and beautiful; endless green savannahs, chequered with coppices of fragrant shrubs, filled the air with the richest perfume. The gaily attired plants which enameled the green had begun to imbibe the pearly dew of evening. Nature seemed silent, and nothing appeared to ruffle the happy moments of evening contemplation; when, on a sudden, an Indian appeared, crossing the path at a considerable distance before me. On perceiving that he was armed with a rifle, the first sight of him startled me, and I endeavored to elude his sight by stopping my pace and keeping large trees between us; but he espied me and, turning short about, set spurs to his horse and came up on full gallop. I never before this was afraid at the sight of an Indian, but at this time I must own that my spirits were very much agitated. I saw at once that, being unarmed, I was in his power; and having now but a few moments to prepare, I resigned myself entirely to the will of the Almighty, trusting to His mercies for my preservation. My mind then became tranquil and I resolved to meet the dreaded foe with resolution and cheerful confidence. The intrepid Seminole stopped suddenly three or four yards before me and silently viewed me, his countenance angry and fierce, shifting his rifle from shoulder to shoulder and looking about instantly on all sides. I advanced towards him and with an air of confidence offered him my hand, hailing him, brother. At this he hastily jerked back his arm with a look of malice, rage, and disdain, seeming every way discontented; when, again looking at me more attentively, he instantly spurred up to me and with dignity in his look and action gave me his hand. Possibly the silent language of his soul during the moment of suspense (for I believe his design was to kill me when he first came up) was after this manner: "White man, thou art my enemy, and thou and thy brethren may have killed mine; yet it may not be so, and even were that the case, thou art now alone and in my power. Live; the Great Spirit forbids me to touch thy life; go to thy brethren, tell them thou sawest an Indian in the forests, who knew how to be humane and compassionate." In fine, we shook hands and parted in a friendly manner, in the midst of a dreary wilderness; and he informed me of the course and the distance to the trading house, where I found he had been extremely ill-treated the day before.

I now set forward again and, after eight or ten miles' riding, arrived at the banks of St. Mary's, opposite the stores, and got safe over before dark. The river is here about one hundred yards across, has ten feet water and, following its course, about sixty miles to the sea, though but about twenty miles by land. The trading company here received and treated me with great civility. On relating my adventures on the road, particularly the last with the Indian, the chief replied, with a countenance that at once bespoke surprise and pleasure, "My friend, consider yourself a fortunate man. That fellow," said he, "is one of the greatest villains on earth, a noted murderer, and outlawed by his countrymen. Last evening he was here, we took his gun from him, broke it in pieces, and gave him a severe drubbing. He, however, made his escape, carrying off a new rifle gun with which, he said, going off, he would kill the first white man he met."

On seriously contemplating the behavior of this Indian towards me, so soon after his ill treatment, the following train of sentiments insensibly crowded in upon my mind.

Can it be denied but that the moral principle, which directs the savages to virtuous and praiseworthy actions, is natural or innate? It is certain they have not the assistance of letters or those means of education in the schools of philosophy, where the virtuous sentiments and actions of the most illustrious characters are recorded and carefully laid before the youth of civilized nations: therefore this moral principle must be innate, or they must be under the immediate influence and guidance of a more divine and powerful preceptor who, on these occasions, instantly inspires them and, as with a ray of divine light, points out to them at once the dignity, propriety, and beauty of virtue.

Cherokee Maidens in the Strawberry Fields Along the Little Tennessee

Proceeding on our return to town [Cowe], continued through part of this high forest skirting on the meadows. Began to ascend the hills of a ridge which we were under the necessity of crossing. Having gained its summit, we enjoyed a most enchanting view — a vast expanse of green meadows and strawberry fields, a meandering river gliding through, saluting in its various turnings the swelling, green, turfy knolls embellished with parterres of flowers and fruitful strawberry beds, flocks of turkeys strolling about them, herds of deer prancing in the meads or bounding over the hills, companies of young, innocent Cherokee virgins, some busy gathering the rich, fragrant fruit. Others, having already filled their baskets, lay reclined under the shade of floriferous and fragrant native bowers of magnolia, azalea, perfumed calycanthus, sweet yellow jessamine, and cerulean glycine, disclosing their beauties to the fluttering breeze and bathing their limbs in the cool, fleeting streams; whilst other parties, more gay and libertine, were yet collecting strawberries, or wantonly chasing their companions, tantalizing them, staining their lips and cheeks with the rich fruit.

The sylvan scene of primitive innocence was enchanting and perhaps too enticing for hearty young men long to continue idle spectators.

In fine, nature prevailing over reason, we wished at least to have a more active part in their delicious sports. Thus precipitately resolving, we cautiously made our approaches, yet undiscovered, almost to the joyous scene of action. Now, although we meant no other than an innocent frolic with this gay assembly of hamadryads, we shall leave it to the person of feeling and sensibility to form an idea to what lengths our passions might have hurried us, thus warmed and excited, had it not been for the vigilance and care of some envious matrons who lay in ambush and, espying us, gave the alarm, time enough for the nymphs to rally and assemble together. We, however, pursued and gained ground on a group of them who had incautiously strolled to a greater distance from their guardians and, finding their retreat now like to be cut off, took shelter under cover of a little grove; but on perceiving themselves to be discovered by us, kept their station, peeping through the bushes; when, observing our approaches, they confidently discovered themselves and decently advanced to meet us, half unveiling their blooming faces, incarnated with the modest maiden blush, and with native innocence and cheerfulness presented their little baskets, merrily telling us their fruit was ripe and sound.

We accepted a basket, sat down and regaled ourselves on the delicious fruit, encircled by the whole assembly of the innocent, jocose sylvan nymphs. By this time the several parties, under the conduct of the elder matrons, had disposed themselves in companies on the green, turfy banks.

My young companion, the trader, by concessions and suitable apologies for the bold intrusion, having compromised the matter with them, engaged them to bring their collections to his house at a stipulated price: we parted friendly.

And now taking leave of these Elysian fields, we again mounted the hills, which we crossed, and traversing obliquely their flowery beds, arrived in town in the cool of the evening.

Apalachucla, Capital Town on the Chattahoochee

[*Coweta was on a plain two and a half miles northeast of Fort Mitchell, Alabama. Apalachucla was about twelve miles south of Coweta. Ed.*]

We repacked and set off again for the Apalachucla town, where we arrived after riding over a level plain consisting of ancient Indian plantations, a beautiful landscape diversified with groves and lawns.

This is esteemed the mother town or capital of the Creek or Muscogulge confederacy, sacred to peace: no captives are put to death or human blood spilt here. And when a general peace is proposed, deputies from all the towns in the confederacy assemble at this capital in order to deliberate upon a subject of so high importance for the prosperity of the commonwealth.

And on the contrary the great Coweta town, about twelve miles higher up this river, is called the bloody town, where the micos, chiefs, and warriors assemble when a general war is proposed; and here captives and state malefactors are put to death.

The time of my continuance here, which was about a week,

was employed in excursions round about this settlement. One day the chief trader of Apalachucla obliged me with his company on a walk of about a mile and a half down the river to view the ruins and site of the ancient Apalachucla. It had been situated on a peninsula formed by a doubling of the river and indeed appears to have been a very famous capital by the artificial mounds or terraces, and a very populous settlement, from its extent and expansive old fields, stretching beyond the scope of the sight along the low grounds of the river. We viewed the mounds or terraces on which formerly stood their town house or rotunda and square or areopagus; and a little behind these, on a level height or natural step above the low grounds, is a vast, artificial terrace or foursquare mound, now seven or eight feet higher than the common surface of the ground. In front of one square or side of this mound adjoins a very extensive oblong square yard or artificial level plain, sunk a little below the common surface and surrounded with a bank or narrow terrace, formed with the earth thrown out of this yard at the time of its formation. The Creeks or present inhabitants have a tradition that this was the work of the ancients many ages prior to their arrival and possessing this country.

This old town was evacuated about twenty years ago by the general consent of the inhabitants, on account of its unhealthy situation, owing to the frequent inundations of the river over the low grounds; and, moreover, they grew timorous and dejected, apprehending themselves to be haunted and possessed with vengeful spirits, on account of human blood that had been undeservedly* spilt in this old town,

---

* About fifty or sixty years ago almost all the white traders then in the nation were massacred in this town, whither they had repaired from the different towns, in hopes of an asylum or refuge, in consequence of the alarm having been timely apprized of the hostile intentions of the Indians by their temporary wives. They all

having been repeatedly warned by apparitions and dreams to leave it.

At the time of their leaving this old town, like the ruin or dispersion of the ancient Babel, the inhabitants separated from each other, forming several bands under the conduct or auspices of the chief of each family or tribe. The greatest number, however, chose to sit down and build the present new Apalachucla town, upon a high bank of the river above the inundations. The other bands pursued different routes, as their inclinations led them, settling villages lower down the river; some continued their migration towards the seacoast, seeking their kindred and countrymen amongst the Lower Creeks in East Florida, where they settled themselves. My intelligent friend, the trader of Apalachucla, having from a long residence amongst these Indians acquired an extensive knowledge of their customs and affairs, I inquired of him what were his sentiments with respect to their wandering, unsettled disposition, their so frequently breaking up their old towns and settling new ones, etc. His answers and opinions were the necessity they were under of having fresh or new strong land for their plantations and new, convenient, and extensive range or hunting ground, which unavoidably forces them into contentions and wars with their confederates and neighboring tribes; to avoid which they had rather move and seek a plentiful and peaceable retreat, even at a distance, than contend with friends and relatives or embroil themselves in destructive wars with their neighbors, when either can be avoided with so little inconvenience. With regard to

---

met together in one house, under the avowed protection of the chiefs of the town, waiting the event; but whilst the chiefs were assembled in council, deliberating on ways and means to protect them, the Indians in multitudes surrounded the house and set fire to it; they all, to the number of eighteen or twenty, perished with the house in the flames. The trader showed me the ruins of the house where they were burnt.

the Muscogulges, the first object in order to obtain these conveniences was the destruction of the Yamases, who held the possession of Florida and were in close alliance with the Spaniards, their declared and most inveterate enemy, which they at length fully accomplished; and by this conquest they gained a vast and invaluable territory, comprehending a delightful region, and most plentiful country for their favorite game, bear and deer. But not yet satisfied, having already so far conquered the powerful Cherokees as, in a manner, to force them to alliance, and compelled the warlike Chickasaws to sue for peace and alliance with them, they then grew arrogant and insatiable and turned their covetous looks towards the potent and intrepid Choctaws, the only Indian enemy they had to fear, meaning to break them up and possess themselves of that extensive, fruitful, and delightful country and make it a part of their vast empire. But the Choctaws, a powerful, hardy, subtle, and intrepid race, estimated at twenty thousand warriors, are likely to afford sufficient exercise for the proud and restless spirits of the Muscogulges, at least for some years to come; and they appear to be so equally matched with the Choctaws that it seems doubtful which of these powerful nations will rise victorious. The Creeks have sworn, it seems, that they never will make peace with this enemy as long as the rivers flow or the sun pursues his course through the skies.

Thus we see that war or the exercise of arms originates from the same motives and operates in the spirits of the wild red men of America as it formerly did with the renowned Greeks and Romans, or modern civilized nations, and not from a ferocious, capricious desire of shedding human blood as carnivorous savages. Neither does the eager avarice of plunder stimulate them to acts of madness and cruelty, that

being a trifling object in their estimation, a duffield blanket,
a polished rifle gun, or embroidered mantle. No, their
martial prowess and objects of desire and ambition proceed
from greater principles and more magnanimous intentions,
even that of reuniting all nations and languages under one
universal confederacy or commonwealth.

Attassee on the Tallapoosa River

I recrossed the river at Tuccabache, an ancient and large
town, thence continued up the river and at evening arrived
at Attassee, where I continued near a week, waiting the
preparations of the traders with whom I was to join in
company to Augusta.

The next day after my arrival I was introduced to the ancient chiefs at the public square or areopagus. In the evening, in company with the traders, who are numerous in this
town, repaired to the great rotunda, where were assembled
the greatest number of ancient, venerable chiefs and warriors
that I had ever beheld. We spent the evening and great part
of the night together in drinking cassine and smoking tobacco.
The great council house, or rotunda, is appropriated to much
the same purpose as the public square, but more private, and
seems particularly dedicated to political affairs; women and
youth are never admitted, and I suppose it is death for a
female to presume to enter the door or approach within its
pale. It is a vast conical building or circular dome, capable
of accommodating many hundred people; constructed and
furnished within exactly in the same manner as those of the
Cherokees already described but much larger than any I had
seen of them. There are people appointed to take care of it,

to have it daily swept clean, and to provide canes for fuel or to give light.

As their vigils and manner of conducting their vespers and mystical fire in this rotunda are extremely singular and altogether different from the customs and usages of any other people, I shall proceed to describe them. In the first place, the governor or officer who has the management of this business, with his servants attending, orders the black drink to be brewed, which is a decoction or infusion of the leaves and tender shoots of the cassine. This is done under an open shed or pavilion, at twenty or thirty yards' distance, directly opposite the door of the council house. Next he orders bundles of dry canes to be brought in. These are previously split and broken in pieces to about the length of two feet and then placed obliquely crossways upon one another on the floor, forming a spiral circle round about the great center pillar, rising to a foot or eighteen inches in height from the ground; and this circle spreading as it proceeds round and round, often repeated from right to left, every revolution increases its diameter and at length extends to the distance of ten or twelve feet from the center, more or less, according to the length of time the assembly or meeting is to continue.

By the time these preparations are accomplished, it is night and the assembly have taken their seats in order. The exterior extremity or outer end of the spiral circle takes fire and immediately rises into a bright flame. How this is effected I did not plainly apprehend. I saw no person set fire to it. There might have been fire left on the earth; however, I neither saw nor smelt fire or smoke until the blaze instantly ascended upwards. The flame gradually and slowly creeps round the center pillar, with the course of the sun, feeding on the dry canes, and affords a cheerful, gentle, and sufficient light until the circle is consumed, when the council breaks up.

Soon after this illumination takes place, the aged chiefs and warriors are seated on their cabins or sofas, on the side of the house opposite the door, in three classes or ranks, rising a little, one above or behind the other; and the white people and red people of confederate towns in the like order on the left hand. A transverse range of pillars supporting a thin clay wall about breast high separates them. The king's cabin or seat is in front; the next to the back of it, the head warrior's; and the third or last accommodates the young warriors, etc. The great war chief's seat or place is on the same cabin with, and immediately to the left hand of, the king, and next to the white people; and to the right hand of the mico or king the most venerable headmen and warriors are seated. The assembly being now seated in order and the house illuminated, two middle-aged men, who perform the office of slaves or servants *pro tempore,* come in together at the door, each having very large conch shells full of black drink, and advance with slow, uniform, and steady steps, their eyes or countenances lifted up, singing very low but sweetly. They come within six or eight paces of the king's and white people's cabins, when they stop together, and each rests his shell on a tripos or little table but presently takes it up again and, bowing very low, advances obsequiously, crossing or intersecting each other about midway. He who rested his shell before the white people now stands before the king, and the other who stopped before the king stands before the white people; when each presents his shell, one to the king and the other to the chief of the white people, and as soon as he raises it to his mouth, the slave utters or sings two notes, each of which continues as long as he has breath; and as long as these notes continue, so long must the person drink, or at least keep the shell to his mouth. These two long notes are very solemn and at once strike the imagination with a religious awe or homage to the Supreme, sounding somewhat like *a-hoo — ojah* and *a-lu-yah.* After this manner the whole assembly are treated, as long as the drink and light continue to hold out; and as soon as the drinking begins, tobacco and pipes are brought. The skin of a wildcat or young tiger stuffed with tobacco is brought and laid at the king's feet, with the great or royal pipe beautifully adorned; the skin is usually of the animals of the king's family or tribe, as the wildcat, otter, bear, rattlesnake, etc. A skin of tobacco is likewise brought and cast at the feet of the white chief of the town, and from him it passes from one to another to fill their pipes from, though each person has, besides, his own peculiar skin of tobacco. The king or chief smokes first in the great pipe a few whiffs, blowing it off ceremoniously first towards the sun or, as it is generally supposed, to the Great Spirit, for it is puffed upwards, next towards the four cardinal points, then towards the white people in the house. Then the great pipe is taken from the hand of the mico by a slave and presented to the chief white man, and then to the great war chief, whence it circulates through the rank of headmen and warriors then returns to the king. After this, each one fills his pipe from his own or his neighbor's skin.

The great or public square generally stands alone, in the center and highest part of the town. It consists of foursquare or cubical buildings, or houses of one story, uniform and of the same dimensions, so situated as to form an exact tetragon, encompassing an area of half an acre of ground, more or less, according to the strength or largeness of the town or will of the inhabitants. There is a passage or avenue at each corner of equal width. Each building is constructed of a wooden frame fixed strongly in the earth, the walls filled in and neatly plastered with clay mortar; close on three sides, that is, the back and two ends, except within about two feet of the wall plate or eaves, which is left open for the purpose of a window and to admit a free passage of the air; the front or side next to the area is quite open like a piazza. One of these buildings is properly the council house, where the mico, chiefs, and warriors, with the citizens who have business or choose to repair thither, assemble everyday in council to hear, decide, and rectify all grievances, complaints, and contentions arising betwixt the citizens; give audience to ambassadors and strangers; hear news and talks from confederate towns, allies, or distant nations; consult about the particular affairs of the town, as erecting habitations for new citizens or establishing young families, concerning agriculture, etc. This building is somewhat different from the other three. It is closely shut up on three sides, that is, the back and two ends; and, besides, a partition wall longitudinally from end to end divides it into two apartments, the back part totally dark, only three small, arched apertures or holes opening into it from the front apartment or piazza, and little larger than just to admit a man to crawl in upon his hands and knees. This secluded place appears to me to be designed as a sanctuary* dedicated to religion or rather priestcraft; for here are deposited all the sacred things, as the physic pot, rattles, chaplets of deer's hoofs, and other apparatus of conjuration; and likewise the calumet or great pipe of peace, the imperial standard, or eagle's tail, which is made of the feathers of the white eagle's

* Sanctorium or sacred temple; and it is said to be death for any person but the mico, war chief, and high priest to enter in, and none are admitted but by permission of the priests, who guard it day and night.

tail* curiously formed and displayed like an open fan on a scepter or staff, as white and clean as possible when displayed for peace, but when for war, the feathers are painted or tinged with vermilion. The piazza or front of this building is equally divided into three apartments, by two transverse walls or partitions, about breast high, each having three orders or ranges of seats or cabins stepping one above and behind the other, which accommodate the senate and audience, in the like order as observed in the rotunda. The other three buildings which compose the square are alike furnished with three ranges of cabins or sofas and serve for a banqueting house, to shelter and accommodate the audience and spectators at all times, particularly at feasts or public entertainments, where all classes of citizens resort day and night in the summer or moderate season; the children and females, however, are seldom or never seen in the public square.

The pillars and walls of the houses of the square are decorated with various paintings and sculptures; which I suppose to be hieroglyphic and as an historic legendary of political and sacerdotal affairs: but they are extremely picturesque or caricature, as men in variety of attitudes, some ludicrous enough, others having the head of some kind of animal, as those of a duck, turkey, bear, fox, wolf, buck, etc., and again those kind of creatures are represented having the human head. These designs are not ill executed; the outlines bold, free, and well proportioned. The pillars supporting the front or piazza of the council house of the square are ingeniously formed in the likeness of vast speckled serpents ascending upwards; the Ottasses being of the snake family or tribe. At this time the town was fasting, taking

* Vultur sacra.

medicine, and I think I may say praying, to avert a grievous calamity of sickness which had lately afflicted them and laid in the grave abundance of their citizens. They fast seven or eight days, during which time they eat or drink nothing but a meager gruel made of a little corn flour and water; taking at the same time by way of medicine or physic a strong decoction of the roots of the Iris versicolor, which is a powerful cathartic. They hold this root in high estimation; every town cultivates a little plantation of it, having a large artificial pond, just without the town, planted and almost overgrown with it, where they usually dig clay for pottery and mortar and plaster for their buildings, and I observed where they had lately been digging up this root.

In the midst of a large oblong square adjoining this town (which was surrounded with a low bank or terrace) is standing a high pillar, round like a pin or needle; it is about forty feet in height and between two and three feet in diameter at the earth, gradually tapering upwards to a point; it is one piece of pine wood and arises from the center of a low, circular, artificial hill, but it leans a little to one side. I inquired of the Indians and traders what it was designed for, who answered they knew not. The Indians said that their ancestors found it in the same situation when they first arrived and possessed the country, adding that the red men, or Indians, then the possessors, whom they vanquished, were as ignorant as themselves concerning it, saying that their ancestors likewise found it standing so. This monument, simple as it is, may be worthy the observations of a traveler, since it naturally excites at least the following queries: for what purpose was it designed? its great antiquity and incorruptibility — what method or machines they employed to bring it to the spot, and how they raised it erect? There is no tree or species of the pine whose wood, i.e., so large a portion of the trunk, is supposed to be incorruptible, exposed in the open air to all weathers, but the long-leaved pine, and there is none growing within twelve or fifteen miles of this place, that tree being naturally produced only on the high, dry, barren ridges, where there is a sandy soil and grassy wet savannahs. A great number of men, uniting their strength, probably carried it to the place on handspikes or some such contrivance.

On the Sabbath Day, before I set off from this place, I could not help observing the solemnity of the town, the silence and the retiredness of the red inhabitants; but a very few of them were to be seen, the doors of their dwellings shut, and if a child chanced to stray out, it was quickly drawn indoors again. I asked the meaning of this and was immediately answered that, it being the white people's beloved day or Sabbath, the Indians kept it religiously sacred to the Great Spirit.[3]

Observations on the Creek and Cherokee Indians

[In response to questions put to him by the American Ethnological Society. Ed.]

Philadelphia, Dec. 15, 1789.
Thus you have, Sir,

My observations and conjectures on these matters, with all the truth and accuracy that my slender abilities will admit of, and without reserve. If they should not answer your wishes and expectations, I desire you will ascribe it to my misapprehension of the queries or lack of knowledge, etc., etc.

I doubt not but you will readily excuse bad writing, composition, and spelling. My weakness of sight, I hope, will plead for me, when I assure you I have been obliged to write the greater part of this with my eyes shut, and that with pain.

I do not mention this to claim any sort of obligation from you, Sir, for all that I know concerning these matters are due to you and to science.

I remain, Sir,

With every sentiment of respect and esteem, your obliged friend,

Wm. Bartram

The Creek and Cherokee Indians

I. HISTORY AND TRADITIONS OF THE MUSCOGULGES

Query. Have those tribes of Indians which you have visited any traditions concerning their origin, their progress, or migrations, which you consider worthy of notice? If they have, what are those traditions? Which of the nations of which you have knowledge seem to have the most accurate and least suspicious traditions concerning their origin, etc.? Have you any reason for believing that the Cherokees, Creeks, or any other of the Southern tribes with which you are acquainted, crossed the river Mississippi in their progress to the country which they now inhabit? If any of these tribes crossed that great river, do you think it is possible to determine, with any degree of certainty, when they did cross it? Can you form any conjecture which part or parts of the country, bordering on the Mississippi, these tribes passed through in their migrations toward the East?

Answer. The Cricks,* or, as they called themselves, *Muscoges,* or *Muscogulges,* are a very powerful confederacy, consisting of many tribes or remnants of conquered nations united; perhaps about sixty towns, thirty of which speak the Muscogulge tongue and are the progeny or descendants of a powerful band of a nation bearing that name, who, many years since (on their nation becoming very numerous, and filling their native country with inhabitants, by which the game and other necessary produce of their country became scarce and difficult to procure), were induced to separate themselves from, and go in search of, new and plentiful regions. They directed their migrations eastward, leaving with great regret and difficulty their native land, containing their relatives and friends, which was on the banks of a large and beautiful river, called the Red River, from great quantities of red stone, of which they formed their tobacco pipes. Their migrations continued a long time and under great hardships and embarrassments, they being continually attacked by hostile Indian nations, till at length they arrived at the banks of the Great River, i.e., that which they crossed, when they began to think of establishing a permanent residence. But, being assaulted and disturbed by surrounding nations, they pushed eastward as far as the Ocmulgee [Ga.]; when, hearing of the settlements of the white people, i.e., Spaniards, at St. Augustine, they sent ambassadors to treat with them on terms of mutual favor. But not being kindly re-

* Nickname given them by the English. [Ed.]

ceived, and hearing of other nations of white people further
to the northeast, i.e., in Carolina (the English were at this
time founding South Carolina at Charleston), they sent deputies or ambassadors to Charleston, offering their friendship
and alliance, to continue forever (as long as the river flow
and the sun continue his course). A treaty immediately took
place, and they joined their arms with the Carolinians, who
assisted them against the surrounding Indian nations, which
were then in the Spanish interest, whom they at length
subjugated and, in the end, proved the destruction of the
Spanish colony of East Florida. The Muscogulges, by uniting
the remnant tribes of their conquered foes, grew stronger
and daily extended their empire. There are now, beside the
Muscogulge towns, or those towns whose inhabitants speak
that tongue, almost as many languages or dialects as there
are towns. It seems apparent, by this account (this account
I had from the most ancient and respectable men of the
Muscogulge, through the best old traders and good interpreters, at different times and in various towns; and I
believe it to be true as mere tradition can possibly be), that
the Muscogulges crossed the Mississippi somewhere about
the Chickasaw country, below the confluence of the Ohio,
as they mention crossing but one large river, i.e., the Mississippi, or Great River.

They, the Natches, Chickasaws, and Choctaws, seem to
possess a common origin, as they all speak a dialect of the
same country. It is certain they all crossed the Mississippi, as
they say of themselves, and long since the Spanish invasion
and conquest of Mexico; for these Indians, viz., the Choctaws,
say they brought with them across the river those fine horses
called Chickasaw and Choctaw breeds. The Seminole horses

or those beautiful creatures bred amongst the Lower Creeks, which are of the Andalusian breed, were introduced by the Spaniards at St. Augustine.

As to the Cherokees, they are altogether a separate nation from the Muscogulges, of much more ancient establishment in the regions they inhabit. I made no inquiry concerning their original descent or migrations to these parts. But I understood that they came from the West, or sunsetting. Their empire, or confederacy, was once very strong and extensive. Before the league of the Creeks (when I speak of the Creeks and Muscogulges I mean the same people) and Carolinians, their empire extended from within forty miles of the seacoast, northwest to the Ohio, comprehending all the regions lying in the waters of the Cherokee River, quite to its confluence with the Ohio, and also the great east branches of the Ohio, upwards beyond the Cunhawa (Kenhewa), Sante, and Pede, northeastward. And it is remarkable that those great pyramidal or conical mounts of earth, tetragon terraces, and cubican yards are to be seen in all this vast territory. (The largest of these I ever saw stands on the banks of the Savannah River, eight miles above Dartmouth and about eighty miles above Augusta, which was nearly the center of the Cherokee empire, at the most flourishing period of its history.)

There are many artificial mounts of earth along the seacoast through Carolina and Georgia about this distance from it, and in the settlements northwest, which bears the name Cherokee Mounts, particularly one about ten or twelve miles from Savannah, near what are now called the Cherokee Ponds. Here, on the road to Augusta, are many ponds and savannahs. Indeed there are people yet living who remember to have seen Cherokee towns inhabited but a few miles above the city of Savannah and afterwards possessed and inhabited by the Muscogulges.

Yet it is certain they were not the people who constructed them, as they own themselves, nor were they built by the people from whom they took possession of the country. Their language is radically different from that of the Creeks, sounding the letter R frequently; in short, there is not one word in their respective languages alike.

II. Probable Origin and Relations

Query. Have you any reason for believing that any of the tribes of Indians which you have visited were derived from either the Mexicans or the Peruvians? If you have, what are those reasons?

Answer. I have no reason, from what I have observed myself, or from information derived from others, to suppose that any of the nations or tribes came from the old Mexicans or Peruvians, unless we believe the accounts which the Natches give of themselves, as related by M. du Pratz. That account should, I imagine, be understood as referring to New Mexico, because their account of their original country and migrations was from the west, or sunsetting, which would be west from their country on the Mississippi, near about the latitude of Santa Fe, north latitude 34 or 35.

The Spanish invasion of these regions and subsequent colonization, after the discovery of the mines and the establishment of forts, in order to possess the country, work the mines, and extend their researches, would very probably cause many natives to decamp, in search of more peaceful abodes at a distance from such troublesome neighbors, and these nations, by a northeast course, would likely, in their opinion, get at the greatest distance from those dreaded bearded men, their common enemy (not yet having heard of other colonies or invasions of the bearded men), and thus propel one another as waves driven before the winds. The Chickasaws, Choctaws, and Muscogulges appear to have arrived some time since the Natches, particularly the two former tribes, and the Creeks last. The Natches might have come from a region nearest the borders of Old Mexico, because it seems they were the most polished and civilized and were most tinctured with Mexican idolatry and superstitions. (For, although they believed in a Great Spirit, yet they adored the sun and moon. They had a temple dedicated to the sun, where they kept the eternal fire, guarded by a high priest and sacred virgins consecrated for the purpose. And though they did not offer human victims to the sun nor eat human flesh, yet they burnt and otherwise put to death captives taken in war. And though it does not appear that they put to death slaves or other persons at the demise of their princes, sovereigns, or *Suns,* yet slaves, concubines, or relatives offered themselves to death, in order to attend the souls of their sovereigns.) They had a complex system of legislation, their princes were hereditary, their sovereignty was absolute, and their power unlimited. The Natches might have arrived soon after the Spaniards had conquered the Mexican Empire and began to extend their conquests toward the north, for there is no mention of their bringing horses with them, these creatures not being yet so increased as to become wild in the country or so plentiful as to become an article of commerce between the wild Indians and Spaniards. (*Wild Indians* — such nations as were not conquered by the Old Mexicans and made tributary, which they call *Chich-*

macs, aborigines or barbarians.) For, according to Du Pratz, this empire had arrived at a prodigious latitude and strength some years before the French attempted to settle in their country, when it appeared to be greatly on the decline. It must have taken many years to have thus increased from a wretched fugitive band, supposing that they had been frightened away from their original country by the Spanish invasions and conquests.

It seems that the arrival of the Chickasaws and Creeks, as well as Choctaws, might have been about the time that the Spaniards, French, and English began their establishments in New England, Virginia, Carolina, and Florida, which I believe will appear to be about the period of the Spanish invasion, conquest, and establishment of power in New Mexico. The Choctaws, I believe, came the last, and in considerable force. According to the account of Du Pratz, derived from the Natches, they appeared suddenly, as if they rose out of the earth. The Creeks have much the same idea of their arrival — like the arrival and settling of a swarm of bees, as they expressed themselves on the subject. Yet it is certain that all these nations or bands, i.e., the Natches, Chickasaws, Muscogulges, and Choctaws, were derived from the same region; for they all speak dialects of the same language generally so near alike that they are able to converse with each other without the aid of interpreters. Thus we may conclude that their arrival in the country which they now possess was one after another, at so considerable a length of time intervening (perhaps a generation or two), each contending for empire and the honor and glory of their tribes, that they in part forgot or disregarded their ancient lineage and affinity.

III. Hieroglyphical Signs — Picture Records

Query. Have you observed among any of the tribes of Indians which you have visited any paintings superior in execution to those of the northern Indians, as we find them on trees and rocks? If you have, what did those paintings commonly represent? And among what tribes of Indians did you observe them? Are any of the Indian tribes very curious in preserving the memory of events by paintings? If such paintings are made use of by the Indians, do you know, or do you suppose, that they were acquainted with any signs or symbols to denote attributes or qualities of various kinds? Thus, how would these Indians convey an idea of courage or of cowardice, of good will or evil, etc.?

Answer. The paintings which I observed among the Creeks were commonly on the clay-plastered walls of their houses, particularly on the walls of the houses comprising the public square . . . or areopagus. They were, I think, hieroglyphics, or mystical writings, for the same use and purpose as those mentioned by historians to be found on the obelisks, pyramids, and other monuments of the ancient Egyptians, and much after the same style and taste, much caricatured and picturesque. Though I never saw an instance of the *chiaroscuro,* yet the outlines are bold, natural, and turned or designed to convey some meaning, passion, or admonition, and thus may be said to speak to those who can read them. The walls are plastered very smooth with red clay; then the figures or symbols are drawn with white clay, paste, or chalk; and if the walls are plastered with clay of whitish or stone color, then the figures are drawn with red, brown, or bluish chalk or paste.

Almost all kinds of animals, sometimes plants, flowers, trees, etc. are the subjects; figures of mankind in various attitudes, some very ludicrous and even obscene; even the privates of men sometimes represented, but never an instance of indelicacy in a female figure.

Men are often depicted having the head and other members of different kinds of animals as a wolf, buck, hare, horse, buffalo, snake, duck, turkey, tiger, cat, crocodile, etc., etc. All these animals are, on the other hand, depicted having the head and other members of different animals, so as to appear monstrous. (I am sensible that these specimens of their paintings will, to us, who have made such incomparable progress and refinement in the arts and sciences, appear trifling and ludicrous; but as you desire me to be particular and omit nothing, I hope to be excused.) Yet I think they are the wretched remains of something of greater use and consequence amongst their ancestors.

But the most beautiful painting now to be found amongst the Muscogulges is on the skin and bodies of their ancient chiefs and micos, which is of a bluish, lead, or indigo color. It is the breast, trunk, muscular or fleshy part of the arms and thighs, and sometimes almost every part of the surface of the body that is thus beautifully depicted or written over with hieroglyphics. Commonly the sun, moon, and planets occupy the breast; zones or belts or beautiful fanciful scrolls wind round the trunk of the body, thighs, arms, and legs, dividing the body into many fields or tablets, which are ornamented or filled up with innumerable figures, as representations of animals of the chase — a sketch of a landscape, representing an engagement or battle with their enemy, or some creature of the chase — and a thousand other fancies. These paintings are admirably well executed and seem to be inimitable. They are performed by exceedingly fine punctures and seem like *mezzotinto,* or very ingenious impressions from the engravings. They are no doubt hieroglyphics, or mystical writings or records of their tribes or families, or of memorable events, etc., etc.

When I was at Manchac on the Mississippi, at M'Gillvany's and Swanson's trading houses, I saw several buffalo hides with the wool on them. The flesh side of the skins was depicted and painted very beautifully; the performance was admirable — I may say inimitable by the most ingenious artists among Europeans, or people of the Old World, unless taught by the Indians. The painted hides were the work of the Illinois Indians near Fort Chartens, where the Company had trading houses and traders who purchased them from the Indians and sent them down here to go to Europe. I was asked six dollars apiece for them, which I thought cheap, considering their curiosity, but had no opportunity of conveying them home. The subjects or figures in the composition were much like those inscriptions or paintings on the bodies of the chiefs and warriors. Their borders were exceedingly pleasing: red, black, and blue were the colors, on a buff ground.

IV. COMPARATIVE RELIGIOUS ADVANCEMENT

Query. Which of the tribes of Indians visited by you are the most polished in their religion, in their manners, in their language, in their government, etc., etc.?

Answer. If adopting or imitating the manners and customs of the white people is to be termed civilization, perhaps the Cherokees have made the greatest advance.

But I presume, if we are to form and establish our judgments from the opinions and rules laid down by the greatest doctors of morality, philosophers, and divines, either of the ancients or moderns, the Muscogulges must have approbation, and engage our esteem.

Their religion is, perhaps, as pure as that which was in the beginning revealed to the first families of mankind. They have no notion or conception of any other God but the Great Spirit on high, the giver and taker away of the breath of life; which is as much as to say that eternal Supreme Being who created and governs the universe. They worship none else.

They pay a kind of homage to the sun, moon, and planets, as the mediators or ministers of the Great Spirit in dispensing His attributes for their comfort and well-being in this life. They have some religious rites and forms, which are managed by their priests or doctors, who make the people believe, by their cunning and craft, that they have a supernatural spiritual communication with invisible spirits of good or evil, and that they have the power of good and evil. They make the people believe that, by conjuring, they can bring rain, fine weather, heat, cooling breezes, thunder and lightning, bring on or expel and cure sickness, etc., etc.

VII. Physical Characteristics

Query. Which is the fairest and most comely tribe of the southern Indians? Are the Indian women generally fairer than the Indian men? Are the children born with the copper tinge or color? Or does this color first make its appearance some days after birth? We hear much in writers of white and spotted Indians, as at the Isthmus of Darien. Have you ever seen or heard of such white or spotted Indians among any of the tribes with which you are acquainted? If you have, some account of these phenomena will be very interesting to me.

Do you remember the names of any of the plants that the Indians which you have visited make use of in painting or staining their skins? Is the succoon (the *Sanguinaria canadensis* of Linnæus), one of the plants employed by the northern Indians as a pigment, found as far south as the countries of the Cherokees, Creeks, etc.?

Answer. The Cherokees are the largest race of men I ever saw. They are as comely as any, and their complexions are very bright, being of the olive cast of the Asiatics. This is the obvious reason which I suppose led the traders to give them the by-name of the Breeds, supposing them to be mixed with the white people. But, though some of them are evidently adulterated by the traders, yet the natural complexion is tawny.

The women are tall, slim, and of a graceful figure and have captivating features and manners, and I think their complexion is rather fairer than the men's.

The Muscogulges are in stature nearly equal to the Cherokees, have fine features, and are every way handsome men. Their noses are very often aquiline; they are well limbed, countenances upright, and their eyes brisk and fiery; but their complexions are of a dark-copper color.

Their women are very small, in appearance not more than half the size of the men, but they have regular and beautiful features, the eyes large, with high-arched eyebrows, and their complexions little, if any, brighter than those of the men.

There are some tribes in the confederacy which much resemble the Cherokees in stature and color, etc., viz., the Uches, Savannahs, and some of the Seminoles. I have seen Indian infants of a few weeks old. Their color was like that of a healthy male European countryman or laborer of middle age, though inclining a little more to the red or copper tinge; but they soon become of Indian copper. I believe this change comes naturally, as I never, from constant inquiry, could learn that the Indians had any artificial means of changing their color.

The Indians who have commerce with the whites make very little use of colors or paints of the native production of their country, since they have neglected their own manufactures for those supplied them cheaply and in abundance from Europe. I believe they are in general ignorant themselves of their own country's productions. The poccoon, or *Sanguinaria gallium,* bark of the *Acer rubrum, Toxicodendron radicans, Rhustruphydon,* and some other vegetable pigments are yet in use by the women, who still amuse themselves in manufacturing some few things as belts and coronets for their husbands, feather cloaks, moccasins, etc.

I have never heard of any white, speckled, or pied people among them.

It is reasonable to suppose that, anciently, when necessity obliged them, the Indians were more ingenious and industrious in manufactures than now. Therefore, we must seek for their arts and sciences among nations far distant from the settlements of the white people, or recover them by inquiry and experiment of our own.

There is one remarkable circumstance respecting the hair of the head of the Indians which I do not know to have been observed by travelers or historians. Besides the lankness, extraordinary natural length, and perhaps coarseness of the hair of the head, it is of a shining black or brown color, showing the same splendor and changeableness at different exposures to the light. The traders informed me that they preserved its perfect blackness and splendor by the use of the

red farinaceous or fursy covering of the berries of the common sumach (*Rhus glabrum*). At night they rub this red
powder in their hair, as much as it will contain, tying it up
close with a handkerchief till morning, when they carefully
comb it out and dress their hair with clear bear's oil.

But, notwithstanding this care and assiduity, it must at
last submit to old age, and I have seen the hair of the extreme
aged as white as cotton wool. I have observed quantities of
this red powder in their houses.

XI. DISEASES AND REMEDIES

Query. What appears to be the most common diseases
among the tribes of Indians with which you are acquainted?
What are their remedies for those diseases? Have you any
reason for believing that the venereal was known among the
north American Indians before the discovery of the continent by the Europeans? Is it a frequent or common disease
at present among the Indians? If so, do they appear to be
acquainted with any remedy or remedies for it? If any remedies,
what are they?

Answer. The Indians seem in general healthier than the
whites, have fewer diseases, and those they have not so acute
or contagious as those amongst us. The smallpox sometimes
visits them and is the most dreaded of all diseases.

Dysentery, pleurisy, intermittent fevers, epilepsy, and
asthma, they have at times.

The whooping cough is fatal among their children, and
worms very frequent. But (besides their well-known remedy,
Spigelia anthelmintica), to prevent the troublesome and
fatal effects of this disease they use a strong lixivium, prepared from ashes of bean stalks and other vegetables, in all

their food prepared from corn (Zea), which otherwise, they say, breeds worms in their stomachs.

They have the venereal disease amongst them in some of its stages; but by their continence, temperance, powerful remedies, skill in applying them, and care, it is a disease which may be said to be uncommon. In some towns it is scarcely known, and in none rises to that state of virulency which we call a pox, unless sometimes amongst the white traders, who themselves say, as well as the Indians, that it might be eradicated if the traders did not carry it with them to the nations when they return with their merchandise. These contract the disorder before they set off, and it generally becomes virulent by the time they arrive, when they apply to the Indian doctors to get cured.

However, I am inclined to believe that this infernal disease originated in America, from the variety of remedies found amongst the Indians, all of which are vegetable. I imagine that the disease is more prevalent, as well as more malignant, among the northern tribes.

The vegetables which I discovered to be used as remedies were generally powerful cathartics. Of this class are several species of the Iris, viz., Ir. versicolor, Ir. verna. And for the same purpose they have a high estimation of a species of either *Croton* or *Styllingia,* I am in doubt which; I think it is unknown to Europeans (Cr. decumbens); it is in great account in the medicines of Dr. Howard, of N. Carolina, in curing the yaws and is called the yaw weed. A great number of leaning, simple stems arise from a large perennial root; these stalks are furnished with lanceolate, entire leaves, both surfaces smooth. The stems terminate with spikes of male and female flowers. The latter are succeeded by trioecious seed vessels, each cell containing a single seed; the capsule, after excluding the seed, contracts and becomes of a triangular figure, much resembling a cocked hat, which has given that name to the plant, i.e., the "cock-up-hat." In autumn, before the stems decay, the leaves change to yellow, red, and crimson colors before they fall off.

I have been particular in the history of this plant, because it is known to possess very singular and powerful qualities. It is common on the light, dry, high lands of Carolina, Georgia, and Florida.

Several species of Smilax, the woody vines of Bignonia crucigera, some of the bays (Laurus) are of great account with the Indians as remedies.

But the Indians, in the cure of all complaints, depend most upon regimen and a rigid abstinence in respect to exciting drinks, as well as the gratification of other passions and appetites.

The Cherokees use the Lobelia syphilitica and another plant of still greater power and efficacy which the traders told me of but would not undertake to show it to me under twenty guineas' reward, for fear of the Indians, who endeavor to conceal the knowledge of it from the whites, lest its great virtues should excite their researches for it to its extirpation, etc.

The vines or climbing stems of the climber (Bignonia crucigera) are equally divided longitudinally into four parts by the same number of their membranes, somewhat resembling a piece of white tape, by which means, when the vine is cut through and divided transversely, it presents to view the likeness of a cross. This membrane is of a sweet, pleasant taste. The country people of Carolina chop these vines to pieces, together with china brier and sassafras roots, and boil them in their beer in spring, for diet drink, in order to attenuate and purify the blood and juices. It is a principal ingredient in Howard's famous infusion for curing the yaws, etc., the use and virtue of which he obtained from Indian doctors.

The caustic and detergent properties of the white nettle (roots) of Carolina and Florida (Jatropha urens), used for cleansing old ulcers and consuming proud flesh, and likewise the dissolvent and diuretant powers of the root of the Convolvulus panduratus, so much esteemed as a remedy in nephritic complaints, were discovered by the Indians to the inhabitants of Carolina (the white nettle roots are good and wholesome food when roasted and boiled; they are about the size of a large carrot when well grown, but few of them are allowed to become large, the swine are so fond of them).

I was informed by the people that, in order to prepare and administer both these remedies, they dig up the roots and divide and cut them into three pieces, in order for their more speedy drying in the shade, and then reduce them to powder, the former being plentifully spread over the ulcer, and the powder of the latter swallowed with any proper liquid vehicle. They are the most efficacious if used fresh as possible — I suppose losing their virtues by desiccation or being exposed to the air.

Through the emollient and discutient power of the swamp lily (Saururus cernuus) and the virtues of the Hypo or May apple (Podophyllum peltatum) — the root of which is the most effectual and safe emetic, and also cathartic and equally efficacious in expelling worms from the stomach — the lives of many thousands of the people of the southern States are preserved, both of children and adults. In these countries it is of infinitely more value than the Spanish Ipecacuanha. I speak not only from my own experience, having been relieved by it, but likewise from numberless instances where I have seen its almost infallible good effects. The roots are dug up in the autumn and winter and spread to dry in an airy loft, when they are occasionally reduced to powder by the usual trituration (for the roots will retain their efficacy when dried). Thirty grains of this fine-sieved powder is sufficient to operate on common constitutions, and half that quantity on children, but a weak dose is sufficient for a cathartic; either way it never fails to clear the stomach of worms.

In fine, I look upon this and the Saururus to be two as valuable medicines as any we know of, at least in the southern States. The virtues of both were communicated to the white inhabitants by the Indians.

Panax ginseng and Norida, or white root (or "bellyache root"), perhaps Angelica lucida. These roots are of the highest esteem among the Cherokees and Creeks; the virtues of the former are well known. Of the latter, its friendly carminative qualities are well known for relieving all the disorders of the stomach, a dry bellyache, and disorders of the intestine, colic, hysterics, etc. The patient chews the root and swallows the juice, or smokes it when dry with tobacco. Even the smell of the root is of good effect. The Lower Creeks, in whose country it does not grow, will gladly give two or three buckskins for a single root of it.

XII. Food and Means of Subsistence

Query. Does the food of the Indian appear to be principally animal or vegetable? What are the principal vegetables employed for food by them? What vegetables do they cultivate for food besides maize, different species of gourds, etc.? What are the principal vegetables of which they make their bread? Do you think the tribes you visited were acquainted with the use of salt before they became acquainted with the Europeans? If you think they were not, what substances did they employ as substitutes?

Answer. Their animal food consisted chiefly of venison, bear's flesh, turkeys, hares, wild fowl, and domestic poultry; and also of domestic kine, as beeves, goats, and swine — never horse's flesh, though they have horses in great plenty — neither do they eat the flesh of dogs, cats, or any such creatures as are usually rejected by white people.

Their vegetable food consists chiefly of corn (Zea), rice, Convolvulus batatas, or those nourishing roots usually called sweet or Spanish potatoes (but in the Creek confederacy they never plant or eat the Irish potato). All the species of the Phaseolus and Dolichos in use among the whites are cultivated by the Creeks, Cherokees, etc. and make up a great part of their food. All the species of Cucurbita, squashes, pumpkins, watermelons, etc.; but of the cucumeres, they cultivate none of the species as yet, neither do they cultivate our farinaceous grains, as wheat, barley, spelts, rye, buckwheat, etc. (not having got the use of the plough amongst them, though it has been introduced some years ago). The chiefs rejected it, alleging it would starve their old people who employed themselves in planting and selling their produce to traders, for their support and maintenance; seeing that by permitting the traders to use the plough, one or two persons could easily raise more grain than all the old people of the town could do by using the hoe. Turnips, parsnips, salads, etc., they have no knowledge of. Rice (Oryza) they plant in hills on high, dry ground, in their gardens; by this management a few grains in a hill (the hills about four feet apart) spread every way incredibly and seem more prolific than cultivated in water, as in the white settlements of Carolina; the heads or panicles are larger and heavier, and the grain is larger, firmer, or more farinaceous, much sweeter, and more nourishing. Each family raises enough of this excellent grain for its own use.

But, besides the cultivated fruits above recited, with peaches, oranges, plums (Chickasaw plums), figs, and some apples, they have in use a vast variety of wild or native vegetables, both fruit and roots, viz., Diospyros, Morus rubra, Gleditsia, Multiloba, S. triacanthus; all the species of Juglans and acorns, from which they extract a very sweet oil which enters into all their cooking, and several species of *palms,* which furnish them with a great variety of agreeable and nourishing food. Grapes, too, they have in great variety and abundance, which they feed on occasionally when ripe. They also prepare them for keeping and lay up for winter and spring time. A species of Smilax (S. pseudochina) affords a delicious and nourishing food, which is prepared from its vast, tuberous roots.

They dig up these roots and, while yet fresh and full of juice, chop them in pieces and then macerate them well in wooden mortars. This substance they put in vessels nearly filled with clean water, when, being well mixed with paddles, whilst the fine particles are yet floating in the liquid, they decant it off into other vessels, leaving the farinaceous material at the bottom; this, being taken out and dried, is an impalpable powder of farina, of reddish color. This, when mixed with boiling water, becomes a beautiful jelly which, when sweetened with honey or sugar, affords a most nourishing food for children and aged people; or when mixed with fine corn flour and fried in fresh bear's grease, makes excellent fritters.

I conclude these articles with mentioning a vegetable which I had but a slight opportunity of observing just as I left the Creek country, on the waters of the Mobile River. It is a species of Palma. It has no stalk or stem above ground; the leaves spread regularly all round, are flabelliform when fully expanded, otherwise cucullated, their slips very short, scarcely appearing at a slight view; in the center is produced a kind of dense panicle or general receptacle of the fruit, of the size of a sugar loaf. There is a vast collection of plums, or drupes of the size and figure of ordinary plums, which are covered with a fibrous, farinaceous, pulpy coating of considerable thickness; this substance, which, to the best of my remembrance, resembles manna in texture, color, and taste, is of the consistency of coarse brown sugar. It is a delicious and nourishing food and diligently sought after. There were several of these clusters brought into the Ottassee town just before I left, of which I ate freely with the Indians, and think in substance and taste it is the most of anything like manna; it is a little bitterish and stinging on the palate, at first using it, but soon becomes familiar and desirable.

I own I am not able to give an accurate botanical account of this very curious and valuable vegetable, because it was disclosed to my observation just on my departure; and although I saw several plants on the road, yet being obliged to follow the mad career of a man traveling with pack horses, I left the country of its native growth before I had an opportunity or leisure to examine it — an omission which I have severely regretted. I am convinced it is an object of itself worth a journey to those regions to examine.[4]

18. William Bartram's Letters

George Edwards to William Bartram, 1761

Dear Sir:

It being upwards of two years since I had the pleasure of a letter from you, I was willing to trouble you with a few lines, in order to be informed whether or not you have received a parcel directed to you from me. It was that latter part of my works, called *Gleanings,* containing 100 colored prints, with their descriptions in French and English. The book was very finely bound and gilt. It was papered up and delivered to our good friend Mr. P. Collinson in the month of January, *anno* 1760, in order to be sent with shop goods from him to Pennsylvania. It was directed to you not only in the paper in which it was packed but also withinside of the book; I think it was on the back of the title page. I understood, by Mr. Collinson, that the ship in which it was sent arrived safe, but he could not tell me whether you had received the book or not. If you have not received it, it must have been secreted by some person who had no right to it. If you have seen or heard of a book answering the above description, it is certainly of right your property.

I should be very sorry to think it is not come to your hands. I shall be glad to hear of you and your father by packet or any other convenient means, the first opportunity; and if I find you have not received the book in question, I will, by such means as you shall direct, convey to you another copy of the same book in black prints, for if the first miscarried, I cannot afford another neatly colored, as the first was.

These books contain all the small birds you were so good to send me two or three years ago.

Pray my kind respects to your father and all friends, and accept the same for yourself, from

Your obliged friend and servant,

George Edwards

College of Physicians, Warwick Lane,
London, November 15, 1761

(*History of Birds,* 4 volumes, 1743, 1747, 1750, 1751; *Gleanings of Natural History,* 1758, 1760, 1764, containing 600 subjects on Natural History never before delineated.)[1]

William Bartram to Thomas Jefferson

Sir:

I have taken the liberty to cover a Letter for your Excell'y from Mr. Alexander Wilson, accompanying a fine and accurate drawing of two rare birds which he lately procured when on a tour through the northeastern parts of the State of New York to view the Cataract of Niagara. Mr. Wilson showed me the birds well preserved. The Jay seems to differ from Mr. Pennant's Corvus cinereus, Arct. Zool. And the Butcher Bird, Lanius excubitor linn. Mr. Wilson, excited by motives of benevolence from a high opinion of your personal and public character, requests me to convey to you his offering as a testimony of his esteem and affection.

Some time past your worthy friend Doct. Barton, soon after his return home from Virginia, informed us that it was your wish to have the horns of the Stone-buck (Capra gervicapra?). I am directed by my brother to assure you that you are perfectly welcome to them, and should have sent them but, living so remote from Philadelphia, have not yet found a safe mode of conveyance.

We have a horn of a species of Cervus from the coast of Hudson's Bay brought and presented to my father by Capt. Swain, who many years since made a voyage thither when on a discovery of the northwestern passage across our continent. Tho' this horn appears to have belonged to an adult, it is singularly small and light and must have shaded the brow of a very small animal. I beg leave to repeat that you are welcome to both these specimens, and wish for an opportunity of safe conveyance.

I sincerely write with my friend W. and every true American in congratulations for your reelection to the Presidency of the U. States.

And wishing You a long and happy Life, by leave to subscribe

> Your Excellency's
> Sincere Friend
> William Bartram

Kingsess. near Philadelphia
March 18th, 1805

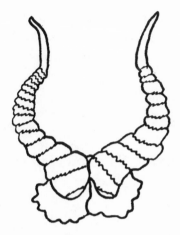

No. 1. Horns of The Antelope as they stood upon a part of the frontal bone of the cranium when we received them but have since parted from each other and may be reunited. They were mutilated when we received them, in the manner they now appear. One horn is yet entire and perfect in figure.

No. 2. The other is a single horn of a species of Cervus from Ter de Labrador or Hudson's Bay. They are small and remarkable in being so flat and thin. This horn is also mutilated, the rats having eat off the points of the antler.

We have added a few other articles to fill the box.

No. 3. Appears to be a species of Chama petrified. It was found in Lower Jersey many feet under the surface of the earth in a heterogeneous stratum of sea shells of various genera and species* combined and cemented into vast, ponderous masses with other recrements of the ocean, together with Aluminous vitriolic and *Ferruginous concrete*.

* Of the great variety of sea shells and other testaceous vermi composing these masses, few appeared to be of the same sorts now found on our seacoast, and don't exist unless in so great depth of water as to elude our researches.

4. *Phytolithus ligni,* a piece of petrified wood said to be holly, found on the banks of Cape Fear River, where I have seen large trees in this state of transmutation.

5. Zoophyla corallina.

William Bartram to Thomas Jefferson

Dear Sir:

At a time when the great and important affairs of the Nation requires so much of your time, I must entreat your Excellency's pardon for this intrusion in covering a letter to you from my friend A. Wilson, the gentleman who formerly communicated to you some drawings of nondescript Canadian birds, which he met with when on a pedestrian journey to view the Cataract of Niagara.

Understanding, Sir, that it is your intention to send abroad parties of ingenious men for the purpose of exploring the regions of Louisiana lying on the Mississippi and its extensive branches and investigating its Natural History, Mr. Wilson having expressed to me his wishes and ardent desire of being employed on that service, I thought it might be pleasing to you to recommend to your notice a character that might be serviceable in this splendid enterprise. Mr. Wilson is in my opinion as well qualified for the department of drawing and painting in Natural History as any person we have. He likewise possesses the art of making preparations in subjects of the productions of Nature in Zoology, Ornithology, etc. Mr. Wilson is a man possessing very liberal scientific acquirements, writes well, of irreproachable moral character, active & indefatigable, a decided and firm republican, agreeable to the genuine principles of the legislative system of the United States.

Sir, duty as well as gratitude impels me to offer to your Excell'y my most sincere thanks and acknowledgments for the distinguished honor and favor extended to me when you were pleased to select me as a suitable person for the department of Nat. History in the voyage up the Red River. The scene was most flattering. But with the utmost regret I was constrained to decline it on account of my advanced age and consequent infirmities (being towards 70 years of age) and my eyesight declining daily. This very flattering mark of your goodness and regard for me has made a deep impression on my mind, and will not be effaced from a heart most sincerely attached.

To

Your Excellency, devoted to your Service

and

Praying for your health and happy long life

William Bartram

Kingsess. Febry. 6th, 1806

William Bartram to Thomas Jefferson

Illustrious President:

Permit me, Sir, to introduce to your notice the bearer hereof, my worthy friend Doctor Benjamin Say; lately chosen Senator in Congress of the U. States, for the City and County of Philadelphia in place of Mr. Clay resigned.

The Doctor is a man of talents, eminent in his profession as a physician, of a fair moral character, and a warm and steady republican, ever since our glorious revolution.

Doctor Say will hand Your Excellency a small packet containing a few seeds of a beautiful flowering tree, together with a catalogue of our collection. The tree is the Mimosa julibruscens (Silk tree), a native of Persia and Armenia; lately brought to us by the celebrated Michaux the elder. The delicate sweet flowers grow in fasciles composed of a number of slender silky threads tipped with crimson anthers. The packet is tied with a silky bark of a species of Asclepias (*Milkweed*), native of Pennsylvania, which should it prove a useful substitute for flax or cotton in linen manufacture, it can be cultivated in any quantities and with less expense, as it is a perennial plant and thrives in almost any soil.

I send you these articles, Sir, as a mark of my homage and respect, not knowing whether they are new to you or of any value.

With every sentiment of esteem,

I pray you may enjoy many days of health and tranquility.

William Bartram[2]

His Excellency
Thomas Jefferson

Kingsess. near Philadelphia
October 29th, 1808

From Thomas Jefferson to William Bartram

Washington, November 23, 1808

Thomas Jefferson presents his compliments to his friend, Mr. William Bartram, and his thanks for the seeds of the Silk tree, which he was so kind as to send him. These he shall plant, in March, and cherish with care, at Monticello. The care of the garden, and culture of curious plants, uniting beauty or utility, will there form one of his principal amusements. He has been prevented, by an indisposition of some days, from having the pleasure of seeing Dr. Say, except on his first visit. An esteem of his character, of very early date, as well as a respect for Mr. Bartram's friendships, will insure to Dr. Say the manifestation of every respect he can show.

He salutes Mr. Bartram with friendship and respect.[3]

From Alexander Wilson to William Bartram

Union School, Dec. 24, 1804

My dear friend:

I have perused Dr. Barton's publication, and return it with many thanks for the agreeable and unexpected treat it has afforded me. The description of the falls of Niagara is, in some places, a just delineation of that stupendous cataract. But many interesting particulars are omitted; and much of the writer's reasoning on the improbability of the *wearing away* of the precipice and consequent recession of the falls seems contradicted by every appearance there; and many other assertions are incorrect. Yet, on such a subject, everything, however trifling, seems to attract attention: the reader's imagination supplying him with scenery in abundance, even amidst the feebleness and barrenness of the meanest writer's description.

After this article, I was most agreeably amused with "Anecdotes of an American Crow," written in such a pleasing style of playful humor as I have seldom seen surpassed; and forming a perfect antidote against the spleen; abounding, at the same time, with observations and reflections not unworthy of a philosopher.

The sketch of your father's life, with the extracts from his letters, I read with much pleasure. They will remain lasting monuments of the worth and respectability of the father, as well as of the filial affection of the son.

Alexander Wilson

From Alexander Wilson to William Bartram

Philadelphia, April 29, 1807

My dear sir:

The receipt of yours of the 11th inst., in which you approve of my intended publication of *American Ornithology,* gave me much satisfaction; and your promise of befriending me in the arduous attempt commands my unfeigned gratitude. From the opportunities I have lately had, of examining into the works of Americans who have treated of this part of our natural history, I am satisfied that none of them have bestowed such minute attention on the subject as you yourself have done. Indeed they have done little more than copied your nomenclature and observations and referred to your authority. To have you, therefore, to consult with in the course of this great publication, I consider a most happy and even auspicious circumstance; and I hope you will, on all occasions, be a rigid censor and kind monitor, whenever you find me deviating from the beauties of nature, or the truth of description. . . .

I hope you are in good health, enjoying in your little Paradise the advances of spring, shedding leaves, buds and blossoms, around her; and bringing in her train choirs of the sweetest songsters that earth can boast of; while every zephyr that plays around you breathes fragrance. Ah! how different my situation is, this delightful season, immured among dusty books and compelled to forego the harmony of the woods for the everlasting din of the city; the very face of the blessed heavens involved in soot and interrupted by walls and chimney tops. But if I don't launch out into the woods and fields oftener than I have done these twelvemonths, may I be transformed into a street musician. . . . [The remainder of the manuscript defaced. Ed.]

Alexander Wilson[4]

THE ROUTE OF WILLIAM BARTRAM'S TRAIL, ACCORDING TO THE *TRAVELS*

This trail does not always coincide with information given in his journal. While certain sections of his journey are still obscure, the general outline of it may be followed with some exactness by present-day travelers in the south. Many of the Georgia and Florida places visited by William on this trip were visited first by him on the journey with John in 1765-1766. In every instance except one, William went farther alone than with his father. Only on St. John's River did they reach an extreme point together, for they went up that river somewhat beyond Lake Harney, having first explored Lake Jessup. They were the first Europeans known to have visited these two lakes.

1773. Sailed from Philadelphia to Charleston.

Reembarked for Savannah, proceeded overland to Sunbury.

Visited St. Catherine's Island (perhaps he meant Colonel's Island, which is much closer to Sunbury).

Attended Midway meeting.

Followed the high road toward Fort Barrington but turned off on the Darien road.

Encountered the swamps of Newport and Sapello rivers, crossing the latter river near the present town of Eulonia.

Followed the northeast side of the Altamaha River to Fort Barrington and crossed on a ferry near that fort.

Followed the "high road" to St. Ille (Satilla) River ferry near the present site of Owen's Ferry.

Continued to St. Mary's River, then returned to Savannah.

Set off for Augusta, Georgia, following the course of the Savannah River.

Joined a surveying party, going from Augusta to Wrightsborough in the northwest part of McDuffie Co.

Arrived at Buffalo Lick, a short distance southeast of Philomath.

Continued along the Great Ridge northward to Cherokee Corner, about nine miles southeast of Athens.

Turned east to the confluence of the Tugaloo and Seneca rivers. Returned to Augusta and Savannah, following the Savannah River.

From Savannah, explored Broughton Island (at the mouth of the Altamaha), bought a canoe there, and went up the river some fifty miles beyond the last settlement.

Returned to Broughton Island and Savannah.

March 1774.

Went overland from Savannah to the Altamaha, descended the river to Broughton Island, followed the south channel to St. Simon's Island (off Brunswick), and visited the settlement and Fort Frederica.

Boarded ship and sailed by Jekyl and Cumberland Islands. Was put ashore on Little St. Simon's Island after receiving news of Indian uprising in Florida, which caused the boat to return to its port.

Walked the beach to point opposite Amelia Island, was taken across by the captain of the fort.

A plantation owner took him by boat through Amelia Narrows to St. John's and up that river to Cowford (Jacksonville), a three-day journey.

Sailed up the river in a small boat to Fort Picolata (Picolata) and on to Charlotia, on the east bank of the river a short distance south of East Palatka, and to Spalding's Lower Store, on the west side of the river about six miles south of Palatka.

Sailed by Mount Hope at Beecher Point, a mile south of Welaka, and Mount Royal on the east side of the river, slightly less than a mile west of Fruitland.

Visited Drayton Island, which almost blocks the exit of Lake George.

Arrived at Spalding's Upper store near the present site of Astor.

From Spalding's Upper Store, sailed on up the St. John's past Battle Lagoon (near the entrance of the river into Lake Dexter) to Lake Beresford and Beresford Plantation on its banks. From that plantation, visited a vast fountain (Blue Springs, west of Orange City), New Smyrna, and Mosquito Lagoon.

Returned to Spalding's Lower Store, detouring up the creek to Six Mile Springs (Salt Springs) as he sailed through Lake George.

Joined a trading company going to the Alachua Savannah (Payne's Prairie, south of Gainesville) and the Indian town of Cuscowilla, located on Tuscowilla Lake just east of Micanopy.

Returned to the Lower Store, following for part of the way the Old Spanish trail that led from St. Mark's to St. Augustine, already grown up in many places with shrubs and trees.

Joined a trading company going to the Little San Juan (Suwannee River).

Followed trail toward Cuscowilla to within a few miles of that town, then took lower trading path, which was the Old Spanish highway to St. Mark's and Pensacola.

Arrived at Talahasochte on the Suwannee, probably on the present site of New Clay Landing on the east bank, a short distance upriver from Manatee Springs (now a State Park).

The traders camped at Long Pond near Chiefland.

Bartram visited the Alligator Hole, which is thought to be Blue Sink near Newberry.

Returned to Spalding's Lower Store.

Again journeyed up the St. John's, pausing at Mount Royal, to the Upper Store.

Returned downriver, embarked at Lower Store for Frederica, Georgia, embarked again, paused at Sunbury, and arrived in Charleston, probably in 1775.

From Charleston to Jacksonburg (Jacksonboro) on the Ponpon

(Edisto) River. Crossed the Savannah into Georgia at Three Sisters' Ferry (almost directly west from Ridgeland), then turned toward Augusta, following the river. Recrossed the river at Silver Bluff to visit Fort Moore on the Carolina shore (12 miles south of Augusta, now engulfed by river).

Returned to Georgia shore and continued to Augusta.

Proceeded to confluence of Broad and Savannah rivers, where Fort James Dartmouth lay on the thin point of land abut a mile from their junction.

Set off toward Fort Prince George, Keowe, above Clemson on the Keowe River (fort built about 1755).

From Keowe, followed Oconee Creek to its head, climbed Oconee Mountain, crossed the Chattooga River, followed War Woman Creek up its narrow, rugged valley, passed Rabun Gap and Estatoah Falls, then followed the Little Tennessee River to Cowe. The site of Cowe beyond West's Mill is indicated by a historic marker.

Started for the "Overhill towns" on the west side of the Jore (Nantahala) Mountains, crossing Jore Mountain (Wesser Bald) to the Nantahala River, then returned to Cowe, Fort Prince George, and Fort James Dartmouth.

From Dartmouth to Fort Charlotte on the Carolina side of the river a mile below Dartmouth, where traders assembled for the Creek Nations.

Camped at Flat Rock, probably beside one of the branches of Brier Creek, between Dearing and Warren.

Followed the Lower Creek Trading Path and Old Horse Trail, pausing at the Ocmulgee Fields (now in the Ocmulgee National Monument), just east of Macon, and arrived at Uche Town in July 1777. Uche lay on the west bank of the Chattahoochee near the north base of the bulge formed by that river as it pushes most deeply into Georgia south of Columbus. Apalachucla was a little south of Uche Town, while Coweta lay north of it, about two and a half miles northeast of Fort Mitchell.

Leaving Apalachucla, followed the Great Trail to the Tallapoosa River, where Bartram visited towns in the general locality of Tallassee, followed the east bank of the Tallapoosa to Coolome, on the south bank of the river about twelve miles east of Montgomery, continued through the present town of Snowdoun, across Route 31, close to Fort Deposit. The trail followed the county line between Conecuh and Monroe, then branched at Burnt Corn Springs. Crossed Little River at Mount Pleasant, going on to the Tensaw River, and somewhere near Stockton he boarded a boat for Mobile.

From Mobile, made some trips up the Tombigbee and Perdido rivers, one to Pensacola, where he went a short distance up the Shambe (Escambe) River.

Embarked for the Mississippi, sailing by Dauphin Island and to the Pearl River. Illness detained him for some time on Pearl Island, then he sailed across Lake Pontchartrain into Lake Maurpas, up the Amite to the Iberville. Ascended the Iberville for a short distance, then disembarked and went overland for about nine miles to Manchac on the Mississippi. (The Iberville River is sometimes called Manchac Bayou.)

From Manchac, went up the Mississippi to Baton Rouge, continued on to Point Coupé (formed when a new river bed was cut at False River in 1722) and the white cliffs of Natchez.

SOURCES OF QUOTATIONS

Chapter 1. Son William Reports on the Life of His Father

1. "Some Account of the Late Mr. John Bartram of Pennsylvania," by William Bartram. *Philadelphia Medical and Physical Journal*, Part I, Vol. 2, 1804.

Chapter 2. John Bartram's Report of a Trip Taken in 1743

1. *Observations on the Inhabitants, Climate, Soil, Rivers, Productions, Animals, and Other Matters Worthy of Notice, Made by Mr. John Bartram, in His Travels from Pensilvania to Onondago, Oswego and the Lake Ontario, in Canada.* To which is annexed a Curious Account of the Cataracts of Niagara, by Mr. Peter Kalm, a Swedish Gentleman Who Travelled There. London: Printed for J. Whiston and B. White, in Fleet-Street, 1751.

Chapter 3. John Bartram's Introduction to Short's Medicina Britannica

1. *Medicina Britannica*, by Dr. Thomas Short, with an Introduction by Mr. John Bartram. Philadelphia: Benjamin Franklin and D. Hall, 1751.

Chapter 4. John Bartram Reports on His Trip to St. John's River, Florida, 1765

1. *Memorials of John Bartram and Humphry Marshall*, by William Darlington. Philadelphia: Lindsay & Blakiston, 1849.
2. *An Account of East Florida, with a Journal Kept by John Bartram, of Philadelphia, Botanist to His Majesty for the Floridas; upon a Journey from St. Augustine up the River St. John's, as Far as the Lakes. With Explanatory Botanical Notes*, by William Stork. London, 1767.

Chapter 5. John Bartram Corresponds with Benjamin Franklin and Other Famous People

1. Original manuscript, Historical Society of Pennsylvania.
2. *Memorials of John Bartram and Humphry Marshall.*
3. Original manuscript, Historical Society of Pennsylvania.
4. *Memorials of John Bartram and Humphry Marshall.*

5. Original manuscript, Historical Society of Pennsylvania.
6. Original manuscript, which hangs on the wall of the Bartram house and near the Franklin stove. The stove was a gift from the inventor to John Bartram.

Chapter 6. *John and William Bartram Discover and Record Some Wonders of the New Continent*

1. *Diary of a Journey Through the Carolinas, Georgia, and Florida from July 1, 1765, to April 10, 1766,* by John Bartram. 1765-1766, Historical Society of Pennsylvania.
2. *Travels Through North & South Carolina, Georgia, East & West Florida, the Cherokee Country, the Extensive Territories of the Muscogulges, or Creek Confederacy, and the Country of the Chactaws; Containing an Account of the Soil and Natural Productions of Those Regions, Together with Observations on the Manners of the Indians,* by William Bartram. Philadelphia, 1791.
3. *Journal of the Travels,* by William Bartram. Field notes written for Dr. John Fothergill, of London. Manuscript in the British Museum (Natural History); photostats of the manuscript in the Historical Society of Pennsylvania.
4. *Travels,* by William Bartram.
5. *Diary of 1765-1766,* by John Bartram.
6. *Travels,* by William Bartram.

Chapter 7. *William Bartram Explores from Charleston, South Carolina, to Augusta, Florida, 1774*

1. Original manuscript, Historical Society of Pennsylvania.
2. *Travels,* by William Bartram.

Chapter 8. *A Journey from Fort Prince George to the Valley of the Little Tennessee River, and the Great Trail Across Alabama*

1. *Travels,* by William Bartram.

Chapter 9. *The Mississippi River Region in William Bartram's Day: August 1777*

1. *Travels,* by William Bartram.

Chapter 10. *Frontier Types in the 18th Century*

1. *Travels,* by William Bartram.

Chapter 11. *Camping Along the Trail*

1. *Travels,* by William Bartram.

Chapter 12. *Earthquakes, Hurricane, Crystal Springs, and Flood*

1. Letter by John Bartram, dated July 18, 1750. Published in *Philadelphia Medical and Physical Journal*, Part I, Vol. 1, 1804.
2. *Journal,* by William Bartram.
3. *Travels,* by William Bartram.

Chapter 13. A Terrifying Battle with Alligators, and Reports on Other Reptiles

1. *Travels*, by William Bartram.

Chapter 14. Fish and Their Enemies

1. *Travels*, by William Bartram.

Chapter 15. The Ways of Insects and Spiders

1. John Bartram in *Philadelphia Medical and Physical Journal*, Part I, Vol. 1, 1804.
2. *Diary of 1765-1766*, by John Bartram.
3. *Travels*, by William Bartram.
4. *Journal*, by William Bartram.
5. *Travels*, by William Bartram.

Chapter 16. William Bartram as an Ornithologist

1. *Journal*, by William Bartram.
2. *Travels*, by William Bartram.
3. *Journal*, by William Bartram.
4. *Travels*, by William Bartram.
5. *Journal*, by William Bartram.
6. *Travels*, by William Bartram.
7. "Description of an American Species of Certhia," by William Bartram, in *Philadelphia Medical and Physical Journal*, Part II, Vol. II, 1804.
8. By Witmer Stone, in *The Auk*, Vol. xxv, No. 3, July 1913.
9. *Philadelphia Medical and Physical Journal*, Part II, Vol. 1, 1804.

Chapter 17. Indian Ruins and Indians of William Bartram's Day

1. *Travels*, by William Bartram.
2. *Journal*, by William Bartram.
3. *Travels*, by William Bartram.
4. *Transactions of the American Ethnological Society*, Vol. III, Part 1. New York: George P. Putnam, 1900.

Chapter 18. William Bartram's Letters

1. Original manuscript, Historical Society of Pennsylvania.
2. Jefferson Papers, Library of Congress.
3. *Memorials of John Bartram and Humphry Marshall*.
4. *American Ornithology*, by Alexander Wilson, Vol. IX. Philadelphia: Bradford and Inskeep, 1828.

GLOSSARY

Abies: probably Hemlock, *Tsuga canadensis.*
Abutilons: Indian mallow.
Acacia: Locust.
Acer negundo: Ash-leaved maple.
———— rubrum: Red, swamp or scarlet maple.
———— saccharum: Silver maple.
———— striatum: Striped maple.
Aconite: Monkshood.
Aconite, blue: Clambering monkshood, *Aconitum uncinatum.*
Adam's needle: *Yucca gloriosa.*
Aesculus: Buckeye.
———— alba: unknown.
———— florida: unknown.
———— pavia: Red or Little buckeye.
———— sylvatica: unknown.
Agave: probably rattlesnake-master, *Manfreda virginica.*
Alachua Savannah: *Payne's Prairie,* south of Gainesville, Florida.
Alligator Hole: Probably *Blue Sink,* about a mile north of New-
    berry, Florida.
Alnus: Alder.
Altamaha River: Georgia.
Althea: Loblolly bay, *Gordonia lasianthus.*
Amaryllis atamasco: Atamasco lily, *Zephyranthea atamasco.*
Amelia Island: off the northeast coast of Florida.
Andromeda: a group in the Heath Family.
———— arborea: Sour wood, *Oxydendrum arboreum.*
———— axillaria: Downy leucothoe, *Leucothoe axillaris.*

Andromeda calyculata: Leather leaf, *Chamaedaphne calyculata.*
——— nitida: Fetterbush, *Neopieris nitida.*
Anemone hepatica: Round-lobed liver-leaf, *Hepatica hepatica.*
——— thalictroides: Rue anemone, *Syndesmon thalictroides.*
Anhinga: Snake-bird, *Anhinga anhinga.*
Annona (Anona): *Annonaceae family.*
——— glabra: Pond apple or custard apple.
——— pigmaea: Probably pawpaw, *Asimina triloba.*
Apalache Bay: *Apalachicola Bay,* Florida.
Apalachucla: Indian town on the Chattahoochee River.
Arethusa: Dragon's-mouth or wild pink, *Arethusa bulbosa.*
Aristolochia frutescens: Snakeroot.
Arundo gigantea: tall perennial grasses.
Augusta, Georgia.
Azalea: a group in the Heath family.
——— coccinea: perhaps Pinkster-flower, *Azalea nudiflora.*
——— flammula: Flame azalea, probably *Azalea lutea.*

Barilla: Sedge.
Barrington, Fort: on the Altamaha River, about four miles north-
    west of Cox, Georgia.
Bartsia: Indian paintbrush, *Castilleja coccinea.*
Batatas (Ipomoea batatas): *Sweet potatoes.*
Baton Rouge, Louisiana.
Bay of Calos: probably off the mouth of the Caloosahatchee River,
    Florida.
Belle Isle: now Hog Island, northwest of Drayton's Island, at the
    north end of Lake George, Florida.
Beresford, Lake: Part of St. John's River. It lies northwest of
    Orange City, Florida.
Betula nigra: Red or River birch.
Bignonia: Bartram often used this term for any trumpet-shaped
    flower.
——— crucigera: Trumpet flower.
——— radicans: Cow-itch, *Tecoma radicans.*
——— sempervirens: Yellow jessamine, *Gelsemium sempervirens.*
Bitterns, little white: probably snowy egrets, *Leucophoyx thula.*

Blackbirds: probably Florida grackles, *Quiscalus quiscula.*

Borgone, Lake: *Borgne Lake,* on the coast of Louisiana.

Bream: fish in the bass family.

————, Great yellow: Warmouth, *Chaenobryttus coronarius.*

Broughton Island, Georgia: off the mouth of the Altamaha River.

Buffalo Lick: southeast of Philomath, Georgia.

Butcher bird: Loggerhead shrike, *Lanius ludovicianus.*

Cactus opuntia: Prickly-pear cactus.

Callicanthus floridus: Sweet shrub, *Calycanthus floridus.*

Callicarpa: French or Bermuda mulberry, *Callicarpa americana.*

Calycanthus: Strawberry or Sweet shrub (see Callicanthus).

Carica papaya: Indian papaya.

———— betula: probably American hornbeam, *Carpinus caroliniana.*

———— ostrya: Hop hornbeam, *Ostrya virginiana.*

Carophyllus: Pink family, *Carophyllaceae.*

Carpinus: Hornbeam.

Cassine: Dahoon holly, *Ilex cassine.*

———— yaupon: probably Cassena, *Ilex vomitoria.*

Castania: Chinquapin, *Castanea ashei* (unknown).

Catalpa: *Catalpa bignonoides.*

Catesby, Mark: author and artist (British), probably the outstanding naturalist to precede the Bartrams in America.

Cedar or Crownbird: Cedar waxwing, *Bombycilla cedrorum.*

Celtis: Hackberry or sugarberry.

Cephalanthus: Buttonbush.

Cercis: Red-bud or Judas-tree.

Certhia: Brown creeper, *Certhia familiaris.*

Chamaerops: low fan palm (a name applied to a Mediterranean species).

Chestnut: *Fagus castanea.*

China brier: Smilax.

Chionanthus: Fringe tree, *Chionanthus virginica.*

Citra: Melons, squash, etc.

Citruls: Melons, *citrullus.*

Citrus: Oranges, etc.

Citrus aurantium: Sweet orange.

Clethra: Sweet pepperbush, *Clethra alnifolia*.

Clitoria: Butterfly pea.

Cochineal: Cochineal insect, *coccinella*.

Cocos nucifera: Cocoa palm or coconut.

Collinson, Peter: English friend and correspondent of the Bartrams'.

Collinsonia: Horse balm.

Conde, Fort: at Mobile, Alabama.

Conti (contee): Red flour made by the Indians from roots of certain species of smilax.

Convalaria majalis: Lily-of-the-valley.

Convolvulus: Bindweed family.

———— batata: Sweet potato, *Ipomea batatas*.

Coolome: Creek Indian town on the Tallapoosa River, Alabama.

Coot: *Fulica americana*.

Cornus: Dogwood.

———— florida: Flowering dogwood.

Corymbus jacobea: see Senecio jacobea.

Corypha: Palms are now *Arecaceae*.

Coupé, Point: on the Mississippi River, about 30.32 degrees, as shown on Ross's 1775 map of the area.

Cowe: Cherokee town on the Little Tennessee, below Wests Mill, North Carolina.

Coweta: Creek or Muscogulge town on the Alabama shore of the Chattahoochee River, south of Columbus, Georgia.

Cowford: Now *Jacksonville*, Florida.

Crane, savannah: Sandhill crane, Grus canadensis (Bartram also called this species "whooping crane").

Crinum: White lily, Crinum, *Crinum americanum*.

Crocodile: Bartram never went far enough south to reach the range of this species, but he used the name interchangeably with that of alligator.

Croton: a group in the Spurge family.

Crow, carrion: Black vulture.

Crying bird (Ephouskyca): Limpkin, *Aramus guarauna*.

Cucumber tree: Magnolia acuminata (*M. macrophylla* and *M. tripetala* are also called Cucumber tree).

Cucurbita: gourds, pumpkins, melons.

Cumberland Island: southernmost coastal island of Georgia.

Cupressus disticha: Bald cypress, *Taxidium distichum.*

———— thyoides: White cedar, *Chamaecyparis thyoides.*

Curlew: Whenever Bartram used the term "curlew," he probably referred to an ibis rather than a shorebird, except on St. Simon Island, when he may have meant a species of *Numenius.*

Curlew, Spanish: White ibis, *Guara alba,* particularly in the immature plumage, are often called Spanish Curlew today.

Cuscowilla: capital town on the Alachua Savannah.

Cypripedium: Lady slipper or moccasin flower.

Cyrilla racemiflora: Southern leatherwood or ironwood.

Darien (Darian), Georgia: near the mouth of the Altamaha River.

Deer (Buck, Roebuck): White-tailed deer, *Odoccileus virginianus.*

Delaware Capes: *Cape Henlopen,* Delaware, and *Cape May,* New Jersey.

Dionea muscipula: Venus's-flytrap, *Dionaea muscipula.*

Dirca palustris: Leatherwood or Moosewood.

Dodecatheon meadea: Shooting Star or American Cowslip.

Dolichose: a group in the Pea family.

Drayton (Draiton) Island: at the north end of Lake George, Florida.

Dye, yellow: from *Xanthorrhiza.*

Eagle, Bald: *Haliaethus leucocephalus.*

————, Fishing: Osprey or Fish Hawk, *Pandion haliaethus.*

————, Greatest gray: Immature bald eagle.

East Lake: Now *Lake Dexter,* west of DeLeon Springs, Florida.

Edwards, George: a British correspondent of Bartram's. William did considerable collecting of birds for him when a boy.

Elysium: Alachua Savannah.

Empertrum: probably Empetrum, a member of the Crowberry family.

Epigea: Trailing arbutus, *Epigaea repens.*
Erythronium: Dog's-tooth violet, *Erythronium americanum.*
Erythryna: perhaps cardinal spear, *Erythrina herbaccea.*
Euonymus Americana: Strawberry bush, *Euonymus americanus.*
Euphorbia: a member of the Spurge family.

Fagus castania (Chesnut): Chestnut, *Castanea dentata.*
———— sylvatica: Beech, *Fagus grandifolia.*
Falling Creek: War Woman Creek, in northeastern Georgia.
Filix: delicate rock fern.
Flat Rock: Camping place in Georgia, this one probably in War-
    ren County south of Messena, on a branch of Brier Creek.
Fort: see
    Barrington.
    Conde.
    Frederica.
    James Dartmouth.
    Manchac (or Iberville).
    Mobile, Louis de la.
    Moore.
    Ninety-Six.
    Picolata.
    Prince George.
Fothergill, Dr. John: A London Quaker physician who subsidized
    the William Bartram expedition to the Carolinas, Georgia,
    Florida, and west to the Mississippi.
Fothergilla gardeni: Fothergilla.
Fragaria: Strawberry.
Franklinia alatamaha: the beautiful shrub collected by the Bar-
    trams in Georgia, near Fort Barrington on the Altamaha
    River. They named it in honor of Benjamin Franklin. It has
    not been found in the wild since 1790.
Fraxinus: Ash, in the Olive family.
———— excelsior: a type species of ash.
Frederica, Fort: on St. Simon's Island, Georgia.
Fusee (Fuzee): flintlock gun.

George, Lake: the largest lake on St. John's River, Florida.

Glass snake (anguis fragiles): a legless lizard, *Ophisaurus ventralis*.

Gleditsia triacanthus: Honey locust, *Gleditsia tricanthos*.

Glycine: Groundnut.

Glycine frutescens: American or Woody wistaria, *Kraunhia frutescens*.

Golphin, George: Galphin, trader at Silver Bluff, Georgia.

Gordonia lasianthus: Loblolly bay.

Gourd: Calabash or dipper gourd.

Gray's Ferry: just north of the John Bartram homestead on the Schuylkill River.

Great Sink: on the northeastern side of the Alachua Savannah, now *Payne's Prairie,* Florida.

Gum, sweet: *Liquidambar styraciflua.*

Halesia: Silverbell or snowdrop tree.

—— tetraptera: Carolina silver bell, *Halesia carolina.*

Halfway Pond: now *Cowpen Lake* in southwest Putnam County, Florida.

Hamamelis: Witch hazel.

Hammock (hummock): generally a group of trees of two or more species.

Hawk, black: Short-tailed hawk, *Buteo brachyurus.*

——, blue: adult male Marsh hawk, *Circus cyaneus hudsonius.*

——, chicken: probably Cooper's hawk, *Accipter cooperi.*

——, fork-tailed: Swallow-tailed kite, *Elanoides forficatus forficatus.*

——, great eagle: Red-tailed hawk, *Buteo jamaicensis.*

Hedera arborea: pepper vine(?), *Ampelopsis arborea.*

—— quinquefolia: Virginia creeper, *Parthenocissus quinquefolia.*

Helianthus: a sunflower.

Heracleum maximum: probably Cow parsnip, *Heracleum lanatum.*

Heron, blue: probably little blue heron, *Florida caerulea caerulea.*

——, little: Snowy egret, *Leucophoyx thula thula.*

Heron, silver-plumed: probably American egret, *Casmerodius albus.*

Hibiscus althea: Rose mallow, probably *Hibiscus moscheutos.*

———— coccineus: native red hibiscus.

Hogehege River: Tennessee River.

Hokio: *Ohio River.*

Hopea tinctoria: Sweetleaf or Horsesugar, *Symplocos tinctoria.*

Humble plant: *Mimosa pudica* (species ?).

Hydrangea quercifolia: Oak-leaved hydrangea.

Hyssopus: Hyssop.

Iberville: see Manchac.

Ibis: see Curlew, Spanish.

Ilex: Holly.

Illicium: yellow anise tree.

———— floridanum: Florida Anise tree or Polecat tree, *Illicium floridanum.*

Indigo: an introduced plant once grown on many southern colonial plantations.

Indigofera: Wilder or Western Indigo plant, *Indigofera leptosepala.*

Ipomoea (Ipomea): a group in the Morning-glory family.

Itea: Virginia willow, *Itea virginica.*

Jack daws: probably Boat-tailed grackle, *Cassidix mexicanus.*

Jacksonburg: now *Jacksonboro,* South Carolina, at the junction of routes 17 and 32 west of Charleston.

James Dartmouth, Fort: at Dartmouth near the confluence of the Broad River and the Savannah.

Jay, blue: *Cyanocitta cristata.*

Jay without a crest: Scrub jay, *Aphelocoma caerulescens caerulescens.*

Jessamine: Yellow jessamine, *Gelsemium sempervirens.*

Jore Mountains: now the *Nantahala Mountains.*

Juglans: the Walnut family.

———— exalta: shellbark hickory, *Hicoria ovata.*

———— nigra: Black walnut.

———— pecan: Pecan, *Hicoria pecan.*

Juniperus americana: perhaps Southern white cedar, *Chamaecyparis thyoides.*

Kalmia: Laurel, a genus in the Heath family.

———— glauca: Swamp laurel, *Kalmia polifolia.*

———— latifolia: Mountain laurel.

Keowe (Keowee) River: The upper part of the Seneca River, which joins the Tugaloo to form the Savannah River.

Kingsessing (Kingsess): The area in which the Bartram Garden and home were located. In 1750 it was about four miles from Philadelphia. Now it is engulfed by that city.

Lagoon near Lake Dexter, Florida, where the great alligator battle took place. This lagoon is probably the one now called *Mud Lake.*

Lagoon, Mosquito: a salt-water lagoon near New Smyrna, Florida.

Lantana: Vervain family; Verbenaceae.

Laurel: Bartram referred to Southern magnolia or *Magnolia grandiflora.* At the present time, *Laurel magnolia* refers to *Magnolia virginiana.*

Laurel, Rose (Magnolia glauca): Rose Laurel, *Magnolia virginiana.*

Laurus borbonia: Sweet bay or Red bay, *Persea borbonia.*

———— sassafras: Sassafras, *Sassafras sassafras.*

Ledum: a genus of the Heath family.

Leontice: probably Blue cohosh, *Caulophyllum thalictroides.*

Lime, Wild (Tallow nut): Tallowwood or Hog Plum, *Ximenia americana.*

Linaria: Toadflax.

Liquidamber styraciflus: Sweet gum, *Liquidambar styraciflua.*

Liriodendron tulipera: Tulip tree, *Liriodendron tulipifera.*

Little Carpenter: Chief or "Emperor" of the Cherokees at the time of Bartram's trip to the valley of the Little Tennessee.

Lobelia cardinalis: Cardinal flower.

Loblolly pine: *Pinus taeda.*

Lonicera sempervirens: Trumpet or Coral honeysuckle.

Lychnis dioica: Red campion or Red bird's-eye.

Lycium Salsum: probably Christmasberry, *Lycium carolinianum.*

M'Intosh: McIntosh, a member of the Highland colony near Darien, Georgia.

Magnolia: Bartram usually referred to the Southern magnolia, *Magnolia grandiflora.*

———— acuminata: Cucumber tree or Mountain magnolia.

———— auriculata: Ear-leaved magnolia, one of William Bartram's discoveries, *Magnolia fraseri.*

———— glauca: Rose laurel, now sweet bay or laurel magnolia, *Magnolia virginiana.*

———— grandiflora: Southern magnolia, Laurel tree or Great magnolia.

———— pyramidata: a rare magnolia discovered by William Bartram in Alabama.

———— tripetala: Umbrella tree.

Malva: Mallow.

Manatee: Sea cow, *Trichechus manatus.*

Manatee (Manate) Spring, now a state park northwest of Chiefland, Florida.

Manchac, Fort (or Iberville): on the Mississippi River about 20 miles south of Baton Rouge.

Maple: see Acer.

Medway: see Midway.

Meleagris occidentalis: Wild turkey, *Meleagris gallopavo.*

Midway Meeting House: at Midway, Georgia.

Mimosa: A family with members ranging in height from a few inches to tall trees.

Mobile, Fort Louis de la: on the Tombigbee River, Alabama.

Moccasin: see Snake.

Mock-bird: Mockingbird, *Mimus polyglottos.*

Momordica: Balsam apple.

Moore, Fort: at Silver Bluff, South Carolina.

Morus: Mulberry.

———— rubra: Red mulberry.

Mount Hope: probably at Beecher Point, about a mile south of Welaka, Florida.

—————— Royal: on the east side of St. John's River, about half a mile west of Fruitland, Florida.

Mud fish: *Amia calva,* found in many Florida rivers.

Muscogee (Muscoges, Muscogulges, Muscogulgees): Muscogulges, or Creek Indians.

Myrica: a genus in the Bayberry family.

—————— cerifera: Wax myrtle.

—————— inodora: Odorless wax myrtle, the only nonaromatic species in the family. Discovered by John Bartram.

Nighthawk: *Chordeiles minor.*

Ninety-Six, Fort: On the high road from Charleston to Fort Prince George, at a distance of 96 miles from the latter, according to traders' estimate.

Nucassee: Indian town on the Little Tennessee.

Nymphaea nelumbo: probably American nelumbo or Lotus, *Nelumbo lutea.*

Nyssa: Tupelo.

—————— aquatica: Large tupelo or Tupelo gum.

—————— sylvatica: Pepperidge or Sour gum.

Oak, Live: see *Quercus sempervirens.*

Ocmulge Fields: ancient Indian ruins now within the Ocmulgee National Monument just east of Macon, Georgia.

Ocmulge River: in Georgia.

Oconee Mountain: The *Oconee* Mountain between the Keowe and Tugaloo Rivers in western South Carolina.

Oenothera grandiflora: a spectacular Evening primrose of the Gulf States discovered in Alabama by William Bartram.

Ogeechee, Great: The Great Ogeechee River lies between the Savannah and the Altamaha Rivers in Georgia.

Ogeechee Mounts: Indian mounds on Amelia Island, Florida.

Olea: Olive family.

Olea americana: probably American wild olive, *Osmanthus ameri-canus.*

Ophrys: A genus in the Orchid family containing several species of Twayblade.

Opuntia: Prickly-pear cactus.

Oriolus: Oriole.

Osmunda: Royal fern family.

Ouaquaphenogaw: The *Okefenokee Swamp* in Georgia and Florida. It is the source of both the Suwannee and the St. Mary's Rivers.

Ounce, called Tiger cat by the Indians: Apparently the Ocelot, *Felis pardalis.*

Painted nonpareil: Painted bunting, *Passerina circis.*

Panax quinquefolium (ginseng): Ginseng or Redberry.

Pancratium: Spider lily, perhaps *Hymenocallis crassifolia.*

Parakeet (Psitacus caroliniensis): Carolina paroquet, *Conuropsis carolinensis.* This species is believed to be extinct.

Pavie: Buckeye.

Pearl Island: lies off the mouth of the Pearl River, which separates southeastern Louisiana and Mississippi.

Persicaria: a genus in the Buckwheat family.

Pewit: Phoebe, *Sayornis phoebe.*

Philadelphus: Syringa.

———— inodorus: Scentless syringa.

Picolata, Fort: on St. John's River, Florida, where Picolata now stands.

Pinus: Pine family.

———— abies: Though Bartram seems to refer to Hemlock when he uses this name, at present *abies* refers to balsam fir.

———— palustris: Long-leaved pine.

———— strobus: White pine.

———— sylvestris: Scotch Pine of northern Europe.

Pistia stratiotes: Water lettuce.

Platanus: Sycamore or Buttonwood, *Platanus occidentalis.*

Point Coupé: on the Mississippi River at about 30.34 degrees.

There were twenty-foot cliffs on the opposite or east shore of the river at that point in 1777.

Polianthus: Amaryllis.

Polymnia: A genus in the Thistle family.

Ponpon River: *Edisto* River, South Carolina. In spite of the use of Edisto on maps, most people of the state still use the old name of Ponpon for the river.

Prince George, Fort: on the Keowe River, approximately fifteen miles above Keowe. The precise location is still a matter of debate.

Prunus: Plum.

Pteris scandens: Climbing fern, probably *Lygodium palmatus*.

Puc-Puggy: Flower Hunter, the Seminole name given to William Bartram.

Pyrus: Pear.

——— coronaria: Narrow-leaved crabapple, *Malus coronaria*.

Quercus: Oak.

——— alba: White oak.

——— dentata: Narrow-leaved wintergreen oak.

——— hemispherica: Species ?

——— niger: Black jack or water oak.

——— phillos: Willow oak, *Quercus phellos*.

——— prinus: Rock chestnut oak.

——— rubra: Red oak.

——— tinctoria: Black oak, *Quercus velutina*.

——— sempervirens: Live oak, *Quercus virginiana*.

——— sinuata: perhaps Turkey or Scrub oak, *Quercus laevis*.

Rhamnus frangula: Alder buckthorn.

——— volubilis: Supple-jack or Rattan vine, *Berchemia scandens*.

Rhododendron: a genus in the Heath family.

——— ferrugineum: the type species for Rhododendron.

Rice bird: Bobolink, *Dolichonyx oryzivorus*.

Ridge, The Great: divides the Savannah River watershed from the Oconee in the Piedmont area of Georgia.

Robinia: The Locust genus in the Pea family.

——— pseudacacia: Locust, or False acacia.

Rosa paniculata (species ?): a rose.

Rudbeckia: the Coneflower genus of the Thistle family.

Ruellia: a genus of the Acanthus family.

St. Augustine, Florida: oldest city in the United States.

St. Ille: The *Satilla* River.

St. Juan: *St. John's* River.

St. Juan, Little: The *Suwannee* River.

St. Mark's, Florida: South of Tallahassee, and once a Spanish port.

St. Simon's Island: now a fashionable winter resort, and lying off Brunswick, Georgia.

Salvia: a genus in the Mint family.

——— coccinea: Red or Scarlet sage.

Sambucus: Elder.

Sanguinaria: a genus in the Poppy family.

Sapindus: Soapberry.

Sarracenia, yellow: Yellow pitcher plant or Trumpet, *Sarracenia flava.*

——— lacunosa: Bartram, very ill when he wrote the description of this plant, apparently confused the characters of two or more pitcher plants. Pitcher p'ants are abundant in the area north and west of Pensacola, where he collected this doubtful species. White top, *Sarracenia drummondii,* is particularly conspicuous.

Senecio: A genus in the Thistle family.

——— jacobea: Tansy ragwort, *Senecio jacobaea.*

Sideroxylon: Mastic or Wild olive, Sapota family.

Silphium: a genus in the Thistle family.

Silver Bluff, South Carolina: on the Savannah River about ten miles south of Augusta, Georgia.

Smilax pseudo-china: Long-stalked greenbriar.

Snake-bird: Anhinga, *Anhinga anhinga.*

Snake, bull: Florida pine snake, *Pituophia melanoleucus.*

——— , chicken: probably four-lined chicken snake, *Elaphe quadrivittala.*

————, coach-whip: *Zamenis flagelliformes.*

————, glass: a lizard, *Anguis fragiles.*

————, green: *Cyclophis aestivus.*

————, ground or bastard rattlesnake: *Sistrunus miliarius.*

————, rattlesnake: *Crotalus adamanteus.*

————, riband (ribbon): the habits described are those of a coral snake, *Elaps julvius,* as are the colors.

Sophora: a genus in the Pea family.

Spalding's Lower Store: on the west shore of St. John's River, about six miles south of Palatka, Florida.

Spalding's Upper Store: near the present site of Astor, Florida.

Staphylea: Bladdernut.

Stewartia: Camellia.

———— malachodendron: Virginia-stuartia or Silky-camellia.

———— montana: Mountain-stuartia, *Stewartia ovata.*

Stillingia: a genus in the Spurge family.

Stork: Whooping crane, *Grus americana.*

Styraciflua: Sweet gum.

Styrax: the Storax family.

Sunbury, Georgia: on the coast near the mouth of the Midway River.

Swallow (Hirundo).

————, bank: *Riparia riparia.*

————, house: barn swallow, *Hirundo rustica.*

Taensa Bluffs: on the Tensaw River, near Stockton, Alabama.

Talahasochte: Indian town on the south bank of the Suwannee River, about four miles upstream from Manatee Springs.

Teal, painted summer: Wood duck.

Three Sisters' Ferry: This ferry across the Savannah River is called Two Sisters' ferry in *Mill's Atlas* of South Carolina, 1825. It is in the Beaufort District.

Thrush, red: Brown thrasher, *Toxostoma rufum.*

————, wood: *Hylocichla mustelina.*

Tilia: the Linden family.

Tillandsia: now Dendropogon.

———— usneaoides: Long or Spanish moss, *Dendropogon usneoides.*

Tortoise, great land: Gopher turtle, *Gopherus polyphaemus*.
————, great soft-shell: Soft-shelled turtle, *Amyda ferox*.
Trillium sessile: Sessile-flowered wake-robin.
Trout: Large-mouthed bass, *Huro salmoides*.
Tumulus: Indian mounds.
Turkey, Wild (Meleagris occidentalis): now *Meleagris gallopavo*.

Ulmus: Elm family.
———— campestris: the type species of elm.
Urtica: a genus in the Nettle family.

Vaccinum: Blueberry and Bilberry.
Viburnam dentatum: Arrowwood.
———— prunifolium: Black haw or Stagbush.
Viola: Violet family.

Wren, golden-crowned: Golden-crowned kinglet.

Index

Acacia. *See* Locust
Academy of Natural Sciences (Philadelphia), 18, 306, 308
Account of East Florida (Stork), 15
Acer. See Maple
Aconite. See Monkshood
Acorn, 73, 85, 129, 285, 366
Adam's needle, 92, 195
Aesculapius, 50
Aesculus. See Buckeye
Aesculus alba, 161
Aesculus florida, 161
Alabama, xxi, 115, 156-162, 182-189, 335
Alabama (Indian village), 165
Alabama Indians, 165
Alabama River, 158, 160, 165, 184
Alachua Savannah. *See* Payne's Prairie
Alder (Alnus), 310
Allegheny, 35
Allegheny River, 24, 32
Alligator, 55, 57, 186, 199, 210, 219, 221, 228-241, 265, 293, 296, 323; *See also* Crocodile
Alligator Hole. *See* Blue Sink
Almond, 69, 138
Alnus. See Alder
Altamaha River, 95, 96, 120, 121, 141, 172, 177, 193-195, 245, 329, 379, 380
Althea. See Loblolly bay
Amaryllis (*Polianthus*), 85, 86
Amelia Island, 121, 174-179, 319, 380
Amelia Narrows, 298, 380
American Ethnological Society, 18, 346
American Geographical Society, xxi
American Naturalists Series, The, xxii
American Ornithology, 376
American Philosophical Society, 17, 18
American Revolution, 16, 17
Amia calva. See Mud fish
Amite River, 164, 383
Amyda ferox. See Turtle, soft-shelled
Andromeda, 162
Anecdotes of an American Crow (Bartram), 18, 311-315, 375
Anemone, 85
Anemone thalictroides. See Rue anemone
Angelica, 85

Angelica lucida. See White root
Anguis fragiles. See Glass snake
Anhinga. See Snake-bird
Anhinga Trail, 228
Anise tree (*Illicium*), 162, 211, 214; Florida (polecat tree; *Illicium floridanum*), 161, 162; star, 63 footnote
Annona (Anona) glabra. See Pond apple
Annona (Anona) pigmaea. See Pawpaw
Antioque Indians, 48-49
Apalache, Bay of. *See* Apalachicola Bay, Florida
Apalachicola Bay, Florida, 122
Apalachucla (Indian town), 157, 335-339, 382
Apollo, 50
Apple, custard. *See* Pond apple
Apple, pond. *See* Pond apple
Apple tree, 42, 312, 313, 366
Aralia, 106
Aramus guarauna. See Limpkin
Arbutus, 85; trailing (*Epigea; Epigaea repens*), 142
Arethusa. *See* Dragon's-mouth
Aristolochia frutescens. See Snakeroot
Asclepias. See Milkweed
Ash (*Fraxinus*), 40, 55, 99, 154, 160, 179, 211; *See also Fraxinus excelsior*
Asimina triloba. See Pawpaw
Astor, Florida, 180, 319, 381
Athens, Georgia, 328, 380
Atlantic Ocean, 179
Attassee, 339-346
Audubon, John James, 290
Augusta, Georgia, 53, 119, 128, 131-132, 136, 206, 225, 227, 273, 328, 339, 350, 380, 382
Auk, The, 306 footnote, 308
Aurora borealis, 93
Azalea, 135, 138, 146, 161, 162, 226, 333; flame (*Azalea flammula; Azalea lutea*), 137, 142

Balm of Gilead, 85
Baltimore, Maryland, 310
Banana, 92
Barilla. See Sedge

405